WALKING IN FRANCE

Rob Hunter

Hamlyn Paperbacks

WALKING IN FRANCE
ISBN 0 600 20442 1

First published in Great Britain 1982
by The Oxford Illustrated Press Ltd
Hamlyn Paperbacks edition 1983

Text © 1982 by Rob Hunter
Maps and illustrations © 1982
by The Oxford Illustrated Press
Hamlyn Paperbacks are published by
The Hamlyn Publishing Group Ltd,
Astronaut House, Feltham,
Middlesex, England

Printed and bound in Great Britain by
Cox & Wyman Ltd, Reading

Line illustrations by John Gilbert Rankin

CONTENTS

ACKNOWLEDGEMENTS

My thanks are due to a very large number of people who helped me on this project, but especially to:

Pauline Hallam and Martine Williams of the French Government Tourist Office, London; Toby Oliver of Brittany Ferries; Samantha Richeley of P & O Ferries; M.Vergier of the FFRP—CNSGR, Paris; Jim Cuthbert of Canvas Holidays; Estelle Huxley; Claude Salgues of the Maison du Tourisme, Perpignan; Kev Reynolds; Colin Glover; The staff of the Institut Géographique National, Paris and the Comité de Tourisme, Dordogne; Madame Pat Villette of Decazeville and the Robert Louis Stevenson Footpath Committee; Tony Pattinson; M.Senn of the CNSGR, Délégation Lozère; M.Michael Wienin of the Drailles en Cévennes; Lawrence Main; Marek Obbink of the Comité Régional du Tourisme, Côte d'Azur; Mauricette Manas; N.Vincent of Waymark Holidays, London; Cris Rees of Romanic Tours; Brian Brett of Dan Air Ltd.

J'ai quitté mon pays, tous mes amis,
J'ai voulu connaître au delà des monts,
D'autres pays, d'autres amis,
de nouveaux horizons ...

This book is dedicated, with varying amounts of affection, to Robin Adshead; Peter Lumley; Claude Salgues; Don Philpott; Cameron McNeish; John Traynor; John Lloyd; Paul Traynor; Paul Hughes; Greg Simmons; Toby Oliver; Philip Pond; Peter Chambers; Keith Spence; Anne Sharpley; Iain Morris; Elfie Tran; with all of whom I have, from time to time, gone . . .

WALKING IN FRANCE

INTRODUCTION

This is a book about France. In it I shall attempt to describe in particular rural France, the *arrière-pays*, the back-country, where most of my leisure time is spent and for which I feel an enduring affection, for both the land and the people. The best way to discover the back-country in any land is to go there on foot, seeing the country at a natural pace.

It might be as well to face the fact that some foreigners have been known to find the French, how shall I say, a little difficult. Personally, I don't find them so and if this is a partisan view, well, I have the will to maintain it. I have lived, travelled and worked in France for many years and can honestly say of my neighbours that if you are prepared to go half way to meet them, then they will come more than half way in return. I like the French and I hope that some of this liking will spill through onto the pages of this book.

As to the book itself, it is concerned with one particular aspect of the country: the activity of walking there. Around this simple pastime lies a whole infrastructure of long trails, little footpaths, campsites, *gîtes*, *auberges*, clubs, touring companies and government organisations. Walking is a popular activity in France, well supported by the nation, and no country in the world has so much to offer the foot-powered traveller.

This book is arranged in four stages. Chapter one contains information on the history and background of France and the French. I don't believe that any country can be enjoyed unless the visitor has some idea of its institutions and how the country works. This chapter also contains information of practical use to any visitor, not only those travelling on foot.

Chapter two describes and explains France for the walker, the organisations and services that support the activity, and where particular information can be obtained. Chapter two also contains advice on using this book and planning walking trips to France.

The subsequent chapters tackle the regions of France and describe the opportunities for walking in each area, again with lots of information and reasons why one area might be more suitable than another. My chapters do not coincide exactly with the official administrative regions, because walking takes little account of political or administrative boundaries.

Finally, there are a number of appendices which include some useful phrases, a bibliography, and an up-to-date list of French topoguides, with distances where available.

Since this is essentially a book of information, some selectivity has been necessary, for information tends to date. I have included detailed information on matters which are unlikely to change such as distances, and general rules on those matters which are likely to change like prices. I have also, after careful checking, included information on projects which are, at time of writing, not yet completed but which I have reason to believe will be completed by publication date or during the lifetime of this particular edition. I have culled this information from a wide variety of differing and sometimes competing sources, and have attempted to reconcile areas of doubt or difference where necessary.

I must at this stage say something on the subject of initials. The French are very fond of using initials to describe their organisations, and in sheer self-defence I have had to do likewise. The thought of writing *Féderation Française de la Randonnée Pédestre — Comité National des Sentiers de Grande Randonnée* several hundred times in the course of this book forces me to adopt FFRP — CNSGR, and even that is hardly brief. All such initials will be fully described at least once.

To prevent this being a catalogue of my own experiences I advertised for help, and many Francophile walkers wrote with suggestions which I have not hesitated to adopt. My thanks to all of them and in particular to Kev Reynolds for his advice on the Pyrénées, and Paul Traynor for gallantly tackling the GR 20 in Corsica and telling me all about it. I hope that the result of this co-operation and much research results in a useful book.

So much for my purpose, so much for my message; what of myself? I have, as I say, spent many years in France. I speak the language and like the people. I have a particular fondness for the country folk, and have been known to bore people to death on the subject of the Auvergne. I have walked extensively in France, in every region and most *départements*, in the Alps and the Pyrénées, along the Norman Coast, across the Massif Central, with friends and alone, in summer and in winter. I do it because I enjoy it, and the purpose of this book is to urge you to do as I have done, with similar happy results.

Bon Voyage.

Rob Hunter
1982

FRANCE AND THE FRENCH

France is the largest country in Western Europe. It covers an area of 550,000 square kilometres (220,000 square miles) and is divided into ninety-five territorial areas or *départements* several of which, although far from the geographic boundaries of Metropolitan France are administered in exactly the same way.

France did not grow to this size overnight, and the fifty-three million French people who make up the country's Metropolitan population are by no means homogenous. France is a diverse country, diverse in scenery, landscape, climate, industry, culture and attitudes, and nowhere more diverse than in her history and inhabitants.

Within the umbrella term 'French', are sheltered Bretons, Basques, Catalans, Corsicans, Provençals, Auvergnats, Poitivians, Alsaciens, and many more, quite apart from the divisions between the people of the north and the *méridional*, the people from the south, or Midi. Regional identities are very strong and the Breton, Basque and Catalan languages are still living tongues, taught and spoken in their home regions. No understanding of France or the French is possible without an appreciation of the background and history of the people, and how they came to combine into the present state.

History

Before the final conquest of the country by Julius Caesar in 52 BC, the country which is now France was occupied by the Gauls, a loose confederation of tribes living to the west of the Loire and usually at war with each other. They united, for the first and last time, in the presence of the legions of Rome, but Caesar defeated their war-chief, Vercingétorix, at Alesia, in what is now Burgundy, in 52 BC and for the next four hundred years Gaul was a Roman province. Towards the end of the Empire various barbaric tribes began to infiltrate the country, notably the Burgundians, who settled along the Saône, and refugee Britons, who settled in 'Armorique', or Brittany. The two major invasions were from the Visigoths, who conquered the south and the Teutonic Franks, who overwhelmed first the north, then drove the Visigoths out into Spain, and finally gave their name to the country of the Franks, France.

Centuries of rule and misrule then followed. The Merovingian dynasty ruled 'France' from the fifth century until AD 751, but they were gradually eased out by powerful subjects known as the Mayors of the Palace, until one mayor, Pepin the Short, usurped the throne.

His descendant, Charles the Great, or Charlemagne, ruled from AD 771 until his death in AD 814. He became Holy Roman Emperor in AD 800 (and married nine times), but the Empire broke up after his death and modern France evolved from the part that lay' west of the Rhône.

Since then France has gradually expanded, but until as late as 1180 the actual territory of the French kings was confined to a small region around Paris, known then and now as the Ile de France. In those days the King of France was more *primus inter pares* than a great feudal landowner, but gradually over the centuries the kingdom grew.

The County of Toulouse was overwhelmed in the Albigensian Crusade of 1209-48, and the old troubadour culture of the Languedoc extinguished. Normandy was annexed in 1208 after the English King John, John Lackland, was defeated at Bovines. The English were finally expelled from Aquitaine in 1453. Anjou, Maine and Burgundy were absorbed after the defeat and death of Charles the Rash, the last Valois Duke of Burgundy, in 1477. Provence was taken in 1481, and Brittany came to the throne by marriage in 1532. The Kingdom of Navarre came to France with the accession of Henri IV. Richelieu, the great Cardinal, captured Roussillon and established a secure southern frontier in 1659. Lorraine was taken and the eastern frontier established on the Rhine in 1766; Corsica was annexed in 1768. Savoie and Nice arrived as late as 1860.

There has, of course, been a certain amount of adjustment. Alsace and Lorraine were annexed by Germany after the Franco-Prussian War of 1870-71, and only returned to France in 1919, to return again to Germany in 1940 and then back again at last to France in 1945.

These large expansions and small contractions were the result of wars, alliances and marriage, but while this was going on the French were fusing together under the influence of several great wars. Between 1345 and 1453 the Valois dynasty fought out the Hundred Years War with their Plantagenet cousins of England, but if the King of the French was there at the start it was the French nation

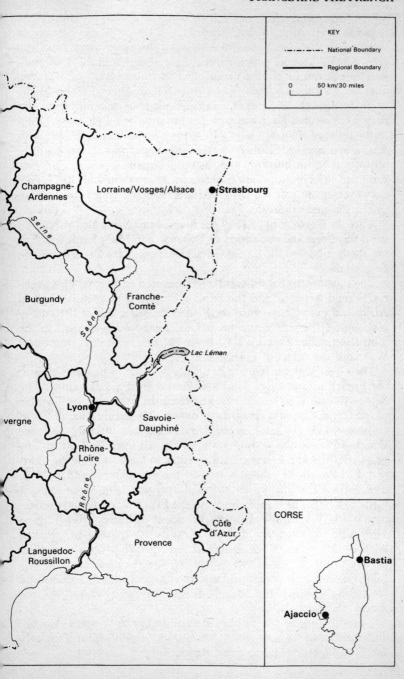

KEY

— ·— ·— · — National Boundary

——————— Regional Boundary

0   50 km/30 miles

Champagne-
Ardennes

Lorraine/Vosges/Alsace   ● Strasbourg

Seine

Burgundy

Franche-
Comté

Saône

Lac Léman

Lyon ●

vergne

Savoie-
Dauphiné

Rhône-
Loire

Rhône

Côte
d'Azur

CORSE

Languedoc-
Roussillon

Provence

● Bastia

Ajaccio ●

which finally triumphed, united by warring against the invader.

In the next century France was ravaged by the Wars of Religion, fought after the advent of Luther between Protestant Huguenots and the Catholic League, which ruined the country until the Protestant heir to the throne of the Valois, the Bourbon Henry of Navarre, adopted Catholicism and was crowned Henri IV of France. Henri acknowledged the liberties of his Protestant Huguenot followers, and they were secured for a while by the granting of religious toleration in the Edict of Nantes. Louis XIII gained Roussillon in the war with Spain, and his son, Louis XIV, the Sun King, was almost continually at war on the northern and eastern frontiers. Louis XIV's Revocation of the Edict of Nantes drove countless thousands of Huguenots overseas and started the Camisard rebellion which flickered on in the Cévennes until the French Revolution.

After the Revolution of 1789 the Napoléonic Wars bled the nation until the defeat and abdication of Bonaparte in 1815, but it was during this period that the fundamental structure of modern France was firmly laid.

The nineteenth century was largely devoted to internal upheavals, the Second Republic and the Second Empire with colonial wars in Africa and Indo-China, until the Franco-Prussian War of 1870 drove Napoléon III from the throne and led to the establishment of the Third Republic. This endured from 1870 right through the Great War until the defeat of France in 1940.

The Great War, the *Guerre de Quatorze*, struck a hammer blow at the French nation. France lost a million men at Verdun alone. The Second World War, which followed from the political consequences of the Great War, also ravaged the nation, but the eventual defeat of Germany, a victory aided by the Free French and internal Resistance forces of France, the *maquis*, restored French hopes and pride. The years after the war, however, saw a return to the usual political disarray. The Fourth Republic lasted only ten years, from 1948 to 1958. The Fifth Republic, which still endures, was largely the work of General Charles de Gaulle, leader of the Free French during the Second World War. De Gaulle was President of France from 1958 to 1968, a period which saw the end of France as a colonial power when Algeria was granted her independence in 1962. Over a million French people, the so-called *pieds-noirs*, were expelled from Algeria following independence, and they have largely settled in the south. De Gaulle resigned after internal disturbances in 1968, but his constitution still stands.

Today France is a Republic, a member of the Western Alliance and the European Economic Community, a political and military force, and a powerful industrial nation.

Political and Administrative Framework

The political and administrative framework of modern France was largely established at the time of the French Revolution of 1789, although later modified by Napoléon, and considerably altered in the following century and a half in the course of the five subsequent Republics.

The centre of power in France is the President of the Republic, who acts through a Government headed by a Prime Minister. The President is elected for seven years, and enjoys the privileges of a Head of State combined with those of an elected official. He appoints the Prime Minister and the Cabinet, is Chief of the Armed Forces, and has powers to dissolve Parliament.

The Government is responsible to Parliament. In France, Parliament consists of a National Assembly, which in turn consists of a Chamber of Deputies, elected by the people for a term of five years, and an upper House, or Senate. Senators are elected every three years by vote of Deputies, general councillors and the delegates for the municipal councils.

Most French Governments are in fact coalitions. The chief political parties in France are the RPR (or Gaullists), and the Republican Party (RP) which occupy the 'Right'; and the Centre Parties, the Social Democrats, the Radical Socialists, and the National Independent Movement. These tend to vote with or for the Centre-Right Government which until the 1981 elections had retained power in France since the war. The 'Opposition' parties are the Socialists; the French Communist Party; the Radical Movement; and the United Socialists. The present government of France is a Socialist coalition.

The administration of France is highly centralised and organised. There are over two million Civil Servants, although nearly half of these are teachers, and government is dispensed to the people through a three-tier system.

The Region

There are twenty-two 'regions' in France. These have been set up since the 1960s and are usually founded in the area and with the name of the former pre-Revolution province; Burgundy, Franche-Comté, Languedoc Roussillon etc. Each region consists of a number of *départements* and the region is designed to provide an overall economic framework. The regional chief, or *Préfect,* is also *Préfect* of the *département* in which the region's capital is situated.

The Département

The *département* is the backbone of the French administrative system. There are ninety-five *départements* in France, each headed by a *Préfect*. The *Préfect* is a powerful public figure, controlling the police and all state services in the department. The *Préfect* is appointed by Central Government. This *département* system was established at the time of the Revolution and, to make a break with old feudal ties, the *départements* were then given local names, usually that of the main local river, thus Seine-Maritime, Loiret, Lot-et-Garonne, and so on, although some, Manche or Finistère, for example, recall a coastal connection. A Frenchman will often use the *départemental* name to describe his birthplace: "I am from Seine-Maritime" for example.

Municipalities (Communes)

There are 37,500 municipalities in France, each administered by a *Maire* and a Municipal Council. The *Maire* and his council are elected for six years. The *Maire* can also perform marriages although, since France is a Catholic country, most civil ceremonies are followed by a Church service. Ninety per cent of the French people are born Catholics but Church attendance has shrunk to about fourteen per cent and is still declining.

Industry and Agriculture

France is among the top six industrial nations in the world, ahead of the UK and rapidly overtaking Germany and the USA. The main industries are engineering, notably cars (Renault, Citroen, Peugeot) and aviation (Aerospatial), textiles, agriculture, food and drink. Banking and finance are also important commercial activities. France was a founder member of the European Economic Community, and is increasingly aligning its agricultural policy to that of other member countries. France is the major producer of wine, butter, milk, wheat and arable crops, and devoted to maintaining the Common Agricultural Policy which protects French farmers and leads to high food prices.

French farms are being rapidly modernised and enlarged but there is a steady drift away from the land. The agricultural population is declining and ageing, a combination of factors which is steadily depopulating the Massif Central, the south-west, and large areas of Languedoc, where abandoned farms and even villages are not uncommon.

Education

As for administration, so for education, which is also highly centralised, even down to the finer details and timings of the curriculum. French children can go to kindergarten from three and start primary education at six for a period of five years. A four-year secondary education then follows, which is followed by high school or *lycée*, which leads to the *baccalaureat*, or School Leaving Certificate. Possession of the *bac* entitles the student to a university place.

There are fifty-seven universities in France and several, the Sorbonne, Toulouse and Montpellier, have an international reputation, although two-thirds of all French students quit without obtaining a degree. The cream of the education system goes on to attend the post-graduate *Grandes Écoles*, and the graduate of a *Grande École* is assured of a high position in public service or industry. The French system is hard working and élitist. School commences at 8 am and finishes at 5 pm. Large amounts of homework are also common and French children always strike the visitor as well disciplined and polite, at least until they become students. All young Frenchmen have to serve one year's National Service.

Art and Culture

France is an intensely artistic and cultural country, remaining a store-house of treasures accumulated during a long history, and is notably rich in architecture, religious and secular. The south is a shrine of Romanesque architecture, while the first and still the greatest Gothic cathedrals were built in the Ile de France. The French Wars have left a legacy of great castles, or *châteaux-forts*, notably on the frontiers of the territory occupied by the perfidious English, such as the Dordogne. The monastic orders built many fine abbeys, some of which, such as Fontenay in Burgundy, and St. Michel de Cuxa in the Pyrénées, still remain, although many others, like Cluny, were destroyed at the Revolution.

The French kings were great builders and when the Religious Wars were over the courtiers followed their example, building palaces along the Loire, in the Ile de France, and as private provincial seats. Chenonceaux, Chantilly, Versailles, Fontainbleau, are all magnificent examples of French architecture and contain priceless collections of objects d'art. Incidentally, in France a *château* can be any large country house, while a medieval castle, with battlements, is a *château-fort*. Most of the *châteaux* of the Loire began as *châteaux-forts*, and some, like Chinon, still are.

Apart from fine architecture, France is full of galleries and mus-

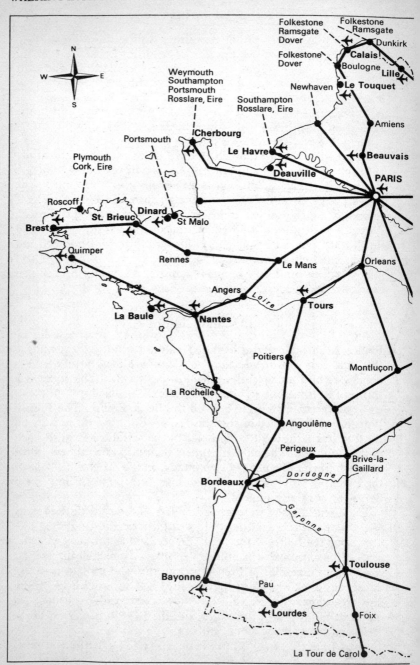

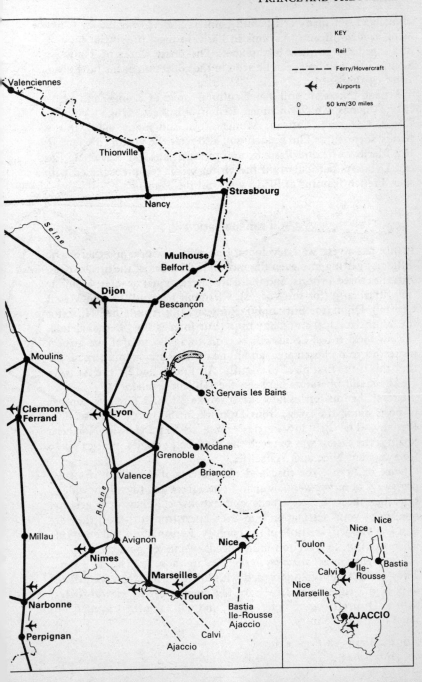

KEY

Rail

Ferry/Hovercraft

Airports

0   50 km/30 miles

eums, and her many artists and painters are represented by collections in magnificent museums in Paris, in most provincial capitals, and especially in their birthplaces. The finest works of Toulouse-Lautrec, for example, can be seen in the collection at his birthplace, Albi, on the Tarn.

Art and letters are still major cultural topics of France, and with a list of names which includes Renoir, Flaubert, Hugo, Voltaire, Dégas, Cézanne, Watteau, Monet, Zola, and many more, this is hardly surprising. The French will also refer the visitor to scientists like Marie Curie and Pasteur, and to musicians like Ravel, Berlioz and Debussy, particularly if the visitor seems too preoccupied with such French features as food, wine and the *can-can*.

Transportation

France has a very well developed transport network, and there is no difficulty getting into even the most remote areas of the *arrière-pays*. Paris has three airports, and there are international or internal flights into Strasbourg (for the Vosges), Clermont-Ferrand (for the Massif Central), Dijon (for Burgundy), Bordeaux (for Aquitaine), Nice (for the Southern Alps) and many more. Air Inter is the internal airline.

Your local travel agent will be able to advise you of the airport nearest to your chosen area, and as new routes are opening up all the time this is the first place to enquire. Air France and British Airways are the major operators between the UK and France.

Cross-Channel ferries now run from the UK and Eire to a number of ports along the coast, from Dunkirk in the north to Roscoff in Brittany. The Brittany Ferries' route to Santander in Northern Spain is the easiest way to reach the Western Pyrénées. Ferries ply to Corsica from Nice and Marseilles.

Once in France the road and rail systems are excellent. Fast expressways or *autoroutes* now span France from end to end and side to side, but these are toll roads and expensive. They may get you quickly to your destination but, even apart from the cost, they are dull and you will see little of the country. Personally, I make it a rule when driving, to travel on minor roads whenever possible.

The main routes, or *routes nationales,* are those with an 'N' prefix. They are fast but often crowded with lorries, which can be difficult to pass in a right-hand drive car. The smaller *départemental* routes, with a 'D' prefix, are quieter, safer, and will take the traveller into some beautiful country.

Speed limits in France are:
Autoroutes   130 km/81 mph

Dual carriageways   110 km/68 mph
Single carriageway   90 km/57 mph
In towns   60 km/36 mph (unless otherwise shown)

To convert kilometres into miles divide by eight and multiply by five: for example, 40 km = 25 miles.

Radar traps operate in France and the French police can inflict on-the-spot fines. Seat belts are compulsory even in towns, children under twelve must travel in the back seat, and the breathalyser, (*Alcool-test*) is increasingly popular. Drivers are advised to carry a red warning triangle in case of an accident or puncture, and to obtain a Green Card level of insurance. Normal UK insurance only provides third party cover abroad.

Rail travel in France is fast and excellent. There are many inter-city services by day and night, and the rural networks are still functioning in many areas, and well worth taking since the routes they follow are very scenic. The little yellow train, the *petit train jaune,* from Perpignan up to the Cerdagne, is just one example of a picturesque rail journey which can take the visitor into fine walking country, while *trains touristiques,* where available, are mentioned in the regional chapters. Tickets for French trains can be bought at any time but must be stamped or *'composted'* before use. Orange *'composter'* machines stand outside every platform.

Many of the remoter areas are served by bus companies which provide the connecting services from the small stations to villages even further back in the hills. Long-distance coach services in France are not common, but local services are quite adequate. A coach in France is a *car,* a car is a *voiture* or, more commonly nowadays, *une auto.*

Banks

French banks are usually open from 9 am to 12 noon, and from 2 pm to 5 pm, although some close at 4 pm. Most will accept sterling notes or travellers' cheques for exchange on production of a passport. Many French banks also participate in the Eurocheque scheme, where an ordinary UK cheque can be cashed on production of a Banker's Card. The daily amount is limited at present to £100. Diners, Access, American Express and Barclaycard (Visa), and Carte Bleu (CB) credit cards are also accepted in many establishments.

Medical Services, Health, Insurance

Normal medical services are available from doctors and hospitals. Chemists (*pharmacies*) can be found in all towns and most villages so, with a cut finger or other minor ailments, go directly to the *pharmacie*, which will be identifiable by an illuminated green cross. *Pharmacie*s will always give first aid. France has a National Health Service similar to that of the UK but the patient has to pay first and then reclaim the money from the State. A visit to a doctor will cost about Fr.40 and it will be fifty per cent more if the doctor makes a house or hotel call. France has reciprocal Health Service arrangements with Britain and travellers should obtain Form No.E111 from the DHSS before travelling, which will cover the large part of all medical bills, at least for those in paid employment.

Unless marked *Eau non potable* all tap water is drinkable, but the normal precautions of washing fruit and avoiding excessive amounts of rich food and wine are advisable.

Police, Fire, Ambulance

The police, fire and ambulance services can be obtained by telephone. The numbers are shown in the public kiosks, but 17 will get the police and ambulance, and 19 will fetch the fire service (*Sapeurs Pompiers*) which is, in fact, a regiment of the French Army.

In mountain districts the *Gendarmerie Montagne* provides Rescue Services in case of emergency, and their patrols can be seen touring the districts, or can be obtained by dialling 17.

Telephone and Postal Services

The French telephone system, after years of difficulty, is now rapidly improving. An STD system is coming into effect and pay kiosks are available for direct dial calls in most towns and villages.

To make an inter-*départemental* call the number must be prefixed with the code number 16. For international calls the same direct dial system applies. To call France from the UK you dial:

010 for an international line, followed by
33 for France, followed by
The *départemental* code (e.g. 1 for Paris), followed by
The subscriber's number.

To dial the UK from France you dial:

19 and wait for an international line (first a bleep and then a continuous tone), followed by
44 for the UK, followed by
The area code (but *without* the initial zero), followed by
The subscriber's number.

Postal services between France and Britain are as secure and rapid as such services are in this day and age.

Mail sent to France can be sent *Poste Restante* or *Poste Centrale* to any town. I have used this to send maps and guides to await my arrival in a particular town, and they were handed over for a small fee on production of my passport. One hint in the event of difficulty is to ask the assistant to check the 'E' pigeon hole — for 'Esquire'.

Conversion Tables

France is entirely metricated and the following conversions will be helpful:

Weights and Measures: 1 kilo = 2.2 lbs
                              1 litre = 1.75 pints
                              1 mile = 1.6 km (8 km = 5 miles).

Temperature: France uses the Celsius (centigrade) system for temperature and to convert this to the more familiar Fahrenheit the following formula is applied:

Temp $0°C \times 2 = X - (1/10 \text{ of } X) = Y + 32° = $ Temp. °F.

or, for example:

$16°$ Centigrade $\times 2 = 32 - 3 = 29 + 32 = 61°F$.

Time: France uses the twenty-four hour clock. For much of the year French time is one hour ahead of Greenwich Mean Time. Both countries have a Summer Time system (*heure d'été*), so that from 6 April to 30 September French time is two hours ahead of Greenwich Mean Time and one hour ahead of British Summer Time. This one hour difference can play havoc with plans for bus or train connections and is worth remembering.

Language

One snag with France for the visitor is that they do tend to speak rather a lot of French there! The pattern may be changing a little but it is fair to say that the French are as bad at learning other languages as the British, but even a few phrases can take the visitor a very long way. A list of words and phrases useful to the walker will be found in the back of this book, and where a French word would be useful I have included it in the text. Walkers in the wild will find few English-speaking people, so some slight knowledge of French plus a good phrase book and dictionary will be very helpful.

French Holidays

In any West European country the vacation period is strongly influenced by the school year. In France the peak holiday time is between

15th July and the end of August. A four-week holiday is the norm in France and a fifth week is becoming increasingly popular. In addition, France has a large number (eleven in all) of public holidays.

Food and Wine

The French have a passion for food, and the country is the world's largest producer of wine. The general standard of cooking in France is very high, and certain regions, Périgord, Normandy, Burgundy and Brittany, are internationally famous for their food. Many other areas have regional dishes which the traveller would be well advised to try, and every province or town will have its own speciality. French cheeses are excellent and very varied and even General de Gaulle lamented over the difficulty of ruling a nation which produced more than three hundred different types of cheese! The seafood is particularly fine along the Atlantic coast, and the mountain areas rejoice in ham, trout, and good thick soups and stews.

The rules for eating well in France, at a reasonable price, are very simple. Seek out restaurants off the main streets, which offer a choice of tourist menu. This is a set bill of fare at prices ranging from 35 francs up to 85 francs, tax and service included, consisting of between four and six courses. The local wine, *vin du pays*, or the *vin maison*, which usually comes in a *pichet*, or small jug, is always good value and usually very palatable. It is customary and polite, when entering a French restaurant, to greet the assembled company with a muttered *'Bonjour Monsieur/Madame'*.

The French tend to eat a light breakfast, a leisurely lunch, and a main meal at dinner. Snack and sandwich bars are not yet popular although reasonably priced snacks are becoming increasingly available in many bars.

You can, of course, eat expensively in France, in which case, if you can afford it, you need no advice from me, but walkers in country districts, eating in small restaurants, hotels of the *Logis de France* network, or *routier* (lorry drivers') cafés, will be pleasantly surprised at the low cost and excellent value.

If you wish to buy food for a picnic, then you must visit the *épicerie* for cheese and ham, the *boulangerie* for bread, the *charcuterie* for pâté or sausage. Fruit and wine can be found in the *épicerie* or in a general food store, *une alimentation*. The prices for local produce are usually very reasonable and in general compare well with Britain, while the weekly markets are always worth attending. French bread is excellent, but goes stale quickly, which is why French bakers bake several times a day.

Tourist Services and Information

Tourism is well organised in France, at Governmental, Regional and local levels. There are French Government Tourist Offices (FGTO) in the capital or major cities of all foreign countries and these offices are the prime sources of information for all tourists to France. Each region has a *Comité Régional de Tourisme*, and their addresses are given in the appropriate chapters of this book. Finally, at the 'grass roots' every town and even every village of any size will have its own tourist office or *Syndicat d'Initiative*. There are over five thousand tourist offices in France and these will have all the relevant local information.

French hotels and campsites are classified on a star system from one star (adequate) to five stars (luxurious), and the prices are fixed annually by the Government. Those prices displayed in every bedroom or campsite office and at the reception desk include taxes and service, and are legally binding. The *Guide Michelin* or the *Guide des Logis et Auberges Rurales de France* will give the visitor accurate current prices. Breakfast is charged separately and usually costs from 8 francs to 12 francs per person. Campsite guides are available by region from the FGTO and are also issued annually by a number of publishers.

This chapter will, I hope, have given the reader some idea of how France functions and how her inhabitants live and are governed. The information contained here will be useful to all travellers in France, and we can now build on this basis to examine the additional facilities available to those who visit France on foot.

WALKER'S FRANCE

France is the ideal country for the walker, the backpacker, and the lightweight camper. The terrain is varied, and the weather largely good and usually reliable. These natural advantages have been supplemented by an excellent and ever increasing range of supporting facilities for walkers which are well maintained and constantly developing.

This does not mean that walking in France is by any means organised or institutionalised. The facilities are there and you can take advantage of them if you wish. If, on the other hand, you prefer to make your own way across the land, you will find the country people unfailingly friendly and always helpful. Providing the walker is also friendly, and behaves with due consideration, the country people in France do not seem to find it necessary to invoke their rights with any vigour and, since the countryside is large and increasingly empty, it is often possible to walk for days, at least in certain areas, without meeting a soul.

Gradings

This is a book for all walkers, and it is necessary to define the types of walking I had in mind when planning the book. Various methods of grading walks do exist, but I have divided walkers into three broad categories.

Backpackers: A backpacker is a walker who camps, carries all the necessary equipment to sustain life, and progresses without outside help or shelter, for up to a week.

Long-Distance Walker: A long distance walker will cover up to twenty miles a day or more, staying in hotels, *gîtes* or hostels. Lighter loads can be carried, although a tent and stove may be necessary in winter as a security measure.

The Day Walker: The day walker prefers to stay in one spot and walk out into the surrounding countryside on a day or half-day basis, carrying only a cagoule and a packed lunch.

I have kept these three categories in mind when analysing information and writing this book, attempting in each region to find areas suitable for each. There is, of course, a considerable degree of overlap, and the terrain and weather will affect the walk wherever you are.

Two methods of grading the actual walks apply and I am grateful to Waymark Holidays, a leading walking tour company with holidays in France, for permission to use their method.

Ungraded: These are holidays in good walking country in the mountains when wild flowers should be at their best. Walks are planned to see flowers and bird life rather than attain passes or summits, which even in mid-summer are still likely to be blocked with snow.

Grade 1: Walking mostly on paths, sometimes rocky, about four hours a day. Good shoes would do, but take boots if in mountains.

Grade 2: Walking as Grade 1, but about five hours a day. Boots preferable.

Grade 3: About six hours a day walking, sometimes off paths. Boots necessary. Comparable with Lakeland summits such as Helvellyn or Snowdon by one of the tracks.

Grade 4: About seven hours a day walking, some scrambling. Across the snow-line at times. Boots essential. Comparable with Ben Nevis, Bidean or the Cairngorms.

Grade 5: Up to eight hours a day walking, some scrambling. Often above the snow-line, depending on the season. Boots essential.

I have stopped at Grade 5 because the Waymark Grade 6 involves mountaineering. The grade shown by each walk refers to the section of the walk described, for over a long walk the terrain and difficulty will vary.

The Touring Club de France (TCF) grade their mountain walks as follows:

R1: Easy route on well marked trail, not too steep and below 2800 m with around 1200 m of ascent.

R2: More difficult, some steep sections, but set below 3000 m and around 1500 m of ascent.

R3: Involves crossing cols at around 3200 m with steep and exposed sections. Around 1700 m of ascent. Some easy icy sections.

R4: High altitude trail, more than 3000 m involving long stages between huts, paths often non-existent, icy sections easy but crevassed.

This method of grading is sometimes found in French guides. The R4 grade, like the Waymark Grade 6, reaches the lower limits of climbing.

When planning a walk, especially abroad, the walker has to decide his own particular grade and preference and match that against the normal rigours of the planned route. Then add in something for the weather and time of year. One constant factor is the terrain, which in France can be very varied indeed.

Terrain

Apart from being the largest country in Western Europe, France possesses an immense variety of terrain with two main mountain ranges, scores of lesser hills in the Massif Central, deep forests, high plateaux and rocky coasts. A general look at the terrain reveals that the north of the country, west from Normandy to Alsace-Lorraine is not too dissimilar from the southern part of the UK. Picardy and Artois, the area around Arras, are farming regions, marred by the coalpits of Arras and Lens, and bordered on the north by the hills of the Ardennes. Normandy is rolling farmland, while the Ile de France and Champagne are noted for great forests and deep river valleys. Most of this is suitable for day or long distance walking and only in the wooded mountainous Vosges does the country become in any sense remote and wild.

Brittany is another agricultural province, largely devoted to market gardening and fishing, similar to Cornwall in appearance, with a splendid coastline and much moorland in the centre. Brittany can cater for all grades of walker in moderate terrain. The great river Loire leads from Nantes up towards Touraine, through perfect walking country, but still well populated and suitable for long distance or day walking. All the western seaboard of France down to the south, as far as the deep forests of the Landes beyond Bordeaux and so into the Pays Basque, where the Pyrénées begin, is perfect for walking. The western coastline runs for 1500 km from Belgium south to the Bidassoa river which marks the frontier with Spain. Plans are currently afoot for a long distance coastal path here, but this coast is really a day- or long-distance walker's area.

Burgundy is a pleasant province, with the great forest of the Morvan as a central core, and plenty of good trails, but the committed walker will really feel a challenge when the Auvergne comes in sight. This area, where the Loire rises, is largely volcanic dominated by the mountains of the Massif Central, an upheaval which affects all central France and sprawls south to the Montagne Noire in distant Languedoc. This area is not particularly high, with the Puy de Sancy at 1886 being the highest peak, but there is snow cover in winter, while the summer can be exceedingly hot. The Auvergne, indeed all the Massif Central, is wild, spectacular walking country which, although catering for all grades, is especially suited to backpackers.

The eastern frontiers of France are marked by three hill and mountain ranges which grow progressively higher as they march south. They are the Vosges, the Jura, and the Alps, the latter containing the highest mountain in Europe, Mt.Blanc (4807 m). The Alps run on south from Lac Léman to the Alpes Maritimes in Provence, where they overlook the Mediterranean and are spanned by the long *Grande Traversée des Alpes* footpath.

South of the Auvergne lies the great plateaux country, the *Causses,* a high flatland at a little over the 1000 m mark, seamed with deep river valleys such as the Tarn. To the south and east lie further hills, the Cévennes, the Éspinouse, outcrops of the Massif Central, and finally, spanning the neck of land between the Atlantic and the Mediterranean, the Pyrénées. The foothills of the eastern Pyrénées, the Corbières and the Aspres, are full of good walks.

We will be looking at the terrain in detail in future chapters, but it is worth noting that although the south is generally warmer than the north, there is sure to be snow cover from November to April *anywhere* over 1000 m. and probably lower and longer in many mountain areas.

Climate

Apart from the terrain, the walker is greatly affected by the climate, (especially when carrying loaded rucksacks), and the weather is certainly a factor to take into account when walking in France.

In France, broadly speaking, the weather is varied but reliable, tending towards extremes, with very hot summers and cold snowy winters in the mountains. The weather is by no means always good but the worst effects can usually be anticipated, and must be taken into account when making plans.

Located between the Atlantic and the Mediterranean and backed by the European land mass to the east, France is subject to three major climatic influences, namely the Continental, the Oceanic (Atlantic) and the Mediterranean.

Brittany, the most westerly province, is greatly affected by the Atlantic, and the northern *départements* tend to be wetter than the southern ones. The temperature band is narrow, averaging 7 °C at Brest (south Brittany) in January, and 17 °C in August. Rainfall is frequent but light and it is *usually* drier in the south of Brittany.

Normandy and the Ile de France, further east around Paris, tend to be colder (2 °C in January) but marginally warmer on average in summer (19 °C in July) and the rainfall diminishes. Picardy and the

Pas de Calais have a climate similar to that of the UK.

Further east, still moving towards the mountains, the westerly airstreams rise, cool, and give further precipitation, so that Lorraine and Alsace tend to be dreary. The Massif Central is wetter and colder than the western regions in winter (below zero for ninety-six days a year in Clermont-Ferrand) but has warmer, dry summers, averaging 25 °C in June and July, and is by and large agreeable, although the snow can lie till April on the hills.

South of the Massif, the Mediterranean inflow heats the air and leads to extremes in the weather. Summers are dry and hot, there is heavy rain in spring and autumn with frequent thunderstorms, and in winter snow cover is over 1500 m. This weather tends towards the dramatic!

The chart below gives average temperatures for the various areas of France:

Av Air Temp °C	Mar-Apr	May-June	July-Aug	Sept-Oct
Brittany	12.9	18.9	22.6	19.6
Paris	13.2	21.1	24.3	18.1
North	12.5	20.5	23.8	17.9
Alsace-Lorraine	12.4	20.9	23.6	17.1
Loire Valley	13.9	21.8	25.4	18.9
Burgundy	5.4	16.9	19.2	15.5
Auvergne	14.3	22.1	25.9	19.0
Dauphiny Alps	15.0	23.2	27.2	20.7
Savoy Alps	13.1	22.0	25.?	18.2
Midi-Pyrénées	7.8	17.5	20.8	18.3
South-west	15.0	22.0	25.7	21.7
Provence	16.8	24.8	29.7	22.6
Riviera	16.8	22.1	27.1	22.9
Pyrénées-Roussillon	16.3	23.1	28.1	22.9
Basque country	14.9	20.1	24.0	21.1
Corsica	17.9	24.7	29.8	24.9

April to October I feel I can rely on good warm weather anywhere along or south of the Loire, including also Burgundy and Dauphiné, but I must quote instances to indicate that one can never rely completely on the climate.

We set out one September to walk the 190 km Robert Louis Stevenson Trail from Le Monastier near Le Puy in the Auvergne to St Jean-du-Gard in the Cévennes. The temperature should have been about 17 °C. In fact it was over 28 °C for most of the week, and we fried!

On another occasion, in October, we walked across the crest of the eastern Pyrénées from Cerdagne to Mont Canigou. We should have had golden autumn weather, but instead we had a blizzard, deep snow, torrential rain, and then, just as we abandoned the route, clear blue skies. On the other hand I have started a May walk in Brittany in a snow storm and finished it four days later by Mont St Michel in shorts and a suntan.

My advice is to study the weather forecasts carefully in the spring and autumn. In the summer you can usually rely on good hot weather (if you feel hot weather is good for walking), and from October to late May be prepared for all sorts of weather and snow cover on the ground anywhere over 1500 m. It is advisable to take shorts and sun oil in spring, and an ice axe in the autumn in the hills. You never know!

The Law for Walkers

Generally speaking the walker is free to roam in France over all footpaths and open tracks. Property is considered 'private' (*Propriété Privée*) and you cannot pass if it is encircled by a wall, ditch or fence and has a *Propriété Privée* or *Défense d'entrer* sign every 20 m., or if the land is cultivated.

No walker would, or should, trample on growing crops but, apart from the obvious example of fields of grain, there may be local by-laws covering the cultivation of mushrooms (*cépes*), snails (*escargots de Bourgogne*) which are cultivated under piles of stones and fed on vine leaves, chestnuts (*châtaigneraie*) and so on.

If any of these or other crops are being actually cultivated, the land is considered in the same way as an orchard *(verger)* and you cannot, or should not, pass over it. It is also common to seal off certain tracks and commune roads (*chemins communaux*) to prevent sheep and cattle straying. On these roads, and across the majority of tracks and footpaths, passage is authorised, or as the French put it, *toléré*. The signs *Reserve de Chasse* and *Chasse Privée* do not mean that walkers are excluded from the path. They simply mean that the shooting is reserved for the owner and his friends.

There are special regulations governing the National and Regional Parks, and the most relevant and usual ones are that wild camping is not permitted if a campsite exists: within one hour's march of a road or village; or under 1600 m. However, I have always found the country people very relaxed over their rights so, if the walker is generally observing the laws and doing no damage, there should be no problem.

The Country Code

The French too have a Country Code *(Code du Randonneur)* which all walkers in France should know and observe:-

1. Love and respect Nature.
2. Avoid unnecessary noise.
3. Destroy nothing.
4. Do not leave litter.
5. Do not pick flowers or plants.
6. Do not disturb wildlife.
7. Re-close all gates.
8. Protect and preserve the habitat.
9. No smoking or fires in the forests. (This rule is essential and actively enforced.)
10. Stay on the footpath.
11. Respect and understand the country way of life and the country people.
12. Think of others as you think of yourself.

Organisations

The principal organisation working for walkers in France is the FFRP -CNSGR, initials which stand for the *Fédération Française de Randonnée Pédestre — Comité National des Sentiers de Grande Randonnée.* This is based at 92 Rue de Clignancourt, 75883 Paris, Cedex 18. Tel: (1) 259-60-40. The FFRP-CNSGR has groups and affiliations all over France.

The CNSGR, as it is popularly called, originated in 1943 and was set up and organised as a national committee in 1947, largely at the instigation of the *Touring Club de France,* (TCF) which from the beginning has supported the aims of the CNSGR. These aims are, in short, to establish a network of long-distance footpaths *(grande randonnée)* all over France, link them with minor local footpaths *(petite randonnée),* supply the GR *(Grande Randonnée)* routes with facilities such as hostels *(gîtes d'étape)* and link the French GR paths with those of other nations.

These GR footpaths are waymarked, publicised in a series of topographic (or Topo) guides, and the CNSGR has succeeded to the point at which there are currently 30,000 km of waymarked *Grande Randonnée* trails and over 130 Topo guides. These Topo guides give a full description of the route, with maps, information on shelters, campsites, transportation, food replenishment points, timings and distances. There are occasional discrepancies between the guide's information and the facts on the ground, but in general they are excellent. Many of the walks have *variants*, or alternative routes. A Topo guide numbered GR14-141, for instance, indicates that the 141 is a *variant* of the main path. A *Tour* is usually a circular walk. The number of guides and footpath kilometres increases all the time. The FFPR-CNSGR also produces a monthly magazine, *Randonnée GR*, which not only gives news on new walks but also contains tear-out pages and sections with which to update your Topo guides.

The CNSGR has a committee of some twenty members, drawn from various organisations interested in the open air life. Apart from waymarking trails, producing guides and a monthly walker's magazine, equipping *gîtes d'étapes*, liaising with everyone on anything connected with walking, (from National Government to local landowners), it is also a major conservationist body.

Touring Club de France (TCF)

This organisation has its address at 65 Avenue de la Grande Armée, 75782 Paris, Cedex 16. Tel: (1) 502-14-00.

As the name implies, the TCF is concerned with all aspects of travel, but has a special interest in walking. The TCF maintains manned hostels open to members and non-members in many remote areas, has TCF rambling groups in most major provincial cities and produces a magazine, *Plein Air*, which if you read a little French, covers all aspects of outdoor activities in France. Membership of the TCF gives access to *gîtes* and shelters at reduced rates. It is possible to join the TCF through the FGTO, London.

Club Alpin Français (CAF)

This organisation is based at 7 Rue La Boétie, Paris 75008. It is primarily an organisation for climbers and mountaineers. The CAF has branches all over France and is affiliated to climbing associations all over the world. There are CAF huts and shelters in the mountain areas of France, open to members and non-members. It is advisable to join the CAF, which can only be done in France, or one of its affiliated organisatons, for this enables the member to reserve a place in a hostel, and to pay reduced rates for accommodation.

British Mountaineering Council

The British Mountaineering Council, Crawford House, Precinct Centre, Booth St. East, Manchester, is currently studying the possibility of introducing a 'Mountain Passport' which will give access to climbing huts everywhere at reduced fees.

Austrian Alpine Club

Huts operated by the *Club Alpin Français* and the *Touring Club de France* are open to all, but spaces can be reserved and rates are cheaper if the walker is a member or belongs to an affiliated club. In the UK the affiliated organisation is The Austrian Alpine Club (UK Section), 13 Longcroft House, Fretherne Road, Welwyn Garden City, Hertfordshire. Tel: Welwyn 31133.

Camping and Hostel Organisations

There are the numerous national organisations, notably:-

Fédération Française de Camping et de Caravanning, 78 Rue de Rivoli, 75004 Paris.

The Camping Club de France, 218 Boulevard St Germain, 75006 Paris.

The Fédération Unie des Auberges de la Jeunesse, 6 Rue Mesnil, 75116 Paris.

This last organisation is the French Youth Hostel Association.

Many outdoor organisations in the UK, such as the YHA and the Ramblers' Association, have contacts and co-membership agreements with similar bodies in France and can supply any necessary membership *carnets.*

In addition to those organisations mentioned above, there are literally scores of other associations concerned with walking. Useful addresses are given in each regional chapter.

Footpaths

The French countryside is criss-crossed with footpaths which are indicated on the 1:50000 IGN *(Institut Géographique National)* maps. All of these may be walked, but this section is concerned only with those trails which are waymarked.

The Grande Randonnée

The *Grande Randonnée* network of long distance footpaths now offers 30,000 km of varied trails for the enthusiastic walker. The basic idea is that a GR route, or Topo guide to a section of a long one, could take anything from three days to three weeks or even longer, depending on the terrain to be covered and the fitness of the walker. The GR 10 Trans Pyrénéan route offers more than 700 km of mountain walking in five guides and more than that if the diversions or *variants* are included. Anyone who can do that across mountains in three weeks has my respect! The GR 65, the Chemin de St Jacques, is even longer, but there are many shorter trails and no part

WAYMARKING OF GRANDE RANDONÉE SIGNS

The signs on GR paths consist of paint marks – horizontal red or white slashes that might either be on rocks, trees or walls. Double signs as shown below, which have arrows, show direction changes. The frequency of the waymarks depends on the terrain. From time to time, small square signboards give the number of the GR, or there are waymark arrows. Examples of GR waymarking are given below.

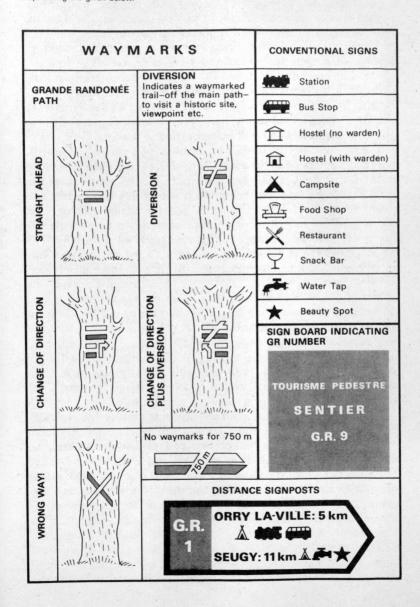

WAYMARKS			CONVENTIONAL SIGNS	
GRANDE RANDONÉE PATH	**DIVERSION** Indicates a waymarked trail–off the main path– to visit a historic site, viewpoint etc.			Station
				Bus Stop
STRAIGHT AHEAD	DIVERSION			Hostel (no warden)
				Hostel (with warden)
				Campsite
				Food Shop
				Restaurant
				Snack Bar
CHANGE OF DIRECTION	CHANGE OF DIRECTION PLUS DIVERSION			Water Tap
				Beauty Spot
			SIGN BOARD INDICATING GR NUMBER	
			TOURISME PEDESTRE SENTIER G.R. 9	
WRONG WAY!	No waymarks for 750 m			
	DISTANCE SIGNPOSTS			
	G.R. 1 ORRY LA-VILLE: 5 km SEUGY: 11 km			

of France is without its GR route or routes and you can find one which suits your style of walking and the time available without difficulty. An up-to-date list of GR routes, actual and planned, is given in the appendices.

GR routes are waymarked *(balisées)* with red and white paint-slashes on trees or posts which, in various combinations, show the route and give directions. GR routes are usually in sections and can be either lateral or circular. Many routes have alternative routes, or *variants,* and some have additional sections as well. The choice is vast and increasing all the time. The major project currently in hand is the French Coastal Path, which will run along the coast from the Belgian frontier to the Spanish frontier, then across the Pyrénées to the Mediterranean and east to Italy. This is developing at the rate of one kilometre a day and will be completed in 1998.

The CNSGR is also devoted to establishing a network of hostels, huts and shelters along the routes of the GRs and it should be borne in mind that the CNSGR and walkers in general are welcomed in rural France because they bring much needed life and income into many depopulated areas. The *gîtes* and the various timings and stages given in the GR Topo guides assume seven hours walking a day as a fair average, at a speed of approximately 4 km per hour. The Topo guides are in French, illustrated with marked maps. While these guides are generally excellent they are not, and probably cannot be, entirely up-to-date. Off the well-beaten trail I always, as a matter of policy, use my compass and am not too surprised to find huts shut or the route invisible. The waymarking can be a little hit and miss and tends to peter out just as you need it.

In mountain areas the Topo guides give timings in hours and minutes, rather than distances, and it should be noted that as French walkers tend to use shelters or *gîtes* rather than camp, the timings assume light loads rather than full rucksacks. Remember that a GR route described as a *Tour* is usually a circular walk.

The CNSGR does not recommend any long trail, or one over difficult terrain, for children under ten years of age.

GR trails are ideal for backpackers or long-distance walkers, depending on the accommodation available en route.

The IGN *(Institut Géographique National)* Map No. 903, shows the *Sentiers de Grande Randonnée,* and the CNSGR produces a brochure, *La France des Sentiers,* which shows all the major paths.

Neither gives details of local footpaths or *drailles.*

Drailles

A *draille* is a drove road. The word *draille* is an Occitan word, deri-

ved from the *langue d'oc*, (the old language of the South) and means a
road or trail used for the *transhumance*, the annual trek of cattle to
and from their summer pasture, high in the mountains. Some *drailles*
form part of GR trails, like the Grande Draille de Languedoc on
Mont Lozère.

They are often clearly marked by centuries of such use, but are
still wild and have often been taken over by the CNSGR. As the
word is Occitan, *drailles* are most common in the South, notably in
the Cévennes, in Lozère, and the Causses, and in the Pyrénées.
There is an *Association Drailles*, Grande Rue, 30360 Vézenobres,
France, which covers the Cévennes and Lozère routes and organises
trips along the *transhumance* trails deep into the *arrière-pays*. I enjoy
draille walks, and recommend them to long-distance walkers who like
getting off the well-trodden footpaths.

Sentiers de Pays

Since there are 30,000 km of GR trails, there must be well over
100,000 km of *sentiers de pays*, or local footpaths. There are very few
areas of France where the local people are not marking out their local
footpaths, and here again the prime source of information is the *Syndicat d'Initiative*. *Sentiers de pays* are ideal for day walking and, since
in any region some areas are clearly more suitable than others, I will
mention good day walking areas in each regional chapter. This list
cannot be exhaustive since it is based on local information and my
own preferences but it will certainly take the day walker to many
beautiful and little-known areas with lots of footpaths to explore.

It should not be thought that *all sentiers de pays* are short. The *sentier de pays* 'Le Tour de l'Aubrac' is currently a *sentier de pays*, but it
would take five or six days' marching to cover it. These long *sentiers
de pays* are organised and often waymarked by local footpath organisations, to spread the word in their own area or fill a local need, but
they are usually adopted by the CNSGR in the end. I have seen them
described in the interval as *GR — Sentiers de pays;* this is done to
confuse us!

Waymarking (Balisage)

The French are very fond of waymarking, and have developed it to
the point at which some control has become necessary. There are
waymarked trails *(routes balisées)* all over the country and all are now
colour coded. GR trails are waymarked with red and white horizontal slashes, or increasingly, where trails overlap, with red and yellow
slashes. Horse riding trails *(sentiers de randonnée équestre)* are waymarked in orange.

Ski touring or cross country skiing trails are waymarked in colours which show the degree of difficulty, green, blue, red, black, in ascending order of difficulty. Even when the snow has gone these marks remain.

All other trails, including *sentiers de pays*, should be waymarked in any combination of yellow, green, blue or black, the favoured waymark being two horizontal slashes in different colours.

The more established local groups, like Club Vosgien or those in the Cévennes, also use signboards, sometimes indicating the routes with illustrations of small animals. These signposts *(jalons)* usually also note time and distance to the end of the stage.

Towpaths

The walker who restricts him or herself to the waymarked trail, may be missing a great deal. I have walked along several towpath trails in France and they have a great deal to offer the walker. They are flat and often shady. The lock keepers are friendly, always ready for a chat, and will supply wine, water, eggs and a pitch for your tent, with very little prompting. Small towns and villages appear at regular intervals and the traffic on the canal is constantly interesting. There are canals all over France, many still in active operation, and I particularly recommend the Canal du Midi in Languedoc, the Canal du Nivernais in Burgundy, the Canal du Rhône in Eastern Languedoc and Provence, the Canal Latéral de la Loire, and the Breton canals. Not all canals have towpaths, as modern canals don't need them, but the historic canals like those mentioned above, date from the time of the horse-drawn barges and are more interesting anyway.

Historic Trails and Pilgrimages

"When in Aprill, the sweete showers fall and pierce the drought of March een to the roote then people longe to goe on pilgrimage . . . ."
. . . and I confess that I am one of them. Robert Louis Stevenson said that he travelled 'but to go', and I sympathise, but walking can be an intellectual exercise as well as the process of putting one foot in front of the other and smelling flowers, and every walk should have an objective.

France is full of pilgrim sites and many footpaths follow the routes of old pilgrim trails and take the foot traveller along the actual trail of his or her ancestors.

Chief of these is the GR 65, the Road to Compostelle, or *Chemin de St Jacques*, which crosses France from Le Puy in the Auvergne to St-Jean-Pied-de-Port on the doorstep of Spain. This is well over 1000 km without diversions *(variants)* but you can do it, as I have, in short stages spread over the years. The GR 65 is covered by several Topo guides.

Burgundy has pilgrim sites on GR trails at Vézelay, at Paray-le-Monial in the South, at Cluny on the GR 76 from Lyon, and at Nevers on the Loire by the GR 3 or 31, where the body of St Bernadette of Lourdes can still be seen at the Convent of St Guildard. In the Dauphiné there is a fine trek of 60 km from Grenoble to the sanctuary of La Salette, set high in magnificent mountain scenery. If the mountains are too testing, the Pilgrimage of Ars in Bresse, in the *département* of the Ain should be suitable. The shrine of St Armadour at Rocamadour in Quercy, near Cahors, in Midi-Pyrénées, is magnificent, containing one of the rare mediaeval Black Virgins, and can be reached on the GR 6 along the Dordogne, or across the hills of Quercy on the GR 46.

Charles Péguy made a memorable pilgrimage to Chartres from Paris across the flat country of the Beauce. Although this is unmarked it is a route well worth following, as many Parisian students still do. In Brittany the GR 34 from Rennes will take the pilgrim walker to the shrine of St Michael on Mont St Michel. France is crammed with such shrines, and they are often set in remote and beautiful places. I recommend a walk across the Aubrac on the GR 65 to the shrine of Ste Foy at Conques, or down the GR 46 to Toulouse and the Cathedral of St Sernin, which contains the shrine of my favourite saint, St Jude, the patron saint of lost causes!

A leaflet, *Pilgrimages in France,* can be obtained from the SNCF (French Railways) in Piccadilly, London.

European Footpaths: Sentiers Européens de Grande Randonnée

There are currently six Trans-European footpaths, part of a network which will, one day, cover the Continent as the GR covers France.

The E 2 from Ostend to Nice enters France from Luxembourg, skirts the German frontier, crosses the Jura, and eventually, via Savoie and Haute Provence, descends to the sea. The distance inside France is around 800 km out of a total distance of some 2000 km.

The E 3 crosses France from Royan on the Atlantic coast, exits through Luxembourg and terminates on the border of Czechoslovakia. The distance inside France is over 1000 km.

The E 4 runs from Puigcerda in the Eastern Pyrénées, through France and as far as Hungary, and again has 1000 km inside France, running from the Pyrénées across some spectacular country in Ardèche and Lozère.

These European footpaths follow the course of existing GR routes, and are indicated in green on the IGN 903 maps.

The walker who uses a little imagination can find walks of all kinds within the framework of France.

National and Regional Parks

There are a great many National and Regional Parks in France. Their aim is to preserve large areas from commercial exploitation and restrict development to those projects which benefit the inhabitants while preserving the flora and fauna in their natural habitat.

These Parks can be found all over France and they are always worth visiting, although some, like the Camargue in the Rhône delta, and the Brière in Southern Brittany, are fairly waterlogged for much of the year. Those parks set in mountain districts are ideal centres for hard day-walking or backpacking.

The Parks contain many hundreds of kilometres of footpaths, and are served by a sensible number of hostels, *gîtes* and refuges. As a general rule, wild camping is not permitted where campsites are available, but in practice, and provided the camper is careful with fire, a small walker's tent on a one-night pitch will not arouse disapproval.

Legislation is currently being introduced to set up a series of 'grands sites', the equivalent of the UK's Areas of Outstanding Natural Beauty. Among such areas are Cap Gris Nez and Blanc Nez, the Crozan Peninsula in Brittany, the *cirque* de Navacelles in Hérault, the Puy de Dôme and the Puy Mary in Cantal. These areas will apparently be cleared of man-made 'improvements' like camping and caravan sites and restored to their natural state.

Tourist Offices and Syndicats

As I have already mentioned, there are tourist offices, *Maison du Tourisme* or *Syndicat d'Initiative* in most villages and in all French towns. These act as a centre for information on all local activities and as a central link for all tourism, often as prime movers in laying out and waymarking local footpaths. It is always a good idea, when arriving in any French town or village, to ask at the *Syndicat*, (the location of which is usually signposted), for any information on local footpaths *(sentiers)* or campsites *(les campings)*. In some areas, and Luchon in the Pyrénées is an example which springs to mind, the local *Syndicat* has excellent facilities available for walkers. I have also found the *Syndicat* helpful when seeking a pitch in a place which has no campsite and, so far anyway, have never failed to find somewhere to pitch my tent. If there is no *Syndicat,* or it is shut, the smallest bar is usually the place to ask for help, information or accommodation.

Accommodation

In most regions, even in the high mountains, it is not always necessary to carry a tent, (although this may sometimes be desirable from the safety angle), as there is a wide variety of accommodation available.

Hotels

Hotels in France are good, numerous and cheap. Cheap, that is, compared with many parts of the world, and often very cheap indeed in country districts. Hotels are graded on a star system from one to five, and in country districts a one or two star hotel should provide adequate accommodation for a walker. Prices have to be declared, pinned to each bedroom door and include service and taxes. It is always advisable to inspect the room and the price before accepting it. The *patron* of the hotel expects this and will not be surprised or annoyed by a request to view the room.

In rural France many of the hotels belong to an organisation called the *Fédération Nationale des Logis et Auberges de France,* and a check through their 1982 handbook reveals no less than 3466 *Logis* and 629 of the cheaper *Auberges.* Their guide book can be obtained from the FGTO, London. Logis are small, one or two star family hotels, and the Auberges, which fall below this category, are simpler and therefore cheaper. Both will usually provide meals and they normally expect the visitor to eat in the hotel as a condition of accepting accommodation.

Chambres d'hôte (Guest Rooms)

Accommodation is always in short supply, so a new scheme sponsored by the *Gîtes de France* organisation is currently being developed, with the aim of providing guest rooms in the smaller villages. The numbers currently available are certain to grow.

Auberges de Jeunesse (Youth Hostels)

There are just over two hundred Youth Hostels in France, but very few outside the larger towns (say 40,000 inhabitants) and hardly any in the country districts. A list can be obtained from the YHA in the UK, or from the *Fédération Unie des Auberges de la Jeunesse,* 6 Rue Mesnil, 75116 Paris.

Cafés

If there is no hotel in the village, and no obvious sign of a *chambre d'hôte*, then head at once for the nearest bar or café. Many smaller villages have cafés which offer rooms and I have in the past year (1981) paid as little as 19 francs for a double room with shower.

The solitary traveller, intending to stay in small hotels and cafés, could currently budget for 75 francs per night for his room and dinner, and be well within this budget in the course of a week. Breakfast is usually extra, costing from 8 francs to 12 francs per person.

Two points are worth remembering when using cafés, guest rooms or hotels. Firstly the *patron* may expect you to eat there. Secondly, never take a room without looking at it first. The *patron* will expect you to do so, and if the room is unsuitable you can ask for another one. You should try to book ahead by telephone, particularly in July and August. Finally, the pillows are in the wardrobe!

Gîtes

Rented holiday homes or *gîtes* are an increasing feature of the French tourist scene. These, however, are usually *Gîtes de France*, holiday cottages, and the walker is more interested in finding *gîtes d'étape*. The phrase is almost untranslatable, but a *gîte d'étape* is best imagined as an unmanned youth hostel.

The CNSGR is attempting to establish *gîtes d'étape* along all the GR trails at distances of around three hours' march apart, and these are listed in the Topo guides. There are various types of *gîtes*. Some are converted barns or stables, others are part of larger hotels or houses. Many are owned by farmers for extra money, some are owned by the local commune, who get a grant from the Ministry of Agriculture towards the cost of building or conversion. *Gîtes d'étape* come in all shapes and sizes and are ideal for the long-distance walker, or to shelter the backpacker in really foul weather.

A typical *gîte* can shelter between ten and thirty people, who sleep in dormitories on bunks and in their own sleeping bags. It will have a common room with tables and chairs, a kitchen, showers and lavatories. The maximum stay is three days and the current price is around 20 francs per night. If the *gîte* has a warden *(le gardien)* he or she may provide a meal.

The *gîtes d'étape* network is constantly expanding and established *gîtes* are listed in the Topo guides. These may not yet include new *gîtes* so here again the *Comité Régional de Tourisme* or the local *Syndicat* should be contacted for current rates and availability. Whenever possible, telephone ahead to reserve a place. Otherwise in summer the *gîte* can be full, and in winter it may be closed.

Refuges or Abris (Shelters)

The mountain regions of France are well supplied with a variety of refuges or *abris*, usually constructed in stone by either the CAF or the TCF. The size varies enormously. Some have wardens and some have not. Some are permanently open, some usually shut. Some cost money, others are free. They offer limited and cramped accommodation, but are usually warm, possess a stove, and if you use them, then except for emergency use, a tent is rendered unnecessary. The sites of refuges are given on most maps in the IGN series and in the Michelin series in scales from 1-200,000 (1 cm = 2 km) upwards. Information on *abris* or refuges is available from local and regional offices of the CAF or TCF. They are usually shown in the Topo guides.

Campsites

France has thousands of campsites, private, municipal, communal, all graded like hotels from one to five stars.

Current prices range upwards from 5 francs per tent per night, and the facilities vary from the spartan to the elaborate. The walker with a small tent can ignore full *(complet)* signs, for a little backpacking tent will usually go in somewhere, and the *gardiens* are normally accommodating. I have never been asked for a camping *carnet* for my little tent, but a group of walkers may need one. Camping *carnets* can be obtained in the UK from the Camping Club, YHA, Cycle Touring Club, etc.

Lists of available campsites are available by region from the FGTO and local *Syndicats*.

Camping à la Ferme

Like the *gîtes d'étape*, the *camping à la ferme* scheme has developed from the need to provide local people in the rural areas of France with a little extra money and some fresh faces. Signs indicating the presence of a *camping à la ferme* site are springing up all over France.

A *camping à la ferme*, or farm camping site, consists of a small area on a farm, able to contain about six tents and provides the camper with simple facilities like running water, sanitation and some farm produce. These sites are often off the normal tourist routes, very quiet and frequently very pleasant, the ideal pitch for a wandering backpacker.

Wild Camping

Wild camping, *camping sauvage* or *à la belle étoile*, is not actively encouraged. In the National and Regional Parks it is actually forbidden, and frowned upon in areas where there is a high fire risk, which means most forests and scrub *(garrigue)* areas below the Loire. Where possible it is advisable to use a *camping à la ferme* pitch, but as usual in France, while there are laws, there are also tacit exceptions for the small tent in the remote areas. As a rough guide, the walker over 1500 m, one hour away from a *gîte,* or clearly keeping out of sight, will probably have no trouble. It does mean, however, that in turn the walker must leave no litter and be very careful with fire and cigarettes.

Maps and Guides

France is serviced by a number of map makers, the chief of which are Michelin, Editions Didier-et-Richard of Grenoble, and above all, the Institut Géographique National, the French equivalent of the UK Ordnance Survey, situated at 107 Rue la Boetie, 75008 Paris. Tel: (1) 225-87-90.

The IGN shop, just off the Champs Elysées, is a mecca for the walker in France for, apart from a wide variety of maps in all sizes, the IGN stocks Topo guides, various guide books and all sorts of walking information. All walking tours in France should begin there.

The basic tool for the walker in France is the IGN 1:100,000 (1 cm = 10 km) Map No. 903, *Sentiers de Grande Randonnée,* which shows all the GR routes in France as well as the National Parks, and gives an excellent idea of the terrain. There are no contours but heights are shown in the mountain areas. This map also acts as the catalogue for the CNSGR Topo guides, showing the routes, although allowances should be made for the fact that it can rarely be completely up-to-date as it is only re-printed every three to four years, while the GR network develops all the time.

The IGN also publishes topographic maps with contours scale 1:50,000 (1¼ inches = 1 mile) or 2 cm = 1 km, and 1:25,000 (2½ = 1 mile) or 4 cm = 1 km. Both are excellent for walking in remote country, show many footpaths other than those waymarked, and give lots of detail. The 1:25,000 is best for the high mountains and recommended for winter use. The CNSGR Topo guides use 1:50,000 extracts to illustrate their routes. The IGN also produces special maps for the National Parks, and a number of favourite outdoor areas like the Cerdagne and Capcir in the Eastern Pyrénées. IGN maps are available all over France and from Stanfords Map Shop, Long Acre, London, and McCarta Ltd., 122 Kings Cross Rd, London WC1X 9DS, tel: 01-278-8278, the IGN agents in the UK.

Map Reading

No one familiar with OS maps will have any real difficulty with IGN maps, but there are certain differences. For example, the interval between contour lines on the 1:50,000 is 20 m and on the 1:25,000 10 m. On some maps both contour intervals are given. Check the contour intervals and conventional signs in the map information panel.

The magnetic variation *(Déclinaison Magnétique)* varieş in different parts of France, and should therefore be checked on each map, with allowances made for annual rate of change. When no variation is known, I set a variation of 5 °W on my compass and this has proved effective and adequate, for the variation across France ranges from between just over 3 °W to just under 7 °W. However, I prefer to use the actual variation if I can find out what it is.

Eastern France, the Alps and Jura are well mapped by Editions Didier-et-Richard of Grenoble. Their 1:50,000 maps, incidentally, use both 10 and 20 m contour intervals and are over printed with GR trails. Michelin maps are not a great deal of use for the off-road walker, who will use IGN, Didier or the Topo guides, but there are many other local maps available in scales from 1:20,000 to 1:50,000, and the best place to find these is in the main local bookshop or newsagent *(librairie* or *Maison de la Presse)*. Not all shops stock maps suitable for walkers but the IGN-CNSGR will have a stockist in the major town of each region, and their addresses are given in the relevant chapters.

The current rage for open air activities has given France a rich store of guidebooks to complement the basic maps. The Michelin 'Green' guides are a useful source of background information and give guidance to favoured outdoor areas.

CNSGR Topo guides are clearly the most useful for GR routes, although not always accurate or up-to-date. Local *Syndicats* can provide maps and folders on the *sentiers de pays* and these are often full of information on weather conditions, campsites, *gîtes,* and the local attractions to be found along the way.

Apart from the CNSGR, good walking guides are available from Fayard, in their *Sentiers et Randonnées* series which covers most of France, from the Club Alpin Français, from Didier-et-Richard, and various French and foreign publishers, notably West Col and Cicerone Press in the UK. These and much other information can be found or obtained in the UK at Stanfords Ltd, 14 Long Acre, London WC2, or from Hachette Ltd., 1 Regent Place, London W1, from McCarta Ltd, from the CNSGR, the IGN shop in Paris, or from local bookshops and *Syndicats* in France. A list of guide books is given in the bibliography and in the relevant chapters.

Health and Hazards

At this point, and before planning any tour, it would be as well to study again the terrain and climate sections at the start of this chapter, for they will affect the rest of this section. Any traveller abroad should also check his or her insurance and have adequate cover for personal injury and loss or theft of equipment.

The walker in France, given some experience in his or her home area, will encounter no particular difficulties, but the following thoughts are worth considering and, as with all physical activity, it pays to be fit before you start. An element of pre-trip training is therefore always advisable.

Heat and Cold

South of the Loire it will certainly be very hot in summer and the risk of heat stroke or heat exhaustion must be considered. Heavy sweating is inevitable, so add some salt tablets to the First Aid kit. Use a sun barrier cream and a lip salve until you face has weathered. A great deal of discomfort will be saved if the walker is fit enough to travel at least the required daily distance without excessive strain and loaded as required, before arriving in France.

From October to May, mountain or hill walkers must be equipped to cope with severe weather, snow and ice, by wearing warm protective clothing and carrying ice-axes and crampons.

Snake Bite

France possesses two varieties of viper and, although bites are very rare, people do die of snake bite every year. Vipers are most common in the Massif Central, the Alps, Provence, and in Languedoc. Each walker would be well advised to carry a snake bite kit, available from chemists *(pharmacies)* in most parts of France. *Serum Anti Venimeux* is available in France in syringes for self-injection and this is effective against the venom of both types of snake. A good knowledge of First Aid, including treatment for snake bite, is essential. If no serum is immediately available and medical help unobtainable at the time, the bite should be opened and the poison sucked or squeezed out. The casualty should stay as still as possible, with cold compresses applied to the area. The casualty must be examined by a doctor as quickly as possible. He or she must not be allowed to rush about in panic as this will disperse the poison through the bloodstream with undesirable effects.

Rabies (La Rage)

Rabies is active in France, but by no means common; I never even think about it when walking there. A bite from a wild animal or farm dog should still be taken seriously, however, for if untreated a rabid bite is fatal and the death an extremely unpleasant one.

The treatment, apart from hurriedly washing the wound with soap and water, is to go *immediately to a doctor,* preferably with the animal that bit you (alive or dead). Tests will reveal if the animal is rabid.

Fortunately a new drug has been developed which, given in one injection, serves as an antidote to the disease, and if given beforehand will serve as a prophylactic, although in the case of a rabid bite, a second injection is advisable. Rabies injections are available from Thomas Cook's Vaccination Centre, Stratton St., London W1 and from other vaccination centres throughout the country.

Clothing and Equipment

Depending on the activity you have in mind, a normal walking, backpacking or lightweight camping scale of clothing and equipment will be adequate but, given the climate and terrain factors, several optional items elsewhere do become either essential or more useful. Reduce this for long distance walking or day walks. However, for France, certain items will always be either essential or very useful:

Essential: A phrase book and dictionary, map *(carte),* compass *(la boussole).*

In summer: Sun cream, lip salve, hat, swimming costume, shorts, sunglasses.

Many walkers now find heavy boots unsuitable and tiring and are wearing light boots or training shoes. A sensible compromise is to take boots and a pair of trainers as well, for use either on the trail or at the campsite. Boots are essential in the Alps and Pyrénées to support the ankle, but the lighter the boots are, the better.

In winter: A warm ear-covering hat, rain- and wind-proof clothing, a change of dry clothing.

In the mountains (over 500 m) from mid-October to April: An ice axe *(piolet),* 10-point crampons, survival kit (see kit list).

If any scrambling or much snow work is even possible, you will also need: A rope and an avalanche cord or *sonde.*

I have carried these last two items with reluctance but there have been occasions when I had cause to be grateful that I had done so. Once you are away from home it is too late to wish you had the equipment, so at the cost of a little extra weight, you will be well equipped should the unexpected happen. A full kit list for walking abroad is given in the appendices.

Walking Holidays

It may be that some people are sensibly cautious about venturing into foreign mountains without some initial guidance. Guides are available locally, but a simple way to start is to take a walking holiday, organised by an activity holiday company. The three main companies specialising in walking holidays are:

Waymark Holidays (Alps, Pyrénées, Cévennes, Provence, R.L.Stevenson Trail), 295 Lillie Road, London SW6, tel: 01-385-5015.

Ramblers Holidays (Auvergne, Brittany, Alps, Normandy, Provence, Picardy), 13 Longcroft House, Fretherne Road, Welwyn Garden City, Hertfordshire AL8 6QP, tel: (07073) 31133.

Countrywide Holidays Association (CHA) (Pyrénées, Auvergne, Alps), Buch Hayes, Cromwell Range, Manchester M14 6HU, tel: (061 224) 2887-8.

First steps in the mountains might be taken with one of these companies, but most of France, including the mountains of the Auvergne and the Alps, is perfectly accessible on your own, although safer with a companion until you gain confidence.

Food

On backpacking trips deep into the back country, I take all my main meals with me in the form of AFD (freeze dried) food from Mountain House, Springlow or Raven, and supplement it by buying wine, eggs, cheese and bread from farms or shepherds, or descending on a village when I feel like a hot fresh meal. Camping Gaz cartridges and 2-star petrol for stoves are obtainable everywhere in France, and prices are no higher and in some cases lower than in the UK, but paraffin and methylated spirits are less readily available.

Planning your Walk

Preparation is the secret of a successful walk (particularly when the walk is made abroad, and perhaps for an extended period), and the key to successful preparation is accurate information.

The first points to decide are, what you are going to do, with whom you are going to do it, where you are going, and when. Walking alone in the mountains, even in summer, has to be discouraged, but elsewhere should pose no special problems.

When you have assessed the possibilities, the main requirement is for accurate information. To gather this, start at the FGTO, 178 Piccadilly, London W1, with a request for information on the region.

(Enclose 50p in stamps to cover return postage). Write also to the local Tourist Offices (see sample letter in the appendices) and study maps, especially the IGN No. 903. Visit bookshops and libraries, and read guidebooks; note relevant magazine articles; talk to anyone who knows your chosen region.

You will therefore need to get information on:-

1. Terrain
2. Weather
3. Getting there (air, train, road)
4. Walks available
5. Relevant maps and guides
6. Accommodation available
7. Kit required (with weights)
8. Health problems
9. Training or skills necessary
10. Food
11. Money and cost — prepare a budget
12. Timings and stages.

The information in this book was collected from many sources, checked and counter-checked, and then condensed into the present format. It will provide the walker with all the basic facts necessary to choose an area of France, and to decide on a suitable walk. It gives sources of any further information necessary for the execution of a particular trip. Each chapter is self-contained, which will avoid searching for a reference in another section. Where an area has some particular feature which I think British walkers will like, then this has been indicated.

Having amassed all the relevant information, you can plan your walk with a fair degree of success and measure the results by achieving what you aimed to achieve and, above all, by enjoying yourself.

THE NORTH OF FRANCE

The walker planning a trip to France might not instantly decide on the Northern provinces. He or she might suspect that the north can be cold and rainy, with a climate and terrain not too different from that of the UK. This is all correct. The walker might then decide that this being so, Northern France is dreary and unsuitable, and this would be quite incorrect.

The Northern frontier provinces: Picardy, Artois (the area around Arras), Ile de France, Champagne and the Ardennes, are rich in history and architecture, set amid fine gentle countryside, with pleasant inns, reasonably good weather, but most important of all, good access via the many Channel ports. This region is ideal for short visits, offering enjoyable walking in attractive countryside.

Historically, the region, battle scarred from the dawn of history to the present day, is full of interest. For much of recorded time it lay outside the demesne of France and was once a centre for the Flemish wool trade. Tapestries came from Arras, cambric from Cambrai. Picardy came to the kingdom as late as the fifteenth century, the English held the Calais *pale* until the mid-sixteenth century, and Louis XIV, in the early eighteenth century, was still at war with the Spanish Hapsburgs to secure these Northern frontiers, long before modern Belgium even existed. The very name of Flanders has spelled doom to foreign armies for over four hundred years.

This northern territory has always been a pathway into France, down which invaders marched on the capital at Paris, so that the names of these northern towns and villages are enrolled on a hundred battle flags. This is the country of Agincourt and Crécy, of Rocroi and Sedan, of the Somme and the Chemin des Dames, of Dunkirk and the Ardennes.

The Region Today

Northern France has a mixed economy. Picardy is farmland, the Artois region is dotted with the coal pits and iron works of an industrial inheritance, and Champagne has, well, champagne. The Ile de France contains the great hunting forests and classical *châteaux* of the French nobility, together with much light industry. Apart from industrial and commercial activities, each region has areas which will appeal to the walker.

These Northern regions have no historic unity and today contain no less than thirteen rural *départements*.

Nord Pas-de-Calais: Pas-de-Calais, and Nord.

Picardy: Somme, Oise, Aisne.

Ile de France: Val d'Oise, Seine-et-Marne, Essonne, and Yvelines (plus three *départements* which are effectively suburbs of Paris).

Champagne-Ardennes: Ardennes, Aube, Marne, Haute-Marne.

The North contains some great cities: Lille, Reims, Châlons, Troyes, Laon, Amiens, Meaux, and many more, all full of architectural and historic interest and providing the perfect starting point for a walking tour. These regions contain a high percentage of the French population but there is still plenty of room, lots of countryside, and a great variety of terrain, enough to enable the walker to be selective, in the choice of route, region and time of year.

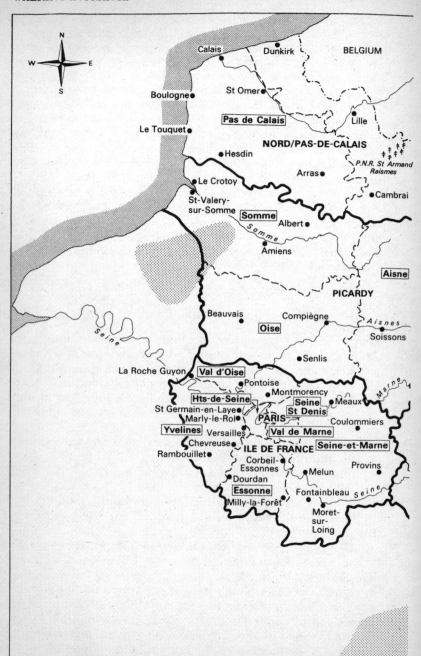

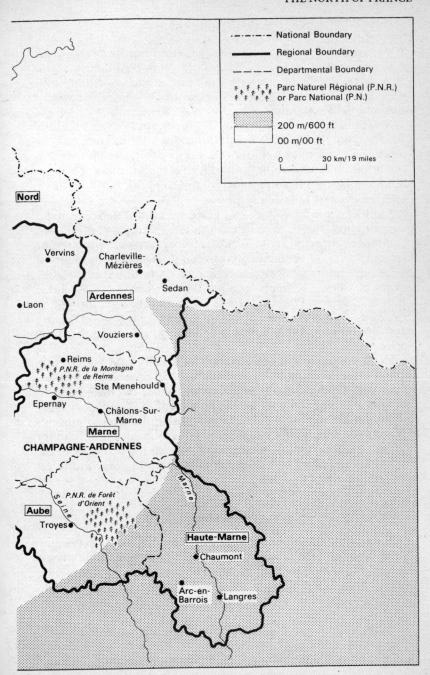

National Boundary
Regional Boundary
Departmental Boundary
Parc Naturel Régional (P.N.R.)
or Parc National (P.N.)

200 m/600 ft

00 m/00 ft

0   30 km/19 miles

Nord

Vervins

Charleville-
Mézières

Sedan

Ardennes

Laon

Vouziers

Reims

P.N.R. de la Montagne
de Reims

Ste Menehould

Epernay

Châlons-Sur-
Marne

Marne

CHAMPAGNE-ARDENNES

Marne

P.N.R. de Forêt
d'Orient

Seine

Aube

Troyes

Haute-Marne

Chaumont

Arc-en-
Barrois

Langres

Physical Description

If we begin in the North, at Calais, our roads run South and West, across the rolling country of the Pas-de-Calais *département,* not so very different from the gentle hills of Kent, to which this region was once joined. The only disruption to this chalky region is caused by the river valleys, running West into the Channel, the Canche, the Authie, and the ominous Somme. There are some crinkles south of St Omer, but the farmland is lightly wooded until we pass the open country of the Somme west of Arras and Cambrai, and turn towards the Belgian frontier and the forested hills of the Ardennes. These are not high hills, being only about 500 m (1,500 ft.), but it is closely wooded country, full of footpaths.

South of the river Somme, we enter the ancient demesne of the French kings, the Ile de France, a forested farming region which completely encircles Paris. There are fine, historically interesting walks in these former hunting preserves, through the vast forests of Fontainebleau up to Compiègne, then to Rambouillet, or along the valley of Chevreuse from Versailles. Further east lie the vine-clad hills of Champagne, where there is excellent walking country south of Reims, in the Parc Naturel Régional, or in the triangle of country that lies between Laon, Reims and Soissons, and along the Aisne river.

Northern France will appeal to those who like gentle day walks, or long-distance walking through a land rich in history and architecture, with plenty of opportunities for day tours, and the enjoyment of food and wine along the way. The walking is all grades 1 and 2, with only the distances in the forests raising the level to grade 3. Having said that, there are some good GR trails and at least one very interesting, long and challenging walk, around the perimeter of the Ile de France, which takes in many of the great *châteaux* and Royal Palaces, the GR 1.

Climate

The climate in this area resembles that of the UK but with two useful differences. Firstly, it is perceptibly drier, as the Atlantic westerlies have shed much of their moisture on the British Isles. Secondly, as we move east, the 'Atlantic' influence gives way to the more extreme 'Continental' weather pattern which gives warmer summers and colder winters.

In the Champagne-Ardennes region for example, the mean summer temperature is 22 °C, and the average winter temperature around 5 °C. The heavier rains fall in the winter, and the Continental influence can produce prolonged dry periods in spring and autumn. The autumn is the ideal time for walking here, especially in the forests when the leaves are changing colour.

Walking in the *Départements*

Even excluding the three *départements* of the Paris *banlieu,* the regions covered in this chapter can still muster the round baker's dozen, most of which contain areas with something to offer.

Pas-de-Calais and Nord

These can be taken together, since they are similar and the Nord *département* is very small. The region runs from the Belgian frontier to the river Authie, below Le Touquet, and provides two main possibilities, either a coastal walk, or a tour along the ridge north of Hesdin, the *collines* (hills) *de l'Artois.* A little north of these hills lies Agincourt, or, as it is more correctly called, Azincourt, (site of the battle of 1415), while to the south of Hesdin, a long ridge marks the site of the battle of Crecy (1346).

Arras is a good centre for exploring the northern battlefields of the 1914-18 war, Vimy Ridge, Loos, Festubert, each an interesting if somewhat melancholy day walk.

Picardy

Picardy musters three *départements,* and is a region made familiar to the British during the Great War. The countryside has recovered from that long devastation, and is now gentle farmland, dotted with little villages and small agreeable towns.

Somme: The Somme is chalkland, and arable farming country. There is interesting coastal walking around Le Crotoy on the Bay of the Somme: ideal for watching seabirds and waders. From Albert, north-east of Amiens, the walker can travel along the Old Front Line of the Great War, which ran from the Channel coast near the present Belgian frontier to Belfort on the Swiss border.

Oise: Much of the Oise is lapped by the Ile de France. Certainly it is tacitly accepted that Senlis, Chantilly and Compiègne have more links with the Ile than with a provincial *département,* but this still leaves some historic and scenically interesting areas around the great castle of Pierrefonds, and pleasant walks towards Normandy and south-east of Beauvais. The great GR 1 Ile de France footpath begins at the *château* of Sceaux, just outside Paris, and then encircles the city, through the great forests.

Aisne: The third *département* of Picardy is the Aisne, where the possibilities for serious walking increase. There is good walking in the Thiérache, around Vervins, a region of castles and fortified churches, or south of Laon along the river Aisne itself. Many way-marked footpaths have been laid out by local *Syndicats,* and all in all this is a good region for day walking, especially if you like military architecture.

Ile de France

Surprisingly, in view of the proximity of Paris, the Ile de France has a great deal of excellent walking. The gems of the Ile de France are the great forests, the hunting grounds of the Bourbon Kings, all of which have waymarked trails, and a number of trans-France GR routes begin here.

Val d'Oise: This north-western *département* adjoins the Picardy *département* of Oise. There is good day walking into the surrounding forests from Compiègne, (which actually lies just inside the Oise), and history lovers will have a feast around Senlis with walks to the beautiful *château* of Chantilly and the ruined abbey at Royaumont. La Roche Guyon, on the Seine, is another good centre, on the frontier between the Ile de France (the French Vexin) and the Norman Vexin, which face each other across the old frontier. These Vexins were the 'marches', which acted as a buffer-zone between the lands of the French King and his vassal, the Duke of Normandy.

Seine-et-Marne: In this *département,* to the east of Paris, the wise walker has a great deal of choice in the farmlands of the Brie, along the Morin, based on Coulommiers. Provins, a walled town on the eastern frontier, allows walking into Champagne, but the real choice must lie between either Moret-sur-Loing, which is my personal favourite, or at Milly-la-Forêt, in the forest of Fontainebleau, a short distance away.

Essonne: This *département* is very residential and only Dourdan, in the Gâtinais country in the south of the *département* is really worth a visit for walkers.

Yvelines: This is a large *département* which runs from historic Versailles to the Beauce, the wide flat plateau around Chartres. There is a very interesting walk from Versailles, north across the woods to Marly (a place beloved by Louis XIV), St Germain and so to Pontoise, an ideal route for a long distance walker. The Vallée de Chevreuse, from Versailles to Rambouillet is also worthwhile, while Chevreuse itself has several good waymarked trails and relics of Racine, who lived and walked hereabouts. This would be a good objective for a long distance walker, or make a fine centre for day walking.

Champagne-Ardennes

Further east, the walking becomes more interesting, because the countryside is more diverse.

The cathedral city of Reims is a good day-walking centre, with easy access to the vineyards of the Montagne de Reims (279 m) and the northern *départements*.

Ardennes: The Ardennes, or *pays de forêts,* as the brochures call it, certainly has forests, with steep valleys, great castles (the one at Sedan is the largest in Europe), and the best walking country in the North of France. This is the *département* for day walkers, with plenty of footpaths at the 500 km level. Charleville-Mézières, or Sedan on the Meuse are good centres.

Marne: The Marne is the Champagne country, cloaked with vines and full of little villages. Epernay, west of Reims, is the champagne centre. The east of the area for walkers who also enjoy good food and wine.

Aube: The *pays d'Othé,* east of Troyes, is the walking area for this *département,* a long forested ridge running for 60 km down to Joigny on the Yonne, and full of little villages; an out of the way area, 'where the tourists don't go.' The *Park Naturel Régional de la Forêt d'Orient* is equally attractive but more crowded.

Haute Marne: The Haute Marne is a heavily forested watershed. Arc-en-Barras is a good walking centre, and Langres is a centre for the country to the north of Burgundy and the Marne lakes. I like the Haute-Marne and usually manage to stop there whenever I am in France, selecting a village at random in which to stay for a couple of days.

The overall view of this entire area is that it is ideal for day walking and long-distance walking over moderate terrain in mild weather. This is not necessarily a backpacking region, since there is ample accommodation. It is recommended for walkers with limited time and an interest in history and the French *douceur de vivre.*

National Parks

Parc Naturel Régional de St Armand-Raismes: This is a small Park of 15,000 acres on the Belgian border, a region of deciduous trees and shallow ponds. It is crossed by the GR 121 and lies a little north of Valenciennes. Much of the park is forested and it contains a nature reserve and a bird sanctuary.

Parc Naturel Régional de la Forêt d'Orient: This Park, six times larger than St Armand, lies to the east of Troyes, circled by GR 24 trails, and contains a huge lake and several rivers. This park is also a bird sanctuary with many species of duck, grebe and heron breeding in the shallow ponds.

Parc Naturel Régional de la Montagne de Reims: This is a small Park just outside Reims, spanning the wine country. The GR 141 circles it and there are plenty of footpaths through the vineyards and across to Epernay. The height hereabouts is only 270 m.

Footpaths

Local Footpaths

This entire region is ideal for day walking to the extent that the FFRP-CNSGR are issuing Topo guides covering day walking in the Ile de France, the first departure from publishing guides exclusive to long-distance footpaths. The first guide, in two volumes, *Petite Randonnée en Ile de France,* lists thirty waymarked paths and offers an exciting two weeks of day walking all over the region. Other guides will follow.

The *Syndicat d'Initiative* in Compiègne produces a guide to walking in the nearby forests, and most of the other forests, such as Rambouillet and Fontainebleau, have waymarked trails. The FFRP-CNSGR have introduced topo-guides here for short walks. P.R. Tome 1 offers 39 circular walks in the Ile de France, while Tome 2 offers a further 60.

The *Comité Départemental des Ardennes* produce a booklet, *Sentiers de Grande Randonnée et Sentiers Pédestres,* covering walks in the Ardennes, and most local *Syndicats* have walking information available for the visitor. A great deal of local information can be collected from the Maison de Tourisme or the FFRP-CNSGR, Rue Clignancourt, 75018 Paris, or the IGN, 7 Rue la Boétie, Paris.

Towpaths

Towpaths are attractive for the walker, especially in a populated region, for canals somehow always manage to run through the remoter parts. These areas are well favoured with canals and there are some 600 km of towpath in Champagne-Ardenne region alone.

There are many canals in the Pas-de-Calais and Nord regions, and all are worth exploring, but the following are particularly interesting, as they run through some fine country: Canal de l'Aisne à la Marne; Canal des Ardennes; and the Canal Calais — St Omer. This canal is an ideal way of crossing otherwise populated farmland, and runs on to Béthune. More of the canals lie in the eastern *départements,* where they feed traffic into the Rhine. Information on towpaths can be obtained from the local *Comités de Tourisme,* or, and this is my method, by studying the brochures of companies who offer canal cruising holidays, *or the Série Verte* IGN 1:100,000 map, which has an adequate amount of detail. It is always advisable to check if the towpath is open all the way, for the newer ones are little more than concrete troughs and often lack towpaths.

Long-Distance Footpaths

In spite of its basic suitability as a day walking area, the North of France has some excellent long distance routes, some of which, by their length alone, provide a challenge to the walker. All of them take in interesting and historic places, and anyone walking in this area should read up on French history before the start.

GR 1 Sentier Tour de l'Ile de France: 605 km encircling Paris and beginning on the steps of the *Musée de l'Ile de France* at the château of Sceaux. A fascinating trip, suitable for long distance walkers, with plenty of accommodation and needing about three weeks to complete. The GR 1 continues right round the Ile, amid forests and through the great tourist centres. **Grade 2.**

GR 11 Sentier de l'Ile de France: These walks, each of which could be a separate trip, are described in a series of five Topo guides, touring in stages around the Ile de France, again from Sceaux. Some of the Topo guides have *variants* or circular tours, off the main trail:

1. Sceaux to Neauphle-le-Château: 48 km or 31 km (two routes).
2. Neauphle to Senlis: 175 km.
3. Senlis to Ferté-sous-Jouarre: 145 km or 60 km or 41 km.
4. Ferté to Fontainebleau: 170 km.
5. Fontainebleau to Neauphle: 164 km.

Any one of these five sections would make a good week's walk and all start and finishing points lie in easy reach of central Paris. There are some short *variants.* **Grades 1 and 2.**

GR 111 Sentier de l'Essone: Milly le Forêt to Gravigny: 215 km. **Grades 1 and 2.**

GR 12-12A Sentier de l'Ile de France — Ardennes: This excellent route runs across the Oise, the Aisne and Ardennes for 302 km with a further 130 km *variant* for the really enthusiastic Francophile. A good two-week trip with the steep bits coming later when the walker is fit. **Grade 1-2.**

GR 120 Tour du Boulonnais: A new circular walk. Topo guide in preparation. **Grade 1-2.**

GR 121-121A Sentier Belgique — Côte d'Opale: This path, the GR 121, runs west from Valenciennes to the coast at Boulogne, just right for catching the UK ferry, and a good 300 km over easy terrain. There is a short 54 km circular *variant,* the 121A from Hesdin, which would make a good weekend walk. **Grade 1-2.**

GR 122: This footpath, with as yet no catalogued Topo guide, is shown on the IGN 903, and runs south from Valenciennes to the GR 12A-E3 near Rethel on the Aisne. An enjoyable walk across the Thiérache country, through a region of fortified churches. **Grade 1-2.**

GR 123 Carlepont — Hesdin: Pas-de-Calais and Somme: Topo guide in preparation. **Grade 2.**

GR 124-124A Folleville — Cire and Bethisy-St-Pierre: A new walk, with a *variant.* Topo guide in preparation. **Grade 2.**

GR 13-132 Sentier Ile de France — Bourgogne: One section in the Ile from Fontainebleau to St Martin-sur-Ouanne in Burgundy, 162 km of good walking, with a *variant* to join the GR 213 at Villeneuve-sur-Yonne. The GR 13 continues south across Burgundy and is one of the classic French routes. **Grade 2.**

GR 14 Boissy St Leger to Dormans, 265 km. **Grade 2.**

GR 14A; GR 14-141 Sentier de la Marne: Two topo guides cover this route. One, the GR 14A runs from Gagny in the Paris suburbs, east to the GR 11 near Meaux, 55 km. The GR 14-141, also the *Sentier de la Marne,* runs on close to Reims in Champagne for another 288 km, but is a very good walk for long-distance walkers, with plenty of accommodation on the way. This topo guide includes the *Tour de la Montagne de Reims.* **Grade 2.**

GR 2-24 Sentier de la Seine: This is a long trail with several alternative routes, from Aix-en-Othe to Châtillon-sur-Seine — a highly recommended 130 km, with a section from Bar-sur-Seine down to Mussy 35 km or 36 km. Visit the treasure of Vix at Châtillon. New Topo guide in preparation. **Grade 2.**

GR 2-213 Sentier de la Seine et de l'Yonne: The Yonne is one of the great rivers of Burgundy and this long trail runs from Les Andelys on the Seine in Normandy, west to Melun and so south. Two Topo guides cover the route, GR 2-213, 196 km, and GR 213 Sentier de la Yonne, 98 km. The Sentier de la Seine *variant,* also on the GR 2 from Triel to les Andelys, is 96 km. Any one of these walks would serve as a good introduction to walking in France. **Grade 1-2.**

GR 22 Sentier Paris — Mont St Michel: Another long trail with one Topo guide covering the section in Yvelines from Orgerus to Mamers, a long 217 km, mostly across the Ile de France and the Parc Normandie-Maine. A good two-week, long-distance, or even a backpacking trip. There are plenty of campsites. **Grade 2.**

GR 24: This footpath, in the Aube south of Troyes, has many *variants,* 24A, 24B, 24C and 24E around the Forêt d'Orient, and pays d'Othé. No Topo guide in the current FFRP-CNSGR catalogue. All the trails and *variants* are waymarked. **Grade 2.**

GR 123 Sentier Ile-de-France — Picardy: This long footpath runs from Carlepont near Compiègne, to Hesdin along the Somme valley and then across Picardy. A good week's walk for the late spring or autumn. **Grade 2.**

GR 125 Sentier de la Baie de Somme au Vexin: A good long walk from St Valéry sur Somme on the Channel coast to Gisors in the Normandy Vexin, or vice-versa. A highly recommended route with a Topo guide in preparation. This would take the long-distance walker about a week. The terrain is fairly gentle and this is ideal country to explore on foot. **Grade 2.**

As you can see, the North of France has some very long and interesting trails fanning out from the capital to all parts of France, and there is no lack of suitable routes for a one or two week trip.

Historic Paths

Two routes, neither of them waymarked nor GR trails, spring to mind in this area, both of interest to the British walker.

In 1415 Henry V marched his army north from Harfleur to the Somme, then along the Somme from Le Crotoy below Amiens, east across open downland to Neslé, and then across the river to Peronne, Albert, Hesdin, and finally to his fateful day at Agincourt. This distance of around 400 km would be a good historic two- to three-week backpacking trip, the later stages leading across the battlefields of the Somme, (a cataclysmic struggle of 1916), and so to Calais. A good history book, like Christopher Hibbert's *Agincourt,* (Batsford), will chart this route.

Further east lies an historic route which dates from some fifteen years after Henry V's march. Joan of Arc campaigned in these parts until her capture by the Burgundians at Compiègne. She left her home in Lorraine in 1430 and her route from Vaucolours to Chinon on the Loire, where she met the 'gentle Dauphin', runs right across the south of this region and would be an interesting route to trace, if a trifle long.

Accommodation

Being heavily populated and, particularly in some areas of the Ile de France, popular with 'package' tours, there is no shortage of accommodation, but it is usually necessary to book ahead anywhere near a tourist centre between July and September.

Youth Hostels can be found in main towns such as Reims, Amiens and even at St-Valéry, but they are not abundant.

A list of hotels is available from the FGTO, London, or local *Syndicats d'Initiative.*

Gîtes and Refuges

There are few 'refuges' in the true sense of the term, since there are no mountains, but all the main GR trails are being equipped with *gîtes*. Details are obtainable in the Topo guides, from the *Comités de Tourisme*, or from:

For Nord and Pas-de-Calais: Fédération Régionale des Associations des Randonneurs, 33 Rue Faidherbe, 59800 Lille.

For Picardy: Association des Gîtes d'Étape de Picardie, 2 bis Rue Charles Dubois, 8000 Amiens.

For Ardennes: CAF des Ardennes, 9 Place Longueville, 08100 Charleville Mézières. Tel: (24) 33-29-56.

Camping

There are scores of campsites, and there should be no difficulty in finding a pitch, except perhaps around the Paris sections of the Ile de France where there are not many sites, and those that there are will often be full with large frame tents; although a small walker's tent will usually fit in somewhere.

Camping à la ferme is growing, and I have found the local farmers and market gardeners are very helpful at finding the walker a pitch.

Wild camping is not permitted in the Ile de France forests, and since the area is intensively cultivated a truly 'wild pitch' is a rarity outside the Ardennes. One alternative available is the *aire naturelle de camping*, a fairly new idea which offers a primitive pitch with very minimal facilities, and a maximum of twenty-five tents over approximately a hectare. Orchards are being adapted for this purpose. Lists of campsites can be obtained from the FGTO and local *Syndicats*, but just looking from about 1600 hrs is usually sufficient.

Transport

Ease of access is one of the great attractions of the North of France. There are ferry and/or hovercraft services to Dunkirk, Calais, Boulogne and Le Havre, connecting with good rail services to Paris and beyond. The bus and local rail networks are also good. There are air connections to Paris (Charles de Gaulle), Beauvais, Le Touquet and Lille.

One under-exploited facility for the walker in France is the *train touristique*. These little trains, frequently steam powered, are entertaining in themselves and can often transport the walker into some little-known part of France, as a starting place for a walking trip. There are several in these regions, and two of these are particularly good:

Chemin de Fer Touristique de la Baie de la Somme: This train is pulled by a turn-of-the-century steam locomotive, which travels around the bay from Le Crotoy or St Valéry-sur-Somme. Information is available from the Station at Le Crotoy.

Chemin de Fer Froissy — Cappy — Dompierre: This train runs from Froissy on the Somme for 14 km to Cappy, across superb downlands, and along river valleys south of Albert. Open in the summer only. Information from the *Syndicat* in Amiens.

Local rail links are very good all over this part of France and the walker should have no trouble getting about.

Maps and Guides

The best introductory maps to the region are the IGN Carte Touristique Série Rouge 1:250,000 No.1 (Pays du Nord) and No.3 Ile de France, Champagne. The IGN also produces a *Picardie (Carte Routière et Touristique)* which shows all the historic sites. 1:100,000 Série Verte are also available and are adequate for walking everywhere outside the Ardennes. A compass would be useful in the large forests of the Ile de France where the visibility is limited.

Most of the books written on this part of France are, unfortunately, concerned with war. Michelin have a Green Guide, in French, to *Nord de la France,* which covers most of the regions mentioned in this chapter, and the Ile de France is covered in Michelin's *Environs de Paris.* Fred Tingey's *North of France* from Spurbooks, covers Picardy, Artois and the Nord. There is an excellent book on the Ile de France in the Collins' Companion Guide series.

To obtain the most accurate information the traveller should stop in Paris, where the latest Topo guides will certainly be available at the IGN shop in the Rue la Boétie. Topo guides can also be purchased in the following shops within the region:

Nord: Au Furet du Nord, Place du Général de Gaulle, 59002 Lille.

Pas-de-Calais: Duminy SA, Angle Rue Faidherbe et Victor Hugo, 62201 Boulogne-sur-Mer.

Somme — Aisne — Ardennes: Papeterie du Nord-Est, 8 Place de Camp, 62500 Hirson.

Oise: Librairie Daelman, 26 Rue des Lombards, 60000 Compiègne.

Val d'Oise: Librairie Akedemos, Place de la Préfecture, 95000 Cergy-Pontoise.

Seine et Marne: Arts et Lettres, 25 Rue St Etienne, Meaux.

Essone: Maison de la Presse, La Ferte-Alais.

Yvelines: Librairie du Jeu de Paume, 5 Rue du Vieux Versailles, Versailles.

Topo guides are stocked in many other shops but those listed here should stock the full range plus other useful maps and guides.

Wildlife

In such a well developed area, large wild mammals are preserved only for sport, and are therefore restricted to the wild boar (*sanglier*) and deer (*cerf*) which live in the forests of the Ile de France and the Ardennes. There is prolific birdlife, and a good place to watch sea-birds and waders is in the Bay of the Somme near Le Crotoy. The Parcs Naturels Régionaux all have bird sanctuaries and the ornithologist will find many attractions both there and in the great forests.

Food and Wine

If compared with Normandy or Burgundy these are not famous gastronomic regions, but there is an abundance of good cooking. Each little town of the Ile de France will have at least one good restaurant and the prices are usually very moderate.

I am very fond of the food of Picardy and if I were asked to choose my favourite dish from that area I would probably settle for a *ficelle picarde,* a rolled pancake of cheese, ham and mushrooms, which is delicious. Picardy soups, based on the excellent vegetables grown in the region, are a real speciality. Arras has excellent sausages of the spicier variety, while in Champagne, which is full of good restaurants, there are few regional specialities except for the *Choucroute de Brienne,* but lots of well-made dishes such as *poulet sauté* or *truite farcie.* In the Ardennes, hunting country, game and fish are popular, and I was concerned to read in a book on local specialities that they even eat squirrels! Fortunately there are also excellent pâtés and stews, with trout from the rivers and, of course, pigeons and pheasants from the local coverts.

The wine should, of course, be champagne, and I know of one well-heeled walker who arrives at his lodging every night panting for 'iced Krug', but champagne is expensive in France. It is often better to settle for some lesser-known *vin du pays,* like the Côteaux Champenois, or even beer. Most French beers are produced in the north of the country and Ardennes beer is excellent.

Information Centres

Ile de France: Comité Régional de Tourisme, 101, Rue de

Vaugirard, 75006 Paris. *Département* offices in Melun (Seine et Marne), Versailles (Yvelines), Corbeil-Essonnes (Essonnes), Montmorency (Val d'Oise).

Champagne Ardennes: Comité Régional du Tourisme, 2 Bis, Bvd. Vaubécourt, 51000 Châlons-sur-Marne. Tel: (26) 68-37-52. There are *départemental* offices in Charleville-Mézières (Ardennes), Troyes (Aube) and Chaumont (Haute-Marne).

Nord Pas-de-Calais: Comité Régional du Tourisme, 157, Bvd. de la Liberté, 59800 Lille. Tel: (20) 57-35-23. *Départemental* offices are at Boulogne (Pas-de-Calais) and in the Square Foch, Lille (Nord). This region has a good footpath organization: FRAR (Nord Pas-de-Calais), 33 Rue Faidherbe, 59000 Lille.

Picardy: Comité Régional du Tourisme BP 0342, 2 bis, Rue Charles Dubois, 80000 Amiens. Tel: (22) 95-65-00. The local footpath organisation, AGEP, has offices at the same address. *Départemental* offices are in Laon (Aisne), Beauvais (Oise) and at 21, Rue Ernest Cauvin, Amiens (Somme).

BRITTANY AND NORMANDY

Although the provinces of Brittany and Normandy have much in common, each has unique features which render it different from the other. Their most immediate attraction to the British walker, however, is that they are not too far away; even the most remote paths in these provinces are only twelve hours away from the UK. Both provinces share cultural and historic links with the British, and if you like feeling at home when you are abroad then this is the place to go. I am very fond of both provinces and recommend them for all varieties of walking, but particularly to those walkers who also enjoy good food, pleasing scenery, and lots of history along the way.

Historically, in the sense of recorded time, Brittany is by far the older province, and retained her independence from the French throne until a much later date. Normandy was gradually colonised by the Viking Northmen from about AD 800 and became a French dukedom in 911, not so very long before Duke William led his forces against the Saxon Harold in the date we all remember, 1066, an event recorded in the great Tapestry at Bayeux.

To begin with Brittany, we must go back to the earliest recorded time: the Roman Conquest of 56 BC by Julius Caesar. He conquered the Celts who lived in Brittany, a land which was then called Armorica, a word meaning the 'land facing the sea'. These were the people who erected the great *menhirs*, the standing stones which dot Brittany and are clustered thickly in Finistère and at Carnac in Morbihan. The Romans ruled Armorica for over four hundred years, but the Saxon pirates, playing their part in those barbarian invasions which destroyed Roman power, eventually drove the Roman-Britons out of Britain and they settled in large numbers in Armorica, overwhelming the native Celts. It is from this time that the land became known as Brittany, or 'little Britain'.

The Northmen followed of course, in the ninth century, but they were eventually defeated by Alain Barbe-Torte, who became Duke of Brittany in 937, and the Dukes of Brittany maintained their independence until the Duchesse Anne married Charles VIII of France in 1488. Brittany became a French possession in 1532. As the last ruler of an independent province, the Duchesse Anne is still remembered all over Brittany. The Bretons were, and still are, stout soldiers and great seamen. Bertrand du Guesclin, the great Constable of France who defeated the English in the Hundred Years War, was born in the beautiful town of Dinan. After his death in 1380 his body went to St Denis, to lie with those of the French kings, but his heart was sent to St Sauveur in Dinan, where it still remains.

Brittany's other famous sons include Peter Abelard, lover of Héloise, Alphonse de Châteaubriant the writer, Jacques Cartier who discovered Canada in 1534, and many fierce corsairs who raided English shipping from the shelter of St Malo.

Brittany is also a mysterious land, with its own language and a folklore full of legends. King Arthur and his Knights sought the Holy Grail here, and it holds the birthplace of Lancelot and the living tomb of Merlin in the forest of Brocéliande. It has great *menhirs*, huge calvaries, Breton ladies in tall *coiffes*, marvellous seascapes, a clear, open, windy land, full of deep meadows, rolling hills, a wave-washed coast, and strange stories of Arthur's knights, Merlin and Morgan le Fé. Delightful!

Normandy, marching north and east along the Breton frontier from the Cousenon river which forms the boundary between the two provinces, is a more dour, martial place, once the home of the warlike dukes, and scene of more recent campaigns in the Second World War.

In AD 911 the Viking Rollo signed a treaty with the King of France, Charles the Simple, and became the first Duke of Normandy. His descendant, William the Conqueror — or the Bastard —

was the sixth Duke, and the Kings of England remained Dukes of Normandy until King John was defeated at Bovines in 1204. The Plantagenets maintained their claim to Normandy throughout the Hundred Years War and, indeed, our present Queen holds the allegiance of the Channel Islands, which the French call the *Iles Anglo-Normandes,* by her right as Duke of Normandy. The Normans were soldiers and travellers and they spread as far away as Palestine and Canada on the rim of the then known world. Quebec was a Norman colony, founded by Samuel Champlain of Dieppe. Normandy has her men of letters, notably Flaubert, Maupassant, Victor Hugo, and such painters as Braque, so there is more to the place than fine cooking and the clash of arms.

Henry V of England made a memorable invasion of Normandy in 1415, in the campaign which took the town of Harfleur and led to Agincourt, and the Norman coast is still marked from the Cotentin to the estuary of the Seine by the invasion beaches of D-Day, 6 June 1944. This open sandy beach is littered with shattered blockhouses and the debris of recent war.

Both provinces suffered terribly in the subsequent fighting. St Malo was totally destroyed, Caen and Brest wrecked by bombing, St Lô ravaged by weeks of street fighting. It says a great deal for the Bretons and their Norman neighbours that they have rebuilt their cities in the ancient style and successfully restored their economies.

The Regions Today

Normandy and Brittany are large provinces, and administratively Normandy in fact consists of two regions, *Haute* based on Rouen, and *Basse* based on Caen. Normandy has five *départements:* Seine-Maritime; Eure; Orne; Calvados; and Manche. Brittany has four: Ille-et-Vilaine; Côtes du Nord; Morbihan; and Finistère, although another *département,* Loire-Atlantique, was only recently severed and is now attached to the new region, Pays de la Loire. Loire-Atlantique remains Breton in spirit and, indeed, contains the ancient capital, Nantes. The present capital of Brittany is Rennes.

Nationalism is strong in Brittany and the region makes some claims to political autonomy. The Breton tongue is now reviving, although it is rarely heard outside Finistère. Breton costume is worn by the old people, especially on feast days and the local pilgrimages or *pardons.* The economy in Brittany is based on agriculture, fishing and tourism. Much of the farm produce comes to Britain and we send them many tourists in return.

Normandy's economy is also biased towards fishing and agriculture, and Boulogne is the premier fishing port of France. Tourism is very important, an area in which the history of the province provides a useful attraction. Tourists flock to see the Tapestry at Bayeux, the great Gothic abbeys of Caen, the Castle of the Conqueror at Falaise. Both provinces enjoy a formidable reputation as gastronomic centres and have certain towns, such as La Baule in Brittany, Deauville in Normandy, which have always been popular with the *Tout Paris*, the rich people of Paris. Rouen, well up the Seine from Le Havre, is a major port, as is Nantes on the Loire and, as communication within the regions is good, their economies enjoy an increasing level of industrial development, notably in petro-chemicals and ship building.

Physical Description

To sum up each province in a descriptive phrase one could say that Brittany resembles Cornwall, and Normandy resembles Sussex. The chief physical difference between the two lies in their coastline. The Breton coast is far more rugged and indented than the Norman one, and there is much more of it, Brittany boasting no less than 1100 km of coastline, stretching from romantic Mont St Michel all the way round to Nantes. This coastal region is the true Armorica, the 'land facing the sea', while the interior of the province is called the Argoat, the 'country of wood'. This is a slight misnomer, for Normandy is far more wooded than Brittany, and full of great forests owned by the local communes.

Both regions have great long beaches, and rocky coves, but for sheer beauty the prize is taken by the coast of Brittany. Beware of the tides and deep bays along the northern coast which make coastal walking difficult, calling for frequent diversions. Except for the Western Cotentin, the Norman coast along the Channel is flatter until the Seine, after which great chalk cliffs run up to the Pas-de-Calais. Southern Brittany is less dramatic than the north or west, but no less beautiful, and contains numerous islands in the *Morbihan*, 'the little sea'.

The provinces are more evenly balanced inland. Brittany offers the wild seascapes of Finistère, the rocky areas around Huelgoat and the great Bay of Morbihan, but Normandy counters with the cliffs of Étretat, the hills of the *Suisse Normande* around Falaise, and the *bocage* of the Cotentin. In truth, both provinces are ideal for those who love breathtaking scenery, much history, and fine food.

Climate

Brittany and Normandy are green lush provinces and face out to the Atlantic westerlies. Therefore it rains. It rains often, but rarely for

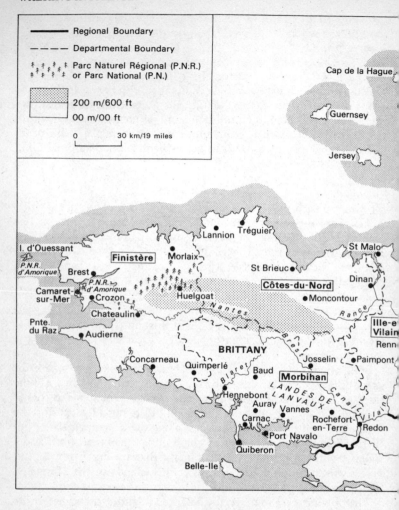

long. I have been on four-day spring walks in both Normandy and
Brittany when we started in snow or heavy rain and finished, four
days later, in shorts and suntans.

Overall in Brittany the weather is more reliable than that of Normandy and, being further south, is a little warmer. If the British
summer is warm, anywhere in Brittany or Normandy will be agreeable. If the British summer is wet, though, then go south, to the
Morbihan. Sea temperatures there are usually several degrees warmer than those along the Channel coast, and sea temperatures rise
because of sunshine.

Walking in the *Départments*

Overall, the walking in either province is not technically difficult. The terrain is gentle and the weather mild. Boots are not usually necessary and shorts and suncream, though useful, are rarely essential. That said, there is a vast choice of walks, long and short, through a wide variety of country, and those walkers who are tired of high mountains, and on balance prefer to walk rather than backpack, will find plenty to occupy them in either region.

Normandy

Seine-Maritime: This *département* is bordered by the Seine and the northern frontier with Picardy. The countryside is rolling and intensively farmed, although Rouen, the capital, is a port. Rouen is a magnificent city, full of medieval churches and, incidentally, the place where Joan of Arc was tried by the Bishop of Beauvais, and executed by the English. *Prenez-garde!*

Seine-Maritime has three distinct regions: the *pays de Caux,* the chalklands from Caudebec on the Seine to the coast, the *Vexin Normand* around Gisors on the eastern frontier with the Ile de France, and the *pays de Bray* further north. There is good gentle walking in the Norman Vexin, near Gisors, and an excellent coastal walk in the *pays de Caux* from Étretat to Dieppe (GR 21).

This *département* also includes the Fôret de Brotonne, now a National Park, and I recommend the day walker to the *pays de Bray,* centred in the Forges-les-Eaux and Gournay. There are several GR trails in the *département,* GRs 21, 225, 211 and 25, with many *variants.* Overall a region for day walking or gentle long distance travel.

Eure: This *département,* south of the Seine, has many delightful river valleys and some fine old towns, notably Pont-Audemer, Evreux and Verneuil. A good centre for day walking is Breteuil, southwest of Evreux, which is on the GR 222 and full of local footpaths. This *département* also contains Richard Lionheart's great castle, Château Galliard, the 'Saucy Castle' near Les Andelays on the GR 2, and there is good walking from here across the Vexin to Gisors. The Eure is well wooded, full of fishing rivers and good for day walking.

Orne: This is, with the exception of the Cotentin, my favourite Norman *départment.* The town of Mortagne in the County of Perche is an excellent walking centre. The valley of the Orne, west of Argentan, is also excellent, while Bagnoles-de-l'Orne is an ideal centre for walks into the Parc de Normandie-Maine. The hills of the *Suisse Normande* lie to the north of this *département,* and there are several GR routes in the east, GRs 22, 22A and 22B.

Calvados: Calvados, as you may guess, is a *département* largely devoted to the cultivation of apples for the *Calvados* brandy. It is also a region rich in history, containing Bayeux, Caen, Falaise, and much of the invasion coast of 1944, with the landing beaches of *Omaha, Gold, Juno* and *Sword* spanning the Côte de Nacre, the Pearl Coast, along the Bay of the Seine. Vire is a good centre for day walking, but the region along the Orne near Clécy, south of Caen would be more interesting, for this is the edge of the *Suisse Normande,* a region of beautiful hills, not very high at about the 250 m mark, but probably the best day walking area in the entire province.

Manche: This is the largest *département,* and full of special interest to the backpacker and long distance walker, with many long, lateral walks. Access to the finger of the Cap de la Hague (a good day-walking area in the Cotentin peninsula), is easy through Cherbourg, and the coastline is dotted with superb little ports and fishing villages. Barfleur, St Vaast and St Pierre-Église are real gems and all are linked on the GR 223 footpath.

I like the village of Ste Mère Église, inland from *Utah* beach, while the headland of Cap de la Hague and the Nez de Jobourg are the places to go if time is short, or for a weekend walk.

Below Carentan, at the base of the Cotentin, lies the *bocage* country, a network of fields and the scene of bitter fighting in 1944. If you want more vivid memories of 1944 you can visit the American Parachute Museums at Ste Mère Église and Carentan.

The western coastline of the Cotentin is rocky, a foretaste of Brittany, leading south through Avaranches to the island of Mont St Michel and the frontier of Brittany on the river Cousenon.

Brittany

Ille-et-Vilaine: The river Cousenon (pronounced *quay-non*) gave Mont St Michel to Normandy by changing course and flowing out to sea on the west side of the island, a fact which the Bretons will never forgive. However, Ille-et-Vilaine, the eastern *département,* has some magnificent medieval sites to balance this loss.

Vitré and Fougères have magnificent castles, and the coastline west from Mont St Michel to St Malo is extremely beautiful. Ille-et-Vilaine is well organised for walking. Fougères is probably the best centre, with Liffré, north-east of Rennes coming in a close second. There are 1000 km of waymarked footpaths in the *département,* several GR trails, GRs 37, 39, 34, with many *variants.* On the western edge lies the Fôret de Paimpont, once known as Brocéliande, home of the Arthurian legends, and all walkers will want to walk into the forest and find the *perron de Merlin,* Merlin's stone, inside which the fairy Vivaine trapped Arthur's wizard. Legend has it that if you sprinkle water on the stone it will immediately rain. Try it!

Côtes-du-Nord: The glory of this *département* is the coastline west from the Rance river, but do not neglect to visit Dinan, birthplace of Du Guesclin, Moncontour in hilly country, or the Ploumanac'h headland, north of Lannion. For coastal walking this *département* is ideal.

Finistère: The Finistère peninsula is archetypal Brittany. Here you will find the calvaries, the people speak Breton, and the ladies wear the *coiffes,* at least on Sundays.

Huelgoat, capital of the Argoat, lies just in Finistère, and is the ideal centre for day walking. Walkers should also visit the calvaries around Morlaix, the Menez-Hom hill and the Crozon peninsula, staying at Camaret, and explore the coast from Concarneau, west towards Audièrne and the wild Pointe du Raz, and north to Châteaulin, a perfect region for the backpacker or the long-distance walker.

This *département* also contains the Parc Naturel d'Armorique, which is an excellent day-walking area, and a number of *Grands Sites*, the equivalent of the UK's Areas of Outstanding Natural Beauty (AONB).

Morbihan: The Morbihan is my favourite *département* in Brittany. The weather is usually warmer than the northern coast, and the area is full of interest for lovers of history. Hennebont on the Blavant is an interesting town, and no visitor should miss seeing walled Vannes or Auray, or touring the Bay of Morbihan in a small boat. It is also possible to visit Belle Isle in the Bay of Biscay off Quiberon, which is a beautiful place. The curious marshland of the Brière lies north of La Baule, while inland lies the great castle of Josselin and, an excellent walker's route, the Brest to Nantes canal towpath. Backpackers will enjoy the Landes de Lanvaux, a long moorland which runs from Baud east to Rochefort-en-Terre.

To conclude, there is good easy-to-moderate walking everywhere in Normandy and Brittany, and the full backpacking routine, while *always* possible, is never necessary. I would personally recommend the Normandy *département* of La Manche, and anywhere in Brittany with slight bias towards Morbihan. Your choice of where to go may be influenced by the weather.

National Parks

Parc Naturel Régional Normandie-Maine: Created in 1975, this large Park straddles the southern boundary of the province and laps four *départements* around Argentan and Alençon. Bagnoles-de-l'Orne is the best centre. The Park contains sixteen campsites, two *gîtes*, and many hundreds of kilometres of footpaths, marked by the *Fédération Ornaise pour le Tourisme de Randonnée*. Day walking centres are at Bagnoles, Sillé le Guillaume in the adjacent region of Western Loire, and Mont St Jean. The GR 36A (Alpes Mancelles) *variant* is another interesting walk.

This is a farming region, richly forested. Details from: Parc Naturel Régional Normandie-Maine, Le Chapître, BP 05, 61320 Carrouges, tel: (33) 27-21-15, or from local *Syndicats*.

Parc Naturel Régional de Brotonne: This Park, which is in two sections, is less than one-fifth the size of the Normandie-Maine, and lies on the Seine between Rouen and Le Havre. It contains the ruins of many fine abbeys, notably Jumièges, and there is good walking in the forest and from Caudebec and Duclair. There are several GR trails across the park. Details from: Maison du Parc Régional de Brotonne, 2 Rond-Point Marbre, 76580 Le Trait, tel: (35) 91-83-16, or from local *Syndicats.*

Parc Naturel Régional d'Armorique: Created in 1969, this lies in Finistère and would provide the perfect setting for a country walking holiday, for it combines a coastal region with some fine inland scenery (and excellent walking). It includes the offshore island of Ouessant (Ushant). Details from: Parc Naturel d'Armorique, Menez-Meur, Hanvec, 29224 Daoulas, tel: (98) 68-81-71, or from local *Syndicats.* The Parc of Brière now lies, officially, in Loire-Atlantique (Pays de la Loire).

Footpaths

Local Footpaths

There are, quite literally, thousands of kilometres of local footpaths in these two provinces, but some areas are particularly suitable for those who prefer walking on a day or half-day basis from a fixed base.

The Norman *départements* are very well organised and each one has its own footpath organisation, with a regional centre at Caen. There is also an organisation called CRAPA (*Circuits Rustiques d'Activité Physique Amenagés*) which waymarks some routes in the Orne, where the major organisation is the FOTPO at 60 Grande Rue, Alençon, tel: (33) 26-18-71. The Association du Tourisme Pédestre, 2 Rue de Puits de la Place, 50400 Granville, does the same for Manche footpaths.

For all information on short routes in **Normandy,** write to FFRP-CNSGR, Chambre Départemental d'Agriculture, 4 Promenade de Madame de Sévigné, 14000 Caen, tel: (31) 84-47-19. This office co-ordinates the footpath information for all *départements* and directly controls the Calvados *département* itself. Other useful addresses are given at the end of the chapter.

For full information on walking in **Brittany,** write for a leaflet to CNSGR-ABRI, 14 Bvd de Beaumont, 35000 Rennes, tel: (99) 79-36-26 or to the local *Syndicats d'Initiatives.*

Towpaths

Brittany is particularly rich in canals, which provide excellent and different walking routes suitable for long-distance walkers, with plenty of canal activity to provide interest. There are some 1500 km of towpaths in Brittany, and they are particularly good for exploring the Argoat. Canals worth inspecting are the Ille-et-Rance, the Nantes-à-Brest, and the Blavet. It is possible to follow the canals from St Malo to Dinan, 38 km along the Rance, and eventually down to Redon 126 km away, right across the province, in easy stages.

Most of the Breton canals date from the Napoléonic era or earlier and are good for walking, but modern sections may not have towpaths.

Apply for information to the Comité de Promotion Touristique des Canaux Bretons, 12 Rue de Jemmapes, 44000 Nantes, tel: (40) 47-42-94.

Long-distance Footpaths

There are currently no less than twenty-one GR trails in Normandy and Brittany, ideal for backpacking or, since accommodation is plentiful, long distance walkers.

Normandy

GR 125: Part of this route circles Gisors (to the west) in the Vexin. The distance is short, a bare 25 km, but it could make an interesting day, and the castle at Gisors is magnificent. **Grade 1.**

GR 2 Sentier de la Seine: A large part of this walk runs through Normandy, covering 186 km from Le Havre to Les Andelys, along the river itself. The centre section from Caudebec would be most interesting and historic, and the great Château Galliard is an excellent finish. **Grade 1-2.**

GR 21-221 Le Havre — Dieppe: This has numerous *variants* but the coastal section, Étretat to Dieppe, is the one I recommend to long-distance walkers and back-packers. **Grade 1-2**

GR 22-22B Paris — Mont St Michel: 288 km of footpath lie inside Normandy and across the Normandie-Maine Park. The 60 km 22B *variant* in the Park would make a good weekend walk. **Grade 1 to 2.**

GR 221-221A: A fairly short 85 km walk across the Cotentin from Coutances into the *bocage*. **Grade 1.**

GR 222 Sentier de l'Eure: 117 km across the *département*, through forested country and interesting town between Verneuil and Evreux. **Grade 1.**

GR 223 Sentier Tour du Cotentin: A long 228 km coastal walk from Avranches to Cherbourg and Barfleur. Splendid scenery, but if time is short the little Val de Saire *variant*, a two-day circuit east from Cherbourg, will be a good weekend. A highly recommended two- to three-week walk. **Grade 2.**

GR 225 Sentier du pays de Bray: A pleasant week for the gentle walker, 104 km from the port of Dieppe inland through agreeable country towards Lyon-le-Fôret. Topo guide in preparation. **Grade 1-2.**

GR 226 Sentier Orne-Baie de Mont St Michel: 154 km across Calvados and Manche with a junction at Carolles on the coast at the foot of the Cotentin. Possibility of diverting, on GR 22, to Mont St Michel, which must be visited, preferably outside the tourist season. Topo guide in preparation. **Grade 2.**

GR 23-23A Sentier La Boulle — Tancarville: Long weekend walk (say three days) in the Norman Abbey tourist circuit, south of the Seine and through the Park of Brotonne. Easy access from Le Havre. **Grade 1.**

GR 25 and Variants — Sentiers de la Région Rouennaise: This is a selection of five routes varying from 9 km to 195 km around the city of Rouen. Depending on the time available, you can walk 9, 11, 89, 115, or 195 km to the north of Rouen. **Grade 1.**

GR 26 Sentier Paris — Vernon-Deauville: Vernon is a frontier town on the doorstep of the Ile de France and this is an interesting route of 160 km, mostly inside Normandy, as far as Deauville on the coast, thus spanning the province from east to north. Topo guide in preparation. **Grade 1-2.**

GR 261 Sentier du Calvados: A short (45 km) but very interesting walk from Caen, north-west to the little fishing village of Port-en-Bessin, with a chance to see Bayeux and the D-Day museum at Arromanches. Recommended for a two-day trip. **Grade 1.**

GR 35 -351 Dreux, Verneuil, Cloyes: A new route, Topo guide in preparation.

GR 36 Sentier Manche — Pyrénées: A long footpath, running the length of France, with sections across the Calvados and the Orne. This section is particularly recommended as a good long-distance walk, south from Ouistreham. Stop where you will . . . **Grade 2.**

Brittany

Brittany is also well served with long-distance footpaths and they may be a trifle more demanding as the countryside is more rugged and the weather warmer. Shorts, light boots, and sun oil recommended.

GR 34 Tour de Bretagne (Tro Briez): This long footpath, with numerous *variants*, takes in all parts of the province and covers in total 841 km in six sections, but would be a good project for a serious walker with a month to spare. The section from walled Vitré to Mont St Michel is an excellent 144 km. **Grade 2 — 3.**

GR 341 Sentier de Bretagne: An excellent 89 km walk along the coast of the Côtes-du-Nord, between St Brieuc and Lannion, round the spectacular Granit-Rose coast. Recommended. **Grade 2.**

GR 342 Sentier de Bretagne: This lies in the south, in the Morbihan, a short 42 km from Quimperlé, but an excellent walk, although not particularly strenuous. It might perhaps best be done as a long-distance walk at the end of a walking holiday.

GR 347 Val d'Oust au pays Gallo: A useful 95 km between the castle at Josselin and the town of Redon, along the Canal de Nantes. A good week's backpacking trip. **Grade 2.**

GR 37 — 37A Sentiers des Alpes Mancelles a l'Argoat: A trans-Brittany route from Crozon in Finistère across the province to Vitré, and so into Normandy. A long but not technically difficult 453 km. Allow three weeks. **Grade 2.**

GR 371 Loudéac — St Brieuc: A new path across the Côtes-du-Nord. Topo guide in preparation. **Grade 2.**

GR 38 Sentier des Landes de Lanvaux: The Landes de Lanvaux is a lightly forested heathland area which runs east-west, north of Vannes. The *total* distance is 304 km, but the eastern section of 154 km to Rochefort-en-Terre is the most interesting. The full route will require backpacking equipment for there are few *gîtes*. This is excellent backpacking country, not unlike Exmoor, but drier! **Grade 3.**

GR 39 and 39A Sentier Manche-Océan: The Manche in this sense means the Channel, not the Normandy *département*. This offers 304 km across Brittany, complete with *variant* (39A). The section from Rennes to Mont St Michel is an interesting 87 km, just right for a four-day walk in spring or autumn.

These Breton and Norman GR trails can be walked at all seasons and by lightly equipped walkers, or backpackers, and the two regions offer excellent walking, especially in June and July or September and October, when the weather is mild and the crowds absent.

Historic Paths

There are several routes which will appeal to history lovers. Henry V of England marched north from Harfleur to Calais, an interesting 400 km for the total route, of which 80 km, from Harfleur to Eu, lies in Normandy. The coastal section from Fécamp is very beautiful, and the route is easily traced.

The GR 39 will lead the walker to the Shrine of St Michel at Mont St Michel, and the GR 26 in Normandy leads to Lisieux, and the shrine of Ste Thérèsa. Quite apart from the objectives, these GR trails take in some fine country.

Castle lovers should take the Brittany trails around Vitré and Fougères, which are really magnificent medieval fortresses, while in Finistère the walker can explore the great Breton calvaries south and west of Morlaix.

Accommodation

As both provinces are well developed tourist areas, there is no short-age of hotel and campsite accommodation outside the main tourist period. July and August could be difficult for day- or long-distance walkers, unless you book ahead.

Normandy

A list of hotels and campsites can be obtained from the FGTO in London. Booking ahead is advisable in summer. Normandy currently has 351 *chambres d'hôte,* and the Gîtes de France organisation or local *Syndicats* have the necessary information. There are only a few *gîtes d'étape* in Normandy and the distribution is uneven along the GR routes. Calvados has only one, Seine-Maritime has nine, but more are being opened and listed in the Topo guides. Suitable cheap overnight accommodation is best sought in cafés, or in a *chambres d'hôte.*

Normandy is full of campsites, and there should be no difficulty in finding a pitch for a small tent. Details on campsites are available from the FGTO, London. A Camping Club *carnet* might be useful on the coastal sites, but I have never been asked to produce mine.

Camping à la Ferme is available and, as the land is intensively farmed, it is best to ask permission before adopting a wild pitch. Wild camping is not theoretically permitted in the forests or Regional Parks because of the fire risk, and smoking in the forests is also discouraged. Both provinces have a good number of *aires naturelles de camping,* which offer a simple pitch, with a maximum of twenty-five tents over a hectare, often in orchards. The facilities are even simpler than on *camping à la ferme* sites; details from local *Syndicats.*

Youth hostels are only available in the major towns such as Bayeux, Dieppe and Caen, and in certain holiday areas along the coast. A list can be obtained from the Auberges de Jeunesse in Paris or the YHA in England.

Brittany

Brittany has always been popular with the British camper, so back-packers will have no trouble finding a pitch. It is, however, quite difficult to find empty hotel accommodation in the high season, but if you travel outside this period, reasonably priced accommodation of all sorts is readily available.

On our Rennes-Brittany walk we paid around £10 for drinks, dinner with wine, bedroom with bath or shower and breakfast. Campsite fees are currently 5 francs (say 50p) per head for tent and one person.

As with Normandy, wild camping is rarely available, without permission, but *camping à la ferme* is definitely on the increase and information is available locally from *Départmental* offices, or *Syndicats*. *Aires Naturelles de Camping* are also available. *Camping à la ferme* prices currently average out at around 3 francs, but are subject to annual revision.

Reservations for *chambres d'hôte* should be made directly with the proprietor, and addresses can be obtained from the *Fédération Nationale des Gîtes de France*. *Gîtes d'étape* are slightly more numerous in Brittany and at prices of between 10 france to 17 francs per night very reasonable as well. In Brittany the maximum stay is two nights. Details by post from ABRI, 14 Bvd. Beaumont, 35100 Rennes, tel: (99) 79-36-26, or from *Départemental* offices.

Transport

Both areas are well served by cross-Channel ferries, hovercraft and jetfoil, running from the UK north to south along the French coast to Dunkirk, Calais, Boulogne, Dieppe, Le Havre, Cherbourg, St Malo and Roscoff. There are good train and bus services from all these ports.

Sealink, Townsend-Thoresen, P & O Ferries and Brittany Ferries have frequent sailings by day and night and the rates available offer the walker considerable opportunities to save money by taking off-peak trips, in seasons more suitable for walking than high summer. Five-day and weekend trips at even lower rates are also available. Details from any good travel agent.

Flights are available from Exeter to Morlaix (Brittany) and from Plymouth to Cherbourg (Normandy) but sea ferries are the most popular link. Details from your travel agent, or the FGTO London.

Within both regions transport is relatively simple. Bus and train services run on an excellent rural network, and are often inter-linked with the cross-Channel ferries.

There is now an *autoroute* from Caen to Paris along the valley of the Seine. Another *autoroute* feeds Rennes and Nantes from the east. There is an excellent N-road network throughout with a link to Le Havre.

Maps and Guides

The basic information for the walker comes from the IGN 903 map, supplemented by the Topo guides, but both regions have plenty of free information available from the Regional Committees and *Syndicats*.

The IGN Cartes Touristiques No 102 (Normandie) and 105 (Bretagne) 1:250,000 (1 cm = 2.5 km) are extremely useful as they show all historic tourist sites and places of interest. Both indicate suitable walking areas, like the Parks, and the *Suisse Normande*.

Michelin 1:200,000 (1 cm = 2.5 km) Nos 54, 58, 59, 63, are good for motoring and do show the main footpath routes, while several of the IGN 1:100,000 Green maps (1 cm = 1 km) cover all parts of the area, as do the Topographic 1:50,000 and 1:25,000 *cartes*. These are useful for day walking, show GR trails, and can be obtained from local IGN and Topo guide stockists.

A great quantity of information is available from the *Syndicats* but visitors will find the following books interesting and useful sources of basic information on the areas. *Brittany* by Henry Myhill (Faber); *History, People & Places in Brittany* by Neil Lands (Spurbooks); *Brittany and the Bretons* by Keith Spence (Gollancz); *Normandy* by Barbara Whelpton (Spurbooks); *Agincourt* by Christopher Hibbert (Batsford); Michelin 'Green' Guides are available for both regions. Walkers will find a lot of walks available described in *Sentiers et Randonnées en Bretagne* (Fayard); *Circuits Pédestres en Seine-Maritime*, published by the Le Havre Chamber of Commerce. Visit your local library or call at Stanfords, Long Acre, London, for guidebooks to the region.

Maps and Topo guides are stocked in the regions at the following centres:

Normandy: Le Nouvel Oeil, 38 Rue aux Ours, 76000 Rouen; Librairie Dombre, 10 Place de l'Hôtel de Ville, 76600 Le Havre; Librairie de la Basse-Normandie, 11 à 15 Rue du Jeudi, 61000 Alençon; Librairie Nicollet, 16-18 Grand Rue, 50100 Cherbourg; Maison de la Presse, 7 Place Littre, 50300 Avranches; L'Eschoher Normand, 50 Rue Paul-Povrier, 50400 Granville; Librairie Générale du Calvados, 98 Rue St Pierre, 14000 Caen.

Brittany: Leperson, 17 Rue St Goneon, 22000 St Brieuc; Librairie de l'Odet, 45 Bvd de Kerguelan, 29000 Quimper; Maison de la Presse, 18 Rue des Fontaines, 56100 Lorient.

The better bookshops in any main town will have a selection of local guides.

Wildlife

Of all animals it is the birds which will attract the naturalist to Normandy and Brittany, and especially the seabirds. The seabird sanctuary on the Pointe du Raz contains a wide variety of gulls and there are puffins on the Sept Iles on the north coast of Finistère. Brittany has no less than 31 bird sanctuaries.

Seabirds swarm along the Channel coast, nesting on the chalk cliffs between Le Havre and Dieppe, wading in the shallow sandy bays of Brittany. There are deer and wild boar (*sanglier*) in the forests, habitat for a variety of birds and small mammals. A good field guide (*Birds of Britain and Northern Europe* published by Collins) and a pair of binoculars would be very useful.

Food and Wine

There is only one wine native to the region, Muscadet, which comes from the Loire Valley around Nantes. Muscadet and *Gros-Plant* wines should be drunk young and well chilled. There is excellent cider (*cidre bouché*) in Brittany, which goes well with seafood, and potent *Calvados* apple brandy from Normandy.

The area has a rich *gastronomie* and the visitor will eat well at modest prices in most restaurants. The vegetables, notably artichokes and asparagus are excellent in Brittany.

Brittany is also justly famous for seafood and shellfish, so that every menu is full of oysters (*huîtres*), sole, crayfish (*langoustine*), crab and lobster (*homard*). The great popular dish of Brittany is the *crêpe* or *galette*, a type of pancake. This comes with many different types of filling, and makes a perfect mid-day snack. Although choice may be limited if you don't like seafood, for price and value Brittany is unrivalled with excellent food at reasonable prices.

The cuisine of Normandy, while equally strong in seafood, is much more varied. Normandy is a true gastronomic region with many dishes of international repute. *Tripes à la mode de Caen* may not appeal to everyone but there is the salt mutton from Mont St Michel, sausages from the Vire, a huge range of pâtes, and excellent cheese, Neufchatel, Pont l'Evêque, Camembert, Livarot, to name but a few. Off the beaten track, where walkers go, you can eat well for under £5 a head at current prices, and that includes four courses and wine.

All native Norman cooking is based on cream from the local dairy herds, so try *Poulet Vallée d'Auge* (chicken), *Canard à la Rouennaise* (duck), *Sole Dieppoise* (fish), *Crème Moules* (mussels), *Tarte aux Pommes* (apple tart). All are local dishes and excellent.

If you become glutted with all this rich food it is customary to take a *trou Normand*, the 'Norman hole', a tot of *Calvados*, between courses, to revive your appetite.

Information Centres

Brittany and Normandy are large, well-populated, well-organised provinces, close to Paris. A great deal of useful information can be obtained from the FGTO London, or the FFRP-CNSGR or IGN offices in Paris. Travel information on ferries and trains can be obtained at any travel agency. The Brittany Ferries Information Bureau, 86 Baker Street, London W1, tel: 01-935 6060 is a good centre for information as is the Comité Régional de Tourisme, 3 Rue d'Espagne, 35000 Rennes, and the local footpath organisation, ABRI-Bretagne, 14 Bvd. Beaumont, 35000 Rennes.

There are *Syndicats* in every town, and *départemental* information is easy to obtain. The following are useful addresses for information: Maison de Bretagne, 17 Rue de l'Arrivée BP 1006, 75737 Paris, tel: (1) 538-73-15; Maison de la Normandie, 342-4 Rue St Honoré, 75001 Paris, tel (1) 260-68-67; Délégation Régionale du Tourisme, 35 Rue Joséphine, 27000 Evreux, tel: (32) 33-25-00.

There are *départemental* offices at Caen (Calvados), Evreux (Eure), St Lô (Manche), Alençon (Orne) and Rouen (Seine-Maritime), Quimper (Finistère), Rennes (Ille-et-Vilaine), and Vannes (Morbihan).

Western France
PAYS DE LA LOIRE
AND POITOU-CHARENTES

It is natural and sensible to follow a chapter on Normandy and
Brittany with one on the two regions which lie directly to the south.
From now on the weather will get warmer and both the terrain and
the climate make increasing acknowledgement to the approaching
Midi, being wilder and milder respectively. Apart from the Vendée,
this is a little-known region, well worth exploring and away from the
crowds which throng the *châteaux* country to the west, or the green
Dordogne further south.

Pays de la Loire is often called Western Loire by the British, but we shall use the French name. It is a new region and, unlike those listed in the last chapter, is an entirely artificial creation with no historic roots. The region around Nantes, north of the Loire, now Loire-Atlantique, once belonged to Brittany. The people there are Bretons and indeed Nantes was once the Breton capital and home of their dukes. Maine, which now forms the Maine section of the *département* of Maine-et-Loire, once belonged, reluctantly, to the Dukes of Anjou, while Poitou and Charente formed part of the great medieval duchy of Aquitaine. The two regions have a lot to offer the walker and provide the perfect introduction to the higher hills and more extreme climate we will encounter from now on.

If we look at the history of the region from the north, in the Mayenne and Sarthe, we stand on the territory of the Counts of Anjou, great rivals of the Dukes of Normandy in the early Middle Ages. One of the Counts, Fulk, was a great hunter and hawker and to improve the cover for game he would carry a few slips of broom in his cap, and plant it in any likely covert. From this habit came one of the most famous surnames in history for, in French, broom or gorse is *genet*, and it is as Plantagenet that the Anjou Dukes are best known to history. Henri II Curtmantle was King of England, Duke of Normandy, and Count of Anjou and, after marrying the beautiful Eleanor of Aquitaine, he ruled Western Europe from the Pyrénées to the Scottish border. Henry II sired such sons as Richard Coeur de Lion and the unlovable King John, whom the French call *Jean Sans-Terre*, John Lack-Land. Anjou, based on Angers, was the home of the Counts of Anjou, Le Mans was their favourite city, and the abbey at Fontevraud their mausoleum. The Plantagenet wars left many castles in the regions, and these dominate the cities along the Loire, such as Angers and Saumur in the *département* of Maine-et-Loire. The largest city in either modern region is Nantes.

The Vendée, south of the Loire, resembles Brittany, and is best known to history as the home of Gilles de Rais, or Bluebeard, who fought with Joan of Arc, and like her was burned alive for witchcraft, which in his case was a not unmerited fate.

The Vendée, Poitou and Charente lie south of the great river Loire, but north of the Gironde. The south of this region is the land of cognac and famous for its vast collection of Romanesque churches. Poitiers to the east is the great city of the region, the place where Charles Martel defeated the Moors in AD 732, and where, much later in 1356, Edward, Black Prince of Wales, crushed a French army and took the French King John into long captivity. This is a gentle sunny region of rich farms and vineyards, bathed in a clear light, dotted with delightful villages.

The long coastline is girdled with islands, such as Noirmoutier, Oleron and Yeu, while inland lie the green and mysterious marshes of the Poitou Marais. All in all this is a marvellously-beautiful, historic and little-known region which I urge any walker who loves history and architecture to visit.

The Regions Today

Pays de la Loire is not a unified region, historically or geographically. It consists of five *départements* which are, from the north-east, Sarthe, Mayenne, Maine-et-Loire, Loire-Atlantique and Vendée.

The Poitou-Charentes lies directly south of this region, although the *département* of Deux-Sèvres is matched to the west by the Vendée.

Poitou-Charentes has four *départements*, Deux-Sèvres, Vienne, Charente and Charente-Maritime. Both regions are very rural and draw much of their income from tourism, agriculture and wine. Nantes is a great commercial city and seaport, and Angers, Poitiers, Saumur and Angoulême are market centres and capitals of their *départements*, but there is no real heavy industry. The Loire wines, Muscadet, Saumur, and Anjou, are excellent and inexpensive, and most of the grapes grown in Charente go to make cognac. Both regions are noted for fine food.

The coast is diverse and fascinating, studded with such town as the Huguenot port of La Rochelle, which is now a major fishing port, like quaint Rochefort and Royan. The Vendée coast is a network of little resorts, and very popular with tourists in the summer.

Physical Description

The *départements* of Mayenne and Sarthe resemble Normandy, with plenty of green, rolling, arable farmland. The Alpes-Mancelles, which are low hills at around 250 m, straddle the *départemental* boundaries and various rivers wind around the hills of this well-watered farming country.

To the south-east lies the Baugeois, below La Flèche. It is a wooded region, and is ideal for those who like solitude, and to walk off the beaten track.

The Loire itself flows along an open valley, with the marshland of Brière (above St Nazaire), as the main physical feature in this western area.

Across the river, in the Vendée, the country becomes more rugged, and this tendency increases as the walker travels south when, in addi-

Regional Boundary

Departmental Boundary

Parc Naturel Régional (P.N.R.) or Parc National (P.N.)

Marsh

200 m/600 ft

00 m/00 ft

0   30 km/19 miles

P.N.R. Normandie-Maine

Mayenne

Mayenne

Laval

Sillé-le-Guillaume

Le Mans

Sarthe

Sarthe

La Châtre sur-le-Loir

La Flèche

Châteaubriant

Loir

Loire-Atlantique

PAYS DE LA LOIRE

Nantes to Brest Canal

P.N.R. de Brière

Seiches-sur-le-Loir

Angers

Guerande

St Nazaire

Nort-sur-Erdre

Erdre

Loire

Champtoceaux

Maine-et-Loire

Le Croisic

Loire

Saumur

Montsoreau

Pornic

Nantes

Fontevraud

Noirmoutier-en-Ile

Cholet

Ile de Yeu

La Roche-sur-Yon

Deux-Sèvres

Châtellerault

Vendée

Parthenay

Poitiers

Les Sables d'Olonne

Mervent

Vienne

Vienne

Lussac-les-Châteaux

Ile de Ré

Marais Poitevin

Niort

POITOU-CHARENTES

La Rochelle

Arailles Limousin

Aigrefeuille d'Aunis

Ile d'Oléron

Confolens

St Trojan

Brouage

Charente-Maritime

Charente

Saintes

Cognac

La Rochefoucauld

Royan

SAINTONGE

Pons

Angoulême

Gironde

Jonzac

Charente

N
W   E
S

tion, the climate warms up appreciably. The coast is sandy though, and the countryside green. These regions present no physical or technical problems to the walker, simply a host of opportunities.

Climate

I always advise visitors to France who want to be sure of warm weather to go south of the Loire. Once you have done so the weather improves perceptibly. Since the coastline is flat, the Atlantic westerlies do not unload their moisture in any great amount, and the sunshine can be guaranteed south from the Vendée. Spring and autumn can be wet, however, and, although the mimosa flowers on the island of Noirmoutier as early as February, the ideal months for walking are April to June, and September to the end of November. July and August will be pleasant and hot but also, alas, crowded, especially in the Vendée. Poitou-Charentes claims less rain and more sun than anywhere else on the Atlantic seaboard.

Walking in the *Départements*

Pays de la Loire

Sarthe: This is farming country, well wooded outside the Parc Normandie Maine, and rolling gently down towards the Loire. The *pays* of the Erve and Vegre rivers, west of Le Mans, is good walking country. The valley of the Sarthe itself, reached from Le Mans, is pleasant easy walking, and the Alpes Mancelles is the region for day walking, with many more challenging routes.

Mayenne: Mayenne is mainly farmland but still agreeable. The north of the *département,* near the towns of Mayenne and Andouille, is the most interesting area with a varied countryside, especially further west towards the Vilaine and around the town of Fougères in Brittany, where the countryside is more broken.

Loire-Atlantique: The Parc de la Brière is largely a marsh, not unlike the Poitivan *marais,* but worth exploring by boat just to see the birdlife. The better walking areas are north of Nantes, around Nort, along the river Erdre, or south of the Loire in the *pays de Retz,* or along the coast from Pornic to Noirmoutier.

Maine-et-Loire: A walk along the Loire takes in great walking country, but along the Western Loire, almost to Champtoceaux, lie docks, wharfs, and all the complex of industrialisation that hovers around a great port. It is necessary to get upstream, past Champtoceaux, before the river becomes attractive. My favourite area here is in the hills around Fontevraud and Saumur, where the Loire takes a great loop before entering the Châteaux country of the Loire.

Vendée: The glory of the Vendée must be its coast, which is quite varied and beautiful. The coast can be followed easily from Pornic south to the Sables d'Olonne. *Sable,* incidentally, means sand. For day walking inland, La Roche-sur-Yon is a good centre. Off the coast lie the islands of Noirmoutier and Yeu.

Poitou-Charentes

This whole region is well supplied with rivers, tributaries of the Loire or the winding Vienne, which itself joins the Loire at Chinon, and has an attractive coastline, some 600 km long. It is agreeable, un-demanding walking country, well wooded, with few large cities but many attractive towns and small villages. The long-distance walker who enjoys covering 25-30 km per day in warm sunshine will enjoy Poitou-Charentes.

Deux-Sèvres: This *département* is mostly famous for the *Marais,* the great marsh sometimes called the *Venise Verte,* the 'green Venice', from the gondola-like craft which ply its waters. It begins west of Niort and spreads up into the Vendée. This is flat country, the towns clustering defensively on the few hills and ridges. The *Marais* can be visited from Coulon and is now protected by the est-ablishment of the *Parc Naturel Régional du Marais.* Parthenay is a good walking centre and very historic.

Vienne: Vienne is my favourite *département* in Poitou-Charentes, mainly because I like Poitiers, but the countryside is very varied, with wide plains and river valleys (notably that of the Vienne itself), huge lakes and rivers and incomparable Romanesque churches. These, incidentally, have nothing to do with the Romans. Romanes-que architecture dates from the period between about 700 AD to about 1200 AD and gets its name from the 'Romantic' carvings often found on pillar capitals, on lintels and in the cloisters.

Châtellerault is the best walking centre for day walking in Vienne, and the river Vienne can be followed south to Lussac, across fine countryside.

Charente: Charente lies against the Limousin plateau, and is de-voted to the distilling of Cognac. La Rochefoucauld is a good centre, dominated by a splendid castle and surrounded by forests, especially to the west towards Angoulême. The countryside, being relatively flat, offers no particular problems to the walker. Such undulations as there are give good views across the vineyards, and Confolens on the Vienne river would be a good centre for day walking.

Charente Maritime: Each region in France has at least one area where all the attractions of that region are seemingly distilled into one delightful mixture. In Poitou-Charentes that distillation is found in Saintonge, south and west of the river Charente and north of Pons. Here is the light, the sun, the churches, the coast, the lot! Many GR trails traverse Saintonge.

The pearls of Charente-Maritime are the offshore islands of Ré and Oléron, but I never miss a chance to visit Brouage, a curious fortified town in the marshland below Rochefort.

Oléron is the biggest French island after Corsica and an excellent place to explore on foot. It has long beaches and rocky headlands and can be reached from Le Chapus. La Côtinière is the best walking centre. The Ile de Ré, further north, is smaller and quieter, but has 25 km of walkable coast, and can be included in a visit to La Rochelle.

Charente-Maritime is an interesting *département*, with good walking in the river valleys of the Charente. The coast at the mouth of the Gironde estuary is particularly beautiful, and indeed called the *Côte de Beauté*. Ronce-les-Bains is the best centre for this region.

Overall, the two regions have more attractions for the long-distance walker than for the backpacker. Tourism is well organised and, except in high season, accommodation is plentiful. This is the place to go with a light pack, walking gently fifteen to twenty miles a day, soaking up the sun and the atmosphere. To rush this area would be a crime, for it is full of delights which need to be savoured rather than gulped.

National Parks

Parc Naturel Régional de Brière: This is a much-drained marshland, north of St Nazaire in the *département* of Loire-Atlantique. The walking is limited but the birdlife is prolific, and the reed-beds can be visited in punts. Not a walker's place, but interesting to the naturalist. The walker would enjoy the nearby *presqu'île* (peninsula) of Le Croisic, and visiting walled Guérande, the 'Carcassonne of the North'.

Information from Maison du Parc, 180 Ile Fedrun, 44720 St Joachim, tel: (40) 45-52-50.

Parc Naturel Régional Normandie-Maine: Most of this lies in Normandy but it laps over into Maine and the Sarthe and is, therefore, mentioned again here. It is good walking country with many kilometres of waymarked footpaths and some GR trails. A recommended area for day walking.

Information from Maison du Parc, Le Chapître, 61320 Carrouges, tel: (33) 27-21-15.

Parc Naturel Régional du Marais Poitevin (Val de Sèvres et Vendée):

This park is not, at the time of writing, officially established but will eventually consist of a region of canals, forests, marshes and reedbeds, ideal for birds. The wetlands of Europe are fast disappearing, but this one should now endure and be worth inspecting.

Information from Parc Naturel Régional de Marais Port, 4 Rue Pasteur, 79000 Niort, tel: (49) 28-38-79.

Footpaths

Local Footpaths

Both regions are making every effort to develop their network of *Sentiers Pédestres*, and in Pays de la Loire they also offer *Sentiers Littoraux*, walks along the coast. All the best areas, Croisic, St Gildas, the Vendée coast south to the Sables d'Olonne, have good waymarked walks.

Clisson has waymarked paths, as does Châteaubriant in the north. Information from *Comité Départemental du Tourisme* in Nantes, or local *Syndicats*.

Information on walking in Sarthe is available from the *Association Sarthe des Petites Randonnées*, at the *Syndicat d'Initiative* in Le Mans. The forest of Bercé is recommended and has a good 20 km waymarked trail, and Sillé-le-Guillaume, just across the border in Normandy, is one of many good centres for the Sarthe.

Many towns in Mayenne and the Vendée have waymarked paths, but nowhere can compete with Saumur in Maine-et-Loire, with no less than 255 km of waymarked trails in the surrounding hills. Information on this excellent walking area is available from the Syndicat d'Initiative, 25 Rue Beaurepair, 49400 Saumur, tel: (41) 51-03-06.

The IGN Cartes Touristiques show good walking areas available in the Collines Vendéenes hills which reach a height of about 250 m around the village of Pouzauges, south of Cholet.

The *Comité Régional de Tourisme* Poitou-Charentes has a booklet with details of all local walks in the region, available from local *Syndicats*. The CRAPA footpath organisation has also marked many trails, and Poitou contains a great many walking groups devoted to clearing and marking more trails. Châtellerault, Saintes, Pons, La Rochefoucaud and Parthenay are recommended centres for day walking, and details on the facilities available are contained in information obtainable from the regional tourist offices and local *Syndicats*. Addresses are given at the end of the chapter.

Towpaths

The great waterside walk is up the Loire, but there is one good towpath walk north from Nantes, along the Erdre to Nort, which is little-frequented by tourists. This river can also be travelled in launches. The river Sarthe is locked and the towpath would make a delightful route across the *département*.

Long-Distance Footpaths

Pays de la Loire

GR 3 Sentier de la Loire: This is a very long footpath following the river from its source in Ardèche, down to the sea. It enters this region at Fontevraud, and follows the river west to Nantes, a distance of approximately 240 km. Do not neglect to visit the Plantagenet tombs at Fontevraud. **Grade 1-3** depending on the area.

GR 3d: An interesting *variant,* or circular walk, south of the river between Saumur and St Aubin-de-Luigne. No Topo guide at present but waymarked, 140 km approximately. Recommended for a good week's walk. **Grade 2**

GR 35 Sentier du Loir: The little masculine (le) Loir is not to be confused with the big feminine (la) Loire. The path follows the course of this lesser river for 120 km approximately, from Seiche-sur-le-Loir (Angers) towards La Chartre-sur-le-Loir, and is a nice long but fairly easy 232 km. A good route for long-distance walking. **Grade 1.**

GR 36 Sentier Manche-Pyrénées: Another long footpath, involving two *département* in this region, Sarthe and Maine-et-Loire. The path comes from Alençon in Normandy, through Le Mans and out into Poitou-Charentes, totalling 453 km in these two regions. Circular *variant* in the north, below Alençon 36A, of 62 km. Two Topo guides cover the GR 36 here, and a separate one covers the GR 36A. **Grade 2.**

GR 364 Lusignan to Olonne-sur-Mer: This runs across the southern Vendée, from the coast inland to join the GR 36 south of Parthenay. Part of the path enters the Marais Poitevin. About 200 km. No Topo guide at present. **Grade 1-2.**

GR 37 Sentier des Alpes-Mancelles à l'Argoat: One long west-east section from near Vitré to Sillé-le-Guillaume in Sarthe. 157 km. Recommended. There is also a 140 km route accompanying sections of the GR 35 from Seiches near Angers to Le Leide, then the GR 36 to Saumur, and the GR 3 back to Erigne near Angers. **Grade 2.**

Poitou-Charentes

Poitou-Charentes has many GR routes and great areas of unexplored country. Several of the GR routes from the north run into Poitou-Charentes and can be followed, if time permits, or picked up locally.

GR 4 Sentier Manche-Océan: Three sections of this long footpath run here and can be tackled in turn or together:

1. Limoges to Puymoyens (Angoulême), 141 km.
2. Angoulême to Saintes, 118 km.
3. Saintes to Royan, 40 km (*variant*).

Together this makes an enjoyable and fairly easy walk, or a good, pleasant two-week backpacking trip. If time is very short then the Saintes to Royon *variant* is the favourite and it could make a two day trip at the end of a week's day walking in Saintonge. **Grades 1-2.**

GR 36 Sentier Manche Pyrénées: A long path which comes in from Pays de la Loire and ends at the south in Roussillon, traversing two *départements* in Poitou-Charente from Parthenay to Périgueux (Dordogne) via Angoulême and it is very beautiful towards Brantôme. An interesting circular route is available: the GR 36 to Brantôme, then north on the GR 436 and then west to Angoulême on the GR 3 (140 km) approximately. **Grades 2-3.**

GR 48 Sentier du Poitou: A route still being extended between Chinon and Limoges, crossing Charentes via Confolens. Currently open from Lussac-les-Châteaux to Availles (42 km) and called the Sentier du Poitou. This is a beautiful part of the region and, when finally open, will be a great trail. A Topo guide is in preparation. **Grade 2.**

GR 360 Sentier de la Saintonge Romane: This route begins near Jonzac and finishes in the region around Saintes in Charente-Maritime, famous for its church architecture. Not too long, at 421 km, with a 180 km *variant* which can be tackled separately. A route for real architecture buffs. **Grade 2-3.**

GR 364 Sentier de la Vendée au Poitou: A marvellous walk crossing the Vendée from Les Sables d'Olonne. Approximately 200 km, across superb country. **Grades 1-2.** (See Pays de la Loire above).

Information on GR routes in both regions is available from the CNSGR, Paris, or from the local CNSGR office, Delegués Départementaux, 79330 St-Varent, tel: (49) 67-52-48.

Historic Paths

One of the pilgrim routes to Compostelle in Spain leads south across Poitou-Charentes through Parthenay and is followed for much of the way by the GR 36. The GR 3 between Saumur and Chinon follows a very historic route, to the castle where Henri II of England died, through a region of castles and very good wine.

Accommodation

Along the Loire valley, in the Vendée or anywhere on the coast, accommodation will be difficult to find in high season, and booking ahead is advisable. At all other times the walker will have no difficulty, although wild camping is not common and the practice often discouraged.

These regions produce an annual register of hotels and 'campings' available from the FGTO or the *Comités Régionaux de Tourisme*. The areas are well supplied with *Logis* hotels offering good accommodation and food, but the *Chambre d'hôte* facilities are still limited, as are the *gîtes d'étape*, with currently only eight in Pays de la Loire, although luckily two are at Fontevraud and Saumur. None is listed in the current guides to Poitou-Charentes, although some certainly exist and will be shown in the Topo guides. This is not critical because there is a wide range of accommodation at an equally wide range of prices.

Campsites are plentiful, and *camping à la ferme* is available inland.

Youth Hostels can be found in the main towns, and larger centres, but these too are not plentiful.

To sum up, there is no lack of accommodation in small hotels, cafés or campsites, but it is advisable to book ahead on the coast or in mid-summer.

Transport

Transport facilities within the region are good. A bridge across the Loire at Nantes gives fast access from the Brittany ports down to the Vendée, and there are fast N-roads or autoroutes to Poitiers (Paris 335 km), Angoulême (Paris 445 km), Niort, and along the Loire. As always in rural France, you are advised to use D-roads whenever possible.

Flights are available from the UK to Nantes and Bordeaux.

There are good rail links to all main centres and the rural rail networks (*réseaux*) are still functioning, with local bus and coach support. There are also *trains touristique* from Montsoreau, to see the troglodyte caves, in Maine-et-Loire, from Sillé-le-Guillaume in Sarthe, Mervent in the Vendée, from Semur-en-Vallon in Sarthe, and on the Ile d'Oleron a little train runs for 14 km across the island from St Trojan.

These little trains do not always cover great distances, but they are a way into some fascinating country, by an unusual route, and always in need of custom.

Both the Brière and the Marais Poitevin can be entered on boats, usually called *chaluttes* or *plattes*, the local punts; details from the respective Maisons du Parc. Ferries run to all the offshore islands, although Oléron and Noirmoutier are now served by bridges.

Maps and Guides

The IGN No 106 (Val de Loire) and 107 (Poitou-Charentes) *Série Rouge* 1:250,000 are good tourist maps. The 100:000 *Série Verte* are also available, and both give a good idea of where the terrain is interesting for walkers. 1:50,000 and 1:25,000 IGN maps are also available. Topo guides are available for most of the GR trails, and local walks are well documented by the local *Syndicat d'Initiative*.

Editions Fayard have two titles, *Sentiers et Randonnées de Poitou-Charentes* by Michel and Françoise Moine, and *Sentiers et Randonnées d'Anjou* by Jean Bellard; the latter gives scores of local walks around Angers.

The Vendée is included in *Brittany* by Henry Meynell (Faber), *Guide 'Bleu'* titles are available to all the areas, and the 'Green' Michelin Guide to *Châteaux de la Loire* and *Côte de l'Atlantique* are useful.

Stanfords and the IGN shop in Paris apart, maps and guides are available within the regions from: Librairie Duchalais, 2 Place St Pierre, 44000 Nantes; Librairie Générale de l'Ouest, 6 Bvd. Le Vasseur, 72000 Le Mans; Librairie de la Pierre, 22 Rue du Jeu de Paume, 53000 Laval; Lacroix, 38 Avenue Georges Clemenceau, 85000 La Roche-sur-Yon.

Information on GR routes in both regions is available from the CNSGR, Paris, or from the local CNSGR office, Delegués Départementaux, 79330 St-Varent, tel: (49) 67-52-48.

Wildlife

In arable, closely cultivated country, the wildlife has a lot of competition. Birds are plentiful, and many seabirds do well along the cliffs of Charentes-Maritime and in the estuary of the Gironde. All the Parks are wildlife centres and worth visiting on that account alone. Wild boar (*sanglier*), and deer are common in the forests. There is good fishing in the river but permits must be obtained from tackle shops or the local *Syndicat d'Initiative*. The Poitevin Marais, north of La Rochelle, is one of the last great wetlands left on the Atlantic coast, and therefore of great interest to the naturalist.

Food and Wine

Both regions, but especially the Loire and Vendée areas, are noted for fine cooking and local dishes. In Pays de la Loire try the *escargots* and *pâtés* from the Loire, with Muscadet, or the *Coq au Vin de Saumur*, or oysters from Marennes. Try seafood along the coast. This region has fine cheese, notably *Port-Salut* from Mayenne, goat's cheese (*Chèvre*) from Maine-et-Loire, and *Cabichou* from Poitou.

Along the Loire the wines from Anjou, notably Saumur, or the ubiquitous Muscadet, are delicious, and you should try the Chinon reds. Poitou-Charente has cognac, and it is possible to visit the distilleries or *chais* and sample the products.

The standard of cooking is excellent. Seafood predominates along the coast, notably *moules*, lobsters and oysters, at very acceptable prices.

In Poitou-Charentes try the *porc farci*, or the stews. *Tournedos macéré au cognac* is excellent.

Information Centres

Pays de la Loire: Comité Régional de Tourisme, 3 Place St Pierre, 44000 Nantes Cedex, tel: (40) 47-39-80; Fédération Régionale des Offices de Tourisme et Syndicats d'Initiative, Office du Tourisme, Place du Change, 44000 Nantes. There are *départemental* Tourist Offices in Angers (Maine-et-Loire), Laval (Mayenne), Le Mans (Sarthe), La Roche-sur-Yon (Vendée).

Poitou-Charentes: Comité Régional du Tourisme, 3 Place Aristide-Briand, 86000 Poitiers, tel: (49) 88-38-94.

Départemental tourist offices (*Office Départemental du Tourism*) are in Angoulême (Charente), La Rochelle (Charente-Maritime), Niort (Deux-Sèvres) and, for Vienne, in the Rue Victor-Hugo, Poitiers.

Central France
VAL DE LOIRE, BURGUNDY, AUVERGNE

In this chapter we move, by three linked but distinct steps, across central France, from the dreamy valley of the Loire which we left at Saumur, through the green and gold country of Burgundy, to the Nivernais on the Nièvre, up to the high volcanic peaks of the Auvergne. Our link, throughout this journey, is the river Loire itself, which rises in the Auvergne and threads its way north-west across all three provinces to the sea.

These three provinces provide marvellous walking country. All are totally French, a change from the Anglo influences of Brittany and Normandy, and, as you move east and south, so the weather becomes warmer and the country more rugged.

The Loire has always been an important river, especially in Berry, Touraine, the Orléanais and Sancerre (ancient names which survive today). The valley contains the great demesnes of the royal dukes of Orléans and Berry, rich in medieval times from their holdings in land and vineyards. The great medieval cities, such as Bourges, Orléans, Tours and Blois, were the focal points for that fine fifteenth and sixteenth century flowering of Italianate architecture which has left the central Loire river perhaps better known today as the Châteaux country. Amboise, Chambord, Chenonceaux, and Azay-le-Rideau, are magnificent Renaissance buildings, a tribute to good taste and the power of artillery, which made the medieval *château-fort* obsolescent; at least until the great Vauban showed how to adapt it as a frontier defence.

Burgundy, the next province to the east, knew its greatest glory a little earlier, in the fifteenth century, during the reigns of the four great Valois Dukes, who ruled here from 1360 until 1477, and were allied with the English during the later stages of the Hundred Years War. These Dukes had lands which stretched from the Scheldt (in what is now Holland) south as far as Provence, but Burgundy was the jewel in their coronet, providing them with troops and the wine trade on which their fortunes were based. The Dukes' southern capital was Dijon, and their former province is a land of great beauty, full of quaint villages, great castles, and splendid walled towns. For the walker, Burgundy is an interesting historic province, blessed with good weather, where the terrain grows more progressively rugged from the Morvan forest south to the Beaujolais.

The Auvergne, the most southern element in this chapter, will delight the walker. To compare the Auvergne with anywhere else is impossible, for nowhere combines so much beauty and variety. The countryside of the Auvergne, occupying the northern segment of the Massif Central, is becoming increasingly depopulated as people leave their villages and go to live and work in the cities, but it is ideal for the walker and backpacker. I warned you I was keen on the Auvergne!

The Auvergne takes its name from the *Arvernii*, a Gallic tribe. Vercingétorix, the last great war chief of the Gauls, was an Arvernii and in this chapter we shall visit the site of his defeat by Caesar at Alésia, which lies today in Burgundy.

During the Middle Ages the Auvergne was a fief of the House of Bourbon which provided kings to the throne of France and, as a frontier zone with Burgundy and Aquitaine, became well studded with *châteaux-forts,* many of which still stand.

The Regions Today

The Val de Loire or Central region now consists of six *départements:* Indre-et-Loire; Indre; Cher; Loiret; Loir-et-Cher and Eure-et-Loir; all named, as usual, from the principal local river, each a tributary of the Loire, although the ancient names, Touraine (based on Tours), Berry, Sancerre, Orléanais, still remain in use by the local people and the Tourist Boards. The northern *départment* of Eure-et-Loire is largely occupied by the plain of the Beauce and, centred on Chartres, owes more to the Ile de France in background than to the historic provinces of Central France.

Burgundy, although much larger than Val de Loire, has far fewer *départements,* which are, from the north, Yonne, Côte-d'Or, Nièvre and Saône-et-Loire, of which the Côte-d'Or is most famous for its wines, and centres on the town of Beaune.

The Auvergne, much wilder than the other two, has four *départements:* Allier; Puy-de-Dôme, the volcanic region; Haute-Loire; and finally, Cantal.

None of the regions is notably industrial, although each contains many thriving market towns and commercial centres. Tourism, wine, arable farming and sheep, make up the bulk of the commerce, although the wild Auvergne does have heavy industry, notably at Clermont-Ferrand, the home of Michelin tyres. Issoire has the largest blast furnace in Europe, while Thiers produces most of France's cutlery. Otherwise it is a region of little towns, with populations around the 50,000 mark, and many small villages.

A word might be said here about the Loire, the great artery of this area. Arriving in summer, the visitor will find the central river reduced to a mere trickle, flowing between sandbanks and low tree-crammed islands. Only in the winter, when the rains come, does the river fill to the brim.

Physical Description

The Val de Loire is gentle country, and the towns occupy any convenient hill. In the north, on the great plain of the Beauce, stands Chartres. The highest part of the region does not exceed 500 m, and the region is best imagined as rolling, well-wooded country, especially in the Orléanais.

Burgundian hills are steeper, and heights in the great forest of the Morvan (which lies east of the Loire, between Nevers and Saulieu) vary from 400 to 900 m, averaging about 500 m elsewhere in the

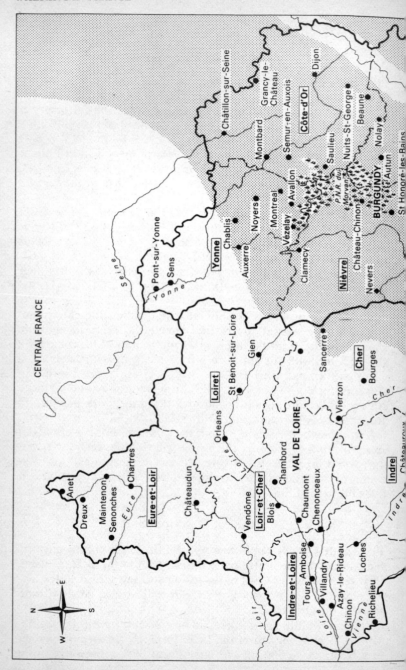

CENTRAL FRANCE

Châtillon-sur-Seine

Grancy-le-
Château

Dijon

Côte-d'Or

Montbard

Semur-en-Auxois

Nuits-St-George

Beaune

Saulieu

Nolay

P.N.R. du

Morvan

BURGUNDY

Autun

Noyers

Montréal

Avallon

St Honoré-les-Bains

Chablis

Pont-sur-Yonne

Sens

Auxerre

Vézelay

Château-Chinon

Yonne

Clamecy

Nièvre

Seine

Yonne

Nevers

St Benoît-sur-Loire

Gien

Sancerre

Cher

Bourges

Loiret

Orleans

Vierzon

Cher

Loire

Châteauroux

Chambord

VAL DE LOIRE

Indre

Chartres

Châteaudun

Eure-et-Loir

Vendôme

Loir-et-Cher

Blois

Chaumont

Chenonceaux

Anet

Dreux

Maintenon

Senonches

Eure

Loir

Amboise

Indre-et-Loire

Tours

Villandry

Azay-le-Rideau

Loches

Chinon

Richelieu

Loire

Vienne

Indre

N
E
S
W

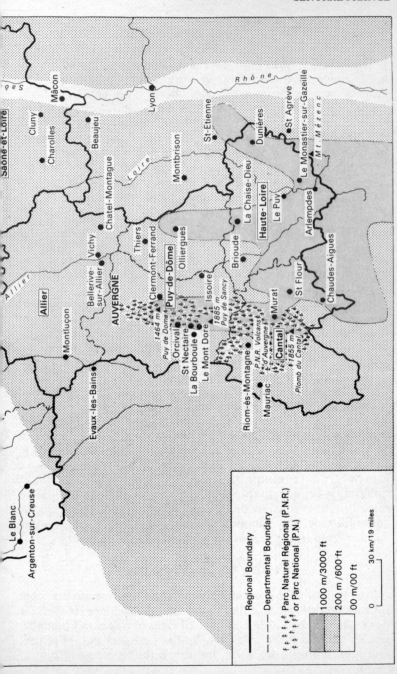

Rhône

Mâcon

Lyon

Saône-et-Loire

Cluny

Charolles

Beaujeu

St-Étienne

Dunières

St Agrève

Le Monastier-sur-Gazeille

Mt. Mézenc

Montbrison

La Chaise-Dieu

Haute-Loire

Loire

Chatel-Montagne

Le Puy

Arlempdes

Thiers

Clermont-Ferrand

Ollierges

Brioude

Chaudes-Aigues

Bellerive-sur-Allier

Vichy

Puy-de-Dôme

Issoire

AUVERGNE

St Flour

Allier

Puy de Dôme ▲ 1464 m

885 m ▲ Puy de Sancy

Murat

Montluçon

Orcival

St Nectaire

La Bourboule

Le Mont Dore

P.N.R. Volcans d'Auvergne

Cantal ▲ 1855 m

Evaux-les-Bains

Riom-ès-Montagne

P.N.R.

Mauriac

Plomb du Cantal

Le Blanc

Argenton-sur-Creuse

— Regional Boundary

- - - Departmental Boundary

Parc Naturel Régional (P.N.R.) or Parc National (P.N.)

1000 m/3000 ft

200 m/600 ft

00 m/00 ft

0   30 km/19 miles

region, but rising to an average 800 m in the Beaujolais, west of Lyon. The Ain is fairly flat. The best walking in the south of Burgundy lies west of the Saône in the Nivernais.

The Auvergne is the central region of France and, indeed, the exact geographical centre of the country is said to be Bruère-Allichamps, between Bourges and Montluçon. Clermont-Ferrand, the capital, is surrounded by mountainous ranges, snow-covered in winter, and running up to 1885 m at the Puy de Sancy, and 1855 m at the Plomb du Cantal. Here the balance tilts from the rural to the wild, and arable farming gives way to sheep and hill country.

The regions, as their départemental names indicate, contain many rivers, great and small, and the countryside offers a wide range of terrain, from flat plain to high snow-covered mountains.

Climate

The Val de Loire has an 'Ocean' climate, with warm summers, up to 25 °C in August and mild weather from March to October. Rainfall is moderate, and sunshine plentiful.

Burgundy has a 'Continental' climate with more extreme weather heat and cold, and is the only place, incidentally, where I have ever had sunstroke. The winters can be very cold and frosty, and the rainfall, especially in the Morvan, is more than adequate to keep the rivers full. The summers though are long and warm, with the occasional thunderstrom to reduce any humidity.

The Auvergne, as part of the Massif Central, has a mixture of climates and adds the 'Mediterranean' to the two already covered. This gives the region hot, dry, cloudless summers, mild, bright winters, but with snow cover over the 1000 m mark, which can lie into May. Thunderstorms are not uncommon, and the rainfall is fairly heavy, at about 1.5 m a year in the uplands, but much less in the eastern part of the country.

Clermont-Ferrand, in the valley, can be much colder, even in summer, than the nearby Puy de Dôme (1465 m). Anyone walking in the Auvergne should be equipped for rapid and extreme changes in the weather, even in the supposedly warm months of summer.

Walking in the *Départements*

All the regions offer good walking but some *départements* are more suitable than others. As a rough guideline, the facilities are ideal for day walkers in the Val de Loire, for all kinds of walker in Burgundy, and for the backpacker in Auvergne. Each category can, of course, find suitable terrain anywhere, but that is the overall picture.

Val de Loire

Eure-et-Loir: Le Loir should not be confused with its larger sister *la* Loire. The Beauce in the north, is a flat plateau and grain country, not ideal for walking, and somewhat monotonous, although the valley of the Eure itself, from Chartres, north through Maintainon to Anet, is pleasant, flat and takes the visitor to some interesting châteaux, notably that of Diane de Poitiers at Anet itself. The southern half of the *département* is more challenging for walkers and Châteaudun is a fine town, from which there are good walks south, along the Loir, to Vendôme.

Loiret: Loiret lies to the east, a small *département,* largely occupied by the *pays Gatinais* around Pithiviers, and the great city of Orléans in the south, where Joan of Arc defeated the perfidious Anglais.

The Fôret d'Orléans, to the north-east of the city, has many fine walks. The countryside is very well wooded, and the smaller towns along the Loire provide great walking centres. Day walkers, who like to change centres and enjoy good weather, history and fine food, will enjoy the Orléanais.

Loir-et-Cher: This is an excellent *département* for the day walker, especially those with an historical turn of mind. The *département* is full of *châteaux,* François I's Chambord, Chenonceaux (which lies, incidentally, on the Cher, not the Loire), Chaumont and Romorantin. The Solange district, north of Romorantin, is particularly agreeable, and has many waymarked *Chemins Ruraux.*

Indre-et-Loire: This *département* is also historically interesting for it adjoins the neighbouring province of Anjou and shares many memories of the Plantagenet wars. Chinon, where the English King Henry II died, is an excellent walking centre, as is Richelieu, and the surrounding countryside has some excellent wines. Further east, Loches on the Indre would be a good base. This *département* contains many *châteaux-forts,* medieval castles or the remains thereof and was a cockpit for strife in the sixteenth century Wars of Religion.

Indre: Châteauroux is the capital of the Indre, a great town of Berry, and a very fine town indeed, but here again I prefer and recommend the day walker to settle in the south, which has much varied countryside, and would suggest the town of Argenton-sur-Creuse, or the lake region between Châteauroux, and Le Blanc on the Creuse river.

Cher: The Cher, south and west of the Loire, is a delightful *département* and the capital, Bourges, the capital of the former Duke of Berri, is worth a day of anyone's time, just to see the magnificent cathedral, and the medieval houses. Walking is popular in Berry, and a network of footpaths, the *Sentiers de Berry*, will take the walker to lots of little-known places.

Local walkers recommend the *pays-fort*, the strong (castle) country in the north of the *département* around Aubigny-sur-Nère. I personally recommend the Sancerre region to the east and the Bec-d'Allier valley as offering the widest range of attractions, including good wine.

Burgundy

Burgundy has fine walking, almost everywhere, and although many parts of Côte-d'Or are largely occupied by vineyards, these occupy only the valleys and the slopes of the *côtes*, leaving the tops open for walking. There are four *départements:-*

Yonne: This is a large *département*, adjoining the Ile-de-France, with fine, varied country-side and many historic towns, like Auxerre and Sens.

My own advice for backpackers and long-distance walkers in the Yonne would be to go to the great pilgrim centre of Vézelay and walk from there west into the Nivernais, or east to Avallon and little Montréal. The walk down the Canal du Nivernais from Auxerre is also very fine, flat and great fun.

Côte-d'Or: The escarpments of the Côte-d'Or and the Côte-de-Nuits run south and north from the wine-drenched little city of Beaune. The eastern face of this escarpment is mostly vineyards, but climb to the top and go west into open country. My favourite area is the *Auxois* from Montbard, or mighty Sémur-en-Auxois. Little Alisé-Ste-Reine, site of Vercingétorix's last stand, is an excellent centre for day walking.

Nièvre: Nevers, on the Loire, is the capital of the rolling Nivernais, in what is now the Nièvre *département*. The Loire valley marks the western frontier of the Nivernais, but the eastern half, around Clamecy is my suggested walking area, with plenty of day walks and an excellent tour possible along the Canal du Nivernais, or the river Yonne.

Saône-et-Loire: This *département* contains much of the Morvan, the great forest of Burgundy, which is now a Regional Park. Château-Chinon is the capital of the Morvan and anywhere between there and Anost is perfect walking country, and full of trails. The Morvan is also surrounded by fine towns, all fairly small: Autun, Saulieu, and Avallon. Within the Park, the Lac de Settons is a good day walking centre.

Further south the Mâconnais and Beaujolais regions are also excellent walking country, good centres being Solutré in the Mâconnais and Beaujeu in the Beaujolais. Both regions have excellent wine, fine weather and rugged terrain — who can ask for more?

Auvergne

When I asked a lady at the Tourist Office in Clermont where I could find the best walking country in the Auvergne she replied simply and accurately, *'Partout'*, 'everywhere'. True enough, but for day-walking centres each *département* has its own favoured area. The most striking features of the Auvergne are the range of scenery and the climate, which varies from volcanic hills to open plateaux and from hot summers to snowy winters.

Allier: This is the ancient 'Bourbonnais' and presently farming country; it is less wild than the other areas, and well forested. Vichy is a famous spa, with lots of gentle walks to the east. The more active will find plenty to do on the Monts de la Madeleine, a little to the east, a long range, snow-capped in winter, at around the 1000 m mark. Châtel-Montagne is the best centre for these hills.

Puy-de-Dôme: My favourite walking country in France begins in the Puy-de-Dôme, a region of lakes and green volcanic hills. These hills date from the 'Hercynian Fold' period, five hundred million years ago, when volcanic eruption shifted the earth to lay out the *grands centres* of the Massif, the Jura, and the Ardennes. The volcanos became extinct some fifty million years ago, but their peaks remain. It is fair to say that anywhere in Puy-de-Dôme will provide the walker with a variety of suitable walking, but especially ridge walking. This region of hills and extinct volcanoes lies east of Clermont-Ferrand and runs up to 1885 m.

Good walking centres are Mont-Dore, Saint-Nectaire where they make good cheese, La Bourboule, and Orcival.

Cantal: If you want wilder walking and fewer people, then move south-west from Puy-de-Dôme and explore Cantal. It resembles a vast cone, tipped at the Puy Mary (1582 m) from which valleys run off in every direction. It is very green, very beautiful, quite remote and I recommend a detailed study of the 1:250,000 IGN Carte Tour-istique to help you select an area. Almost anywhere in the Monts du Cantal would be excellent for backpacking, but little Murat or larger St Flour are good centres, the latter being the jumping-off place for the even more remote Margeride country.

Haute-Loire: Haute-Loire is a very mixed region topographically, and in winter becomes a paradise for the cross-country skier, which is always the sign of a good walking area. Good walking can be found around La Chaise-Dieu, dominated by its great abandoned abbey, in the Vélay around Le Puy and my favourite area in winter, the Margeride, south of St Flour. This is not easy country, being remote and occasionally subjected to storms, but if you stay in Châteauneuf-de-Randon, where du Guesclin died, and explore the country to the north, or walk west into the Gévaudan region, you will find marvellous walking and spectacular scenery.

The overall picture for walkers in these three regions is one of increasing severity, but no real difficulty. In the Val de Loire anyone can walk anywhere all the time. As we move south up to Haute-Loire in the Auvergne, so the terrain becomes more rugged and the weather more extreme until eventually we arrive in areas more suited to the fit, experienced walker in summer, and which should be viewed with some caution in winter, however experienced you are.

National Parks

There are two National Parks, and both offer excellent walking.

Parc Naturel Régional du Morvan: The Morvan park was created in 1970, and straddles a part of all four Burgundian *départements*. It is centred on Château Chinon and Autun, Saulieu and Avallon are the nearest major centres. The park is well wooded, full of rivers and has several artificial lakes, notably the Lac des Settons. The park stands at an average height of 800 m and has numerous footpaths, linking up many small villages and campsites. Details from Maison du Parc, Saint-Brisson, 58230 Montsauche.

Parc Naturel Régional des Volcans: This is a most spectacular park, centred on the extinct volcanic craters of the Puy-de-Dôme and Cantal. These volcanoes have long been extinct, but their topless cones still remain to dominate the landscape. Their heights go up to over 1800 m, and this Park is an excellent walking area. Details from Syndicat Mixte du Parc des Volcans, 28 Rue St.Esprit, 63000 Clermont-Ferrand.

Footpaths

Local Footpaths

Of the three regions covered in this chapter, Burgundy is the finest for day walking. This is not to say that the other areas do not have many good places, but Burgundy can offer a wider choice of objectives for the walker, however wide his or her interests may be, and a greater variety of terrain.

In the Val de Loire, Chinon in Touraine, Romorantin in the Sologne, or Vendôme on the Loir are excellent centres. Berry has many short waymarked trails, the *Sentiers du Berry* organised by

SEPANEC Organisation of 41 Rue Théophile Larry, 18000 Bourges. Details and a guide book are available from the *Syndicat* in Bourges.

In Burgundy, the Morvan is covered by a booklet *Sentiers Pédestres en Morvan*, obtainable from the Park Office at St Brisson.

The Côte-d'Or has waymarked trails around Chatillon and Beaune, while the CAF has no less than thirteen waymarked trails and fifty routes open, all over the Côte d'Or and the Morvan. Details from the CAF, 34 Rue des Forges, 21000 Dijon.

Saône-et-Loire is very well organised, with every area offering local paths, but Solutré in Mâcon, Cluny and Charolle are particularly recommended.

The Yonne is more urban but Noyers-sur-Serin is a town well worth visiting with many medieval houses and lots of good walking round about. I would suggest Noyers as a base, with walks out to Montréal, Chablis, and Avallon.

In the Auvergne, good walking is available everywhere, but I particularly recommend the Puy-de-Dôme for day walking in the volcano area, the Margeride and, a little off the beaten track, Monastier-sur-Gazielle in Haute-Loire, for walks to Mont Mézenc and along the infant Loire, through Arlempèdes. This is delightful country in late spring, the land where all the clichés come true. There really are flower-filled meadows of narcissi and daffodils, shepherdesses do play pipes to their flocks, and cattle pull the ploughs.

Towpaths

One of the nicest walks I know is along the Canal du Nivernais from Auxerre to Clamecy. There are a number of long canals in the area which offer gentle interesting walking through areas of great peace and beauty.

The Canal du Nivernais is only one of several in Burgundy. The Canal de la Burgogne can be picked up in Dijon and followed west to the *Auxois* around Semur or south to the Saône. In the Val de Loire walkers can explore the Canal-latéral-de-la-Loire or the Canal due Centre from Marseille-les-Aubigny. I recommend canal towpaths to those who like the type of walking which combines remote areas with fairly gentle progress. Canals seem to have a knack of producing halts at the appropriate moment, and are suitable for all kinds of walker.

Long Distance Footpaths

Commanding vast tracts of Central France, these three regions are blessed with a very wide variety of long-distance footpaths, circular, lateral, or as part of some trans-France route.

Val de Loire

GR 3 Sentier de La Loire: This is a very long footpath descending the Loire from the Auvergne and covered by several Topo guides. From the west it enters Val de Loire from Anjou at Chinon and runs along the river and round into the Nivernais. Two Topo guides cover this section. GR 3 Saumur to Orléans 255 km, and Fontevraud to Pont-de-Mauves 188 km. These two are excellent walks along the river, with much of historical interest and many *variants*. **Grade 2, and 3** in Auvergne.

GR 3c: A new footpath, the GR 3c is in course of preparation and will run across Berry from Villesavin to Gien and link up with the new GR 41. **Grade 1.**

GR 3-32: A new path, a *variant* off the GR 3 Orléans to Males-herbes in Loiret. Topo guide in preparation. **Grade 2.**

GR 31 Sentier du Sancerrois et de la Solongne: This runs through the finest walking country in the Val de Loire region, from Nièvre to Vierzon, 165 km. It could be accomplished in about a week and is highly recommended. The 31 — 307 section which runs west to east, north of Bourges, is also excellent. The latest 1981 GR list shows a second Topo guide in preparation for the GR 31, covering the trail between La Charité-sur-Loire and the château at Chambord. **Grade 2.**

GR 35 Sentier du Loir: This path covers the *départements* traversed by the Loir river, running through Anjou and Maine, taking in Eure-et-Loire, Loir-et-Cher, Sarthe and Maine-et-Loire, 232 km in total. **Grade 1-2.**

GR 351 Sentier de la Blaise: A short footpath of only 50 km from Dreux in Dure-et-Loir to Senonches. **Grade 1.**

GR 41 Sentier St Etienne-Chinon: This route will eventually run across the regions of Auvergne and Val de Loire through Berry from St Etienne to Chinon. Two Topo guides currently cover the route Cézallier to Mont-Dore (90 km) and Super-Besse to Evaux-les-Bains (145 km). The total distance will require about three weeks of walking, and would appeal to backpackers. **Grade 2.**

Burgundy

Burgundy has rather more GR footpaths and a greater variety of terrain, including the wooded region of the Morvan.

GR 13-131-132 Sentier Ile-de-France-Bourgogne: Most of this long footpath runs across Burgundy and each of the three sections has a Topo guide. GR 13 runs from St Martin-sur-Ouanne to Mont Beuvray (where Julius Caesar once camped) across the Morvan (208 km). The 132 is a short *variant* of 37 km off this route. The main trail would be a good two-week walk through steadily tougher country and will lead from the Ile-de-France to Vézelay, a place no walker should miss, for Vézelay is still a pilgrim centre.

The GR 13-131 goes on from Mont Beuvray to Signal du Mont, south of Autun across Saône-et-Loire and, depending on the route taken, offers either 60 km or 54 km of good walking in hilly country. An ideal one-week backpacking trip for a spring or autumn break. **Grade 2-3.**

GR 2-213 Sentier de la Seine et Yonne: The Seine and the Yonne both rise in Burgundy and join forces at Montereau on the edge of the Ile-de-France. The GR 2 is a long footpath running down the Channel coast from Le Havre to the heartland of Burgundy, and supplied with a number of *variants* along the way. Four Topo guides cover the entire route, but only one affects this chapter.

The GR 2-213, from Pont-sur-Yonne to Auxerre and Melun to Troyes, is made up of two footpaths, the Sentier de la Seine (196 km) and the Sentier de la Yonne (98 km). I recommend both, for they take the walker to some marvellous towns across splendid country. Sens has a magnificent cathedral and there is fine country between there and Auxerre, which Walter Pater described as the prettiest town in France, a judgement with which I cannot disagree. **Grade 2.**

GR 2-24 Sentier de la Seine: The walker on the GR 2-24 finishes at Châtillon, and should visit the museum there which contains the fabulous gold treasure from the Gallic tombs at Vix. The Seine is often thought of as existing only from Paris to Le Havre (rather as the Loire exists in people's minds only as the *Châteaux* country), but this is the Upper Seine and very beautiful. This is a pleasant 130 km route, with two *variants* of 35 km and 36 km. **Grade 1.**

GR 3 Sentier de la Loire: This footpath continues through Burgundy with two more Topo guides. The first, Pont-de-Diou to Pierre-sur-Haute, covers 200 km, and the second begins at Pont-de-Diou and goes on to Neuvy-sur-Loire, in the Nivernais (209 km). I recommend this latter walk for a pleasant ten-day trip as it also offers, as a *variant,* a 30 km *Tour of the Puisaye,* a region south-west of Auxerre. **Grade 2.**

GR 7 and 7-76 Sentier Vosges-Pyrénées: Yet another very long path running the full length of the country, entering Burgundy in the north at Langres, and exiting into the Ardèche country, south of Lyon. This path has numerous *variants* and two Topo guides, one for the Côte d'Or, and one for Seine-et-Loire. I recommend the Côte d'Or section from Grancey-le-Château to Nolay, for Nolay is a marvellous gem-like little town near Beaune, which would make a fine finish. At 129 km this is a good week's walk. **Grade 2-3.**

The GR 7-76 continues the path south from Nolay to Mont St

Rigaud which is further and tougher. 236 km for the GR 7, and 60 km for the GR 76. **Grade 2-3.**

GR 760 Tour du Beaujolais: This is a good walk absorbing part of the GR 7 and 76 and circling the fine vine-cloaked hills of Beaujolais in the *Clochemerle* country just north of Lyon. **Grade 2-3.**

Auvergne

The Auvergne is fine walking country, with many excellent GR trails within the region as well as sections of longer trails. Any walker, whatever his or her particular persuasion, will be delighted with the Auvergne.

GR 3 Sentier de la Loire: This long path, which we have met again and again in the last chapters, cuts through the Allier *département* in the section from Pont-de-Diou to Pierre-sur-Haute (200 km). The Allier section is short, but attractive, in fine backpacking country. **Grade 3.**

GR 30 & 33-331 Sentiers du Massif Central: This *sentier* network consists of two paths. The GR 30 *Tour des Lacs d'Auvergne* (170 km), is a beautiful walk in the Mont-Dore region and a challenging ten-day trip for the fit long-distance walker or backpacker.

The GR 33-331 is also in the Puy-de-Dôme, is longer at 201 km, but equally interesting, covering a variety of scenery across the country from St Alvard to Pierre-sur-Haut, and the GR 3.

GR 330 Tour du Livradois: A circular walk in the Puy-de-Dôme, a perfect route for backpackers. 260 km, say ten days. **Grade 3.**

GR 4 Sentier Mediterranée-Océan: This long footpath crosses Cantal and Puy-de-Dôme. This section from Pont-St-Esprit to St Flour is 225 km, and then St Flour to Aubusson in the Limousin, 267 km. Two Topo guides describe the routes. **Grades 2-3.**

GR 40 Tour du Velay: This is a marvellous circular backpacking or long-distance walk of 160 km in Haute-Loire around the town of Le Puy. This is moderately hilly country of between 800 to 1500 m high and covers the hills of Velay and Mézenc, two beautiful areas. Anyone looking for the perfect two-week trip should cover this route. **Grade 3.**

GR 400 Sentier à travers le Volcan Cantalien: 146 km in the Plomb de Cantal. A challenging, highly scenic walk, and a perfect one-week or ten-day task for a fit walker. The volcanoes are now green, cone-shaped hills, spectacular to visit and a challenge to climb. **Grade 3.**

GR 41 Sentier Saint-Etienne to Chinon: When completed, this will be a great walk. Two sections in the Auvergne are already open. There are two Topo guides covering the Mont-Dore, one from Brioude to la Bourboule (90 km) and another from Super-besse to Evaux les Bains (145 km). These routes are practical from the end of April to November, for this is skiing country in winter. **Grade 2-3.**

GR 412 Sentier des Monts du Livradois: This is a short (54 km) walk in Haute-Loire from Olliergues to la Chaise-Dieu. I did it comfortably in three days, although the Topo guide divides it into eleven stages. The Monts du Livradois are not very high, the Signal de Monts at 1218 m being the highest peak, but it is wild country and a satisfactory walk. **Grade 2-3.**

GR 4-43-44: Pont St Esprit — St Flour, 250 km. **Grade 3.**

GR 65 Sentier de Saint Jacques de Compostelle: A great and historic route, the old pilgrim trail has one section in Auvergne, from Le Puy south and west to the Aubrac (140 km). It is long and hot in summer, but well waymarked, an ideal backpacker or long-distance walker's route. **Grade 3.**

I once covered this section in six days and I wish it had taken longer. From the Aubrac the trail continues across Aveyron to Conques and Figeac.

GR 7-72-73 Sentier Vosages-Pyrénées: This trail enters the Auvergne at Mont Pilat in the Parc du Pilat and runs across Haute-Loire to exit at Mont Aigoual in Lozère. There are two short *variants* to this route. **Grade 3-4.**

This is a lateral north to south walk, of great variety, suitable for long-distance walkers or backpackers, and would take about ten days.

GR 441 Tour de la Chaîne des Puys: This is a short (108 km) circular tour of the Parc des Volcans, just west of Clermont-Ferrand. The scenery is splendid with views over some 40 extinct volcanoes and this is the perfect one-week walk in the Puy-de-Dôme *département*. There are plenty of *gîtes,* but even a day walker could tour this region with ease, for there is no lack of that accommodation which makes short trips possible. **Grade 2-3.**

The Loire Valley, Burgundy and Auvergne are all splendid walking areas. Looking over the three, it is easy to see that while they collectively offer a great deal to the long-distance walker, the Auvergne is the region with the greatest range of challenging walks, and will appeal particularly to the backpacker.

Historic Paths

The history lover will have a feast in these three areas. The GR 3 along the Loire, which runs through all these regions and on to Ardèche, is a pageant of the past, as it weaves through the châteaux country. You just choose an area and walk, but Fontevraud, Chinon, Saumur and Villandry are just four places which must be seen.

Burgundy is full of castles. Vézelay, where St Bernard preached the Second Crusade, is one of the great pilgrim centres of France, and one of the assembly places for pilgrims heading for Compostelle.

The GR 13-131 Vézelay to Autun follows their route and you will see the *coquilles de St Jacques*, the symbol of St James, on the cathedral at Autun.

Accommodation

There is no problem with accommodation anywhere in this area, provided the walker is prepared to book, and preferably travel a little out of the high season, or off the too-well beaten tracks. This entire region is extremely popular with all types of tourist, and in the Auvergne especially with walkers, so that although there is plenty of accommodation, there is no lack of clients in the high season. The Loire Valley and Burgundy have plenty of hotels at all prices, while in the remoter Auvergne, the walker may have to rely more on campsites and then *gîtes* on GR trails. The Loire Valley lists 563 hotels, 147 *Logis* and 42 *auberges:* Burgundy has even more. The Auvergne has developed a number of *Stations Vertes de Vacances,* which are towns, villages, or hamlets where good, comfortable accommodation is the base for outdoor activities in areas of particular beauty. Bellerive-sur-Allier, Etreuil, Chaudes-Auges, Mauriac, Rion-en-Montagnes and St Flour are just a few *Stations Vertes.* There are twenty-seven more in the Loire Valley and a full list is available from the *Comité Régional du Tourisme* or the FGTO, London. *Gîtes d'étape* are most common in the Auvergne, and cluster thickly in the volcano regions. In summer they will be crowded so booking ahead is advisable.

The centre for information on walking in the Auvergne is CHAMINA, 5 Rue Pierre le Vénérable, 63000 Clermont-Ferrand. Their office is open every afternoon from 1500 hrs. to 1900 hrs. The ATRPA *(Association du Tourisme de Randonnée Pédestre de l'Allier)* at 13 Avenue de la République, 03300 Moulins, is the information centre for the Northern Auvergne.

Burgundy has very few *gîtes d'étape,* only one on the GR 7 and three CAF huts on the GR 13, although more are planned. There is plenty of accommodation, although at a higher price, in small hotels, or at a cheaper rate in the campsites. Details are available from the CAF, 34 Rue des Forges, 21000 Dijon.

The Loire Valley has even fewer *gîtes d'étape,* but there are a few along the GR 3.

Youth Hostels can be found only in the main towns of each region, Bourges, Dijon, Châlon, although there is one in Vézelay, on the pilgrim track to the abbey at Fontenay. There are plenty of campsites, both large and small, and an increasing number of *chambres d'hôte.* Campsite information is available from the FGTO and *chambre d'hôte* addresses from the local *Syndicats*. *Camping à la Ferme* is possible in all regions and with permission it is possible to camp anywhere in the Loire Valley and Burgundy. The Auvergne has far more wild places, and wild camping in the true sense of the term is possible in every *département*, but especially in Cantal and Eastern Haute-Loire, on the borders of Ardèche.

Transport

All areas are well covered by transport services. International airlines fly in to Clermont-Ferrand, and Lyon. Air Inter serves even more local airfields from Paris (Orly). Road access is easy from the Channel ports to the Loire Valley, and down the A 11, A 10 and A 6 autoroutes. These are toll roads *(péage)*. The 'N' roads will be cheaper, and the 'D' roads more interesting.

Trains run south from Paris (Austerlitz) to the Loire Valley, Burgundy and Auvergne, and from Paris (Montparnasse) to Chartres (Eure-et-Loir). The internal coach services are good, and the rural train network quite adequate. Details from the FGTO and French Rail.

The *Trains Touristique* trains may not run every day or out of the high season, mid-May to mid-September being the most popular periods, but as swift ways into the back country by an uncommon route, they cannot be bettered. The *Chemin de Fer de Bligney-sur-Ouche* in the Côte-d'Or is very short, only 3 km, but the Ouche is an attractive valley, west of Dijon. The Auvergne has a much longer run, from Dunières in Haute-Loire to St Agreve in Ardèche, 37 km across the Velay gorges, a splendid trip. Details from the *Compagnie des Chemin de Fer* at St Etienne.

The Loire Valley offers 20 km of a *train touristique* route from Richelieu to Chinon. Details from the station at Richelieu.

Maps and Guides

The IGN 1:250,000 Série Rouge 1 cm = 2.5 km covers the areas with four maps: 106 (Val de Loire); 108 (Nivernais-Bourgogne); 109 (Bourgogne-Franche Comté); and 111 (Auvergne).

1:100,000 (Serie Verte maps) are adequate for the Loire Valley and Burgundy, excluding the Morvan, but 1:50,000 maps are advisable for the Auvergne, and 1:25,000 scale is advisable in winter when snow is certain on the tops.

There are a number of footpath guides available for the Morvan, Côte-d'Or, Auvergne and Loire Valley.

Good general guide books are very useful, especially in order to understand the fascinating complex history of the Loire Valley and Burgundy. The Michelin Green guides to the *Loire* (in English), *Burgundy* and *Auvergne,* are excellent.

Collins' Companion Guides have *The Loire Valley* by Richard Wade, and *Burgundy* by Robert Speight. Spurbooks have *History, People and Places in Burgundy* by Neil Lands, and *The Auvergne* by Norman Brangham. *Portrait of the Auvergne* by Peter Graham, published by Robert Hale, is very readable, while *The Loire* by Vivien Rowe from Eyre Methuen is an interesting guide to the whole river.

Detailed local information on visiting the gardens, the *châteaux,* the *son-et-lumière* performances and other local attractions can be obtained from the Tourist Offices in the main towns, local *Syndicats* or the FGTO, London.

Topo guides are stocked at: Librairie Legrand, 1 Place de la Libération, 21000 Dijon; Delaunay, 40 Avenue des Etats-Unis, 63000 Clermont-Ferrand; Defloux, 11-15 Rue de Paris, Auxerre; Aurlelia, 4 Rue de la Cerche, 4500 Orléans; Le Masque et La Plume, 6 Rue Michelet, 37000 Tours; Librairie Regal, 21 Rue de la Tonnellerie, 28004 Chartres.

Wildlife

The area is full of interest for the naturalist, with plenty of birds and mammals. Wild boar and deer are common in the Morvan, while the Col de la Tournoel (1104 m) north of Clermont-Ferrard is a noted place for such raptors as red kite, booted eagle, buzzards and Montagues harrier. I have seen a dozen hawks following a threshing machine in the Nivernais, waiting for small animals to rush from the shelter of the corn, and the Loire Valley is ideal for warblers, small waders, and such smaller birds as buntings, red-backed shrike, redstarts, and crested tits. A good field guide and a pair of binoculars would be useful and add enjoyment to the trip.

Food and Wine

Burgundy is one of the great gastronomic regions of France, the Loire Valley has fine restaurants and the Auvergne will give you an appetite.

The Loire Valley offers some excellent fish, including salmon and trout, asparagus from the Sologne, strawberries from the Orléanais, cheese from St Benoit and Vendôme, sausages *(andouillettes* or *rilletes)* from Vouvray and Touraine, and inexpensive excellent wine from Chinon, Bourgueil, Sancerre and Vouvray, inexpensive that is if purchased locally and if possible from the *hyper-marché*.

Recommended dishes include the *volaille du Gâtinais, pigeon à la crapaudine*, venison, *gibier de sologne, poulet en barbouille* or, from the Beauce, *cul de Veau aux petits pois*.

Burgundy has so many great wines that for a walk through the villages of the Côte-d'Or or Côte-de-Nuit, a wine list would be more useful than the conventional guide book! Pommard, Nuits-St-George, Montrachet, Clos Vougeot, are all there, but far from cheap. However, good wine at reasonable prices can be obtained from the local supermarkets, and I recommend the walker to seek out the less well-known local wines like the Irancy reds from near Chablis, or the wines of Mâcon and Beaujolais. In the Beaujolais incidentally, it is the custom to serve red wines *chilled*, so don't send your bottle back in exchange for one just off the boil!

Dijon is the gastronomic centre of Burgundy, and famous for its mustard, which is said to be named after the motto of the Valois dukes, *Moult me tard* (I take my time). The town is also noted for gingerbread and a little honey cake, the *pain d'épices*. Other specialities are snails, *escargots de Bourgogne*, fed on vine leaves, *jambon persillé*, and from the Saône the fish stew or *pochuse*. Morvan ham and beef from the Charollais are also excellent, while in the Ain, the corn-fed *poulet de Bresse*, and *bleu de Bresse* cheese are excellent.

A favourite *apéritif* now found all over the Midi is the *kir*, a glass of white wine with a dash of *crème de cassis*. It can be a trifle sweet so *pas trop de cassis* — not too much cassis!

In the Auvergne, try the ham, *jambon cru*, the excellent cheese *bleu d'Auvergne*, or that from Cantal. There is good mutton, and the Auvergne stews or *potées* of meat and vegetables are delicious. Auvergne wine is practically unknown outside the province, but you can buy a palatable Côte d'Auvergne red in Clermont and a Côte du Forez near Montbrison. Like most mountainous areas the Auvergne has its own brand of firewater, and the strong can try the *Verveine du Velay* or the gentian-based *Arvèze*. Personally I would stick to a *kir*, or a little Armagnac.

Information Centres

Val de Loire: Comité Régional au Tourisme, 10 Rue du Colombier, 45032 Orléans. *Départemental* offices are in Chartres (Eure-et-Loir), Tours (Indre-et-Loir), Châteauroux (Indre), Orléans (Loiret), Blois (Loir-et-Cher), Bourges (Cher). Walkers can also apply to Chamina, 5 Rue Pierre-le-Vénérable, 63000 Clermont Ferrand.

Burgundy: Comité Régional de Tourisme, 55 Rue de la Préfecture, 21000 Dijon, tel: (80) 32-81-68. *Départemental* offices are in Nevers (Nièvre), Mâcon, (Saône-et-Loire), Auxerre (Yonne).

Auvergne: Maison d'Auvergne, 53 Avenue Franklin Roosevelt, 75008 Paris, tel: (1) 225-17-57; Comité Régional du Tourisme, 45 Avenue Julien, 63000 Clermont-Ferrand, tel: (73) 93-04-03. (Also Puy-de-Dôme département). *Départemental* offices are in Moulins (Allier), Le Puy (Haute-Loire), Aurillac (Cantal).

Eastern France
ALSACE-LORRAINE, FRANCHE-COMTÉ, RHÔNE-LOIRE

The eastern frontier of France, even after excluding the Alpine *départements* which are covered in chapter twelve, is still a vast area running from the German border south for hundreds of kilometres into Provence. This chapter will cover three modern regions and no less than fourteen *départements* but, while each region contains excellent walking, some of the *départements* can be virtually excluded, if only because their walking facilities are greatly overshadowed by those of other *départements* nearby. The Alpine *départements* of Drôme and Isère in the Savoie-Dauphiné region are covered in chapter twelve, 'Mountain France'.

Historically, this part of France, the eastern frontier, is a fairly recent addition to the national inheritance, Alsace-Lorraine being re-attached as recently as 1945, after annexation by Germany on three occasions in the previous eighty years.

Franche-Comté belonged for hundreds of years to the Holy Roman Empire. Here stood the County of Burgundy, facing and often opposed to the great Dukedom across the Saône. The Rhône valley was itself a frontier, and contained the Vivarais, which is now the Ardèche *département,* a very wild area, and by way of contrast, the great trading city of Lyon. This entire region is waymarked by the fortress cities designed by the great Vauban, military architect to Louis XIV. This chapter will cover three regions with great and currently much under-used outdoor potential. All are hilly and in some parts mountainous. The land gets higher and drier as the walker travels south, and for anyone who likes the less-known, uncrowded trails, these three regions are worth exploring.

The Regions Today

Covering so large an area, these regions are very diverse in climate, terrain and thought. Alsace and Lorraine are industrial regions, rich with iron and coal, much influenced by their German past, and the closeness of the Rhine. Franche-Comté is green, hilly and beautiful, the Jura range running out of nearby Switzerland to influence the landscape. The Rhône valley is a great waterway, dominated by Lyon, the second city of France, but also contains some of the most perfect and undiscovered walking country in France which lies between this valley and that of the Loire.

Physical Description

In the north, Alsace and Lorraine lie parallel — with the rolling wooded hills of the Vosges lying in between.

Alsace lies to the east, and abuts the Rhine itself, and is flatter than Lorraine which descends from the Vosges and ripples west to the Marne, and north to the hills of the Ardennes. The northern part of Lorraine is industrial, the south is farmland. Great rivers thread the region and the Moselle links the great cities of Metz and Nancy.

The chief outdoor area in this north-eastern part of France lies in the hills of the Vosges; perfect for walking in summer and for ski touring in winter. These hills run north to south, their height rising during the journey, and covered in huge forests of beech and pine. The hilltops are dotted with ruined castles, and the whole landscape is lightened by many lakes. The Vosges rise to around 1500 m, but the rise is gradual and the hills rounded, (similar to the South Downs in places). These rounded hills are called locally *ballons,* or, an echo from the German past, *kopfe.* The hills get more rugged further south, beyond Colmar. Obernai is a good centre for the northern Vosges and can be reached from Strasbourg.

In Franche-Comté lies the Jura, a long, curving range of hills, dating from the 'Jurassic' period, a geological era which takes its name from hereabouts, and again, like the Vosges, this is excellent cross-country skiing and walking country. The Jura winds north-east to south-west across the two *départements* of Doubs and Jura, straddling the Franco-Swiss frontier, and may be reached with ease from the capital, Besançon, which is dominated by a huge Vauban frontier fortress. These hills are under snow for much of the winter and, although there are several downhill alpine resorts, the region is a known centre for cross country skiers. The Jura hills are not particularly high, at around 1000-1500 m, lightly wooded, and full of lakes and waterfalls, of which the great falls of Hérisson, and the Lac de Chalain are particularly fine. This is a marvellous area for ridge walking, north to south along the grain of the hills.

The Rhône-Loire region is drained by the river Rhône, which joins with the Saône at Lyon. The high Alps lie to the east in Savoie and, excluding them until later, most of the walking lies on the west bank in the beautiful *départements* of Ardèche, Loire, Rhône and Ain. These areas are almost unknown, for they lie in 'No-Man's Land', between the Auvergne and the Alps, but because of this they will attract the walker who likes to explore little-known territory, with fine weather virtually guaranteed, in a landscape of great beauty.

Climate

The climate changes rapidly as the walker moves south, a fact attributable to the local effect of the various ranges of hills. Springtime is the ideal season in the north, where it tends to be rainy, but the Vosges can offer fine summers and beautiful autumn weather, when the beech leaves are on the turn.

Franche-Comté is influenced by the same 'Continental' air streams, and this, plus the varied terrain, has a profound effect on the climate. Spring can arrive six weeks later on the hilltops than in the valley, with snow on the tops when the flowers are well advanced in the fields below. There is snow cover in the Jura for five months of the year, so summer and autumn are the ideal walking seasons, when the traveller on the ridges can enjoy the green countryside and see full rivers below, rushing down to over eighty lakes. The hills of the Jura are, at the moment, much neglected by the foreign walker and I recommend them.

Along the Rhône, the climate is milder and sunnier along the west

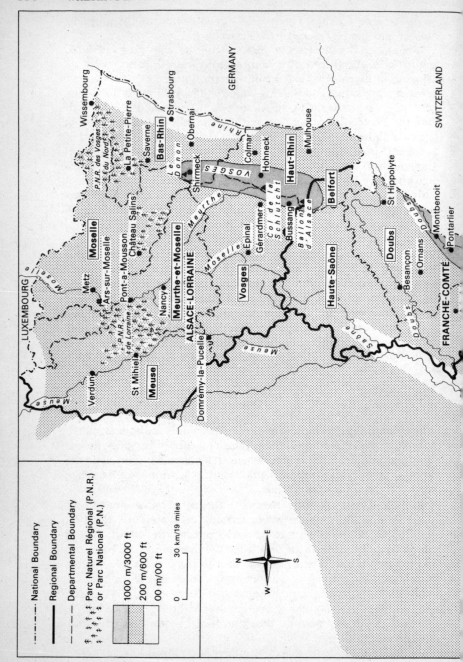

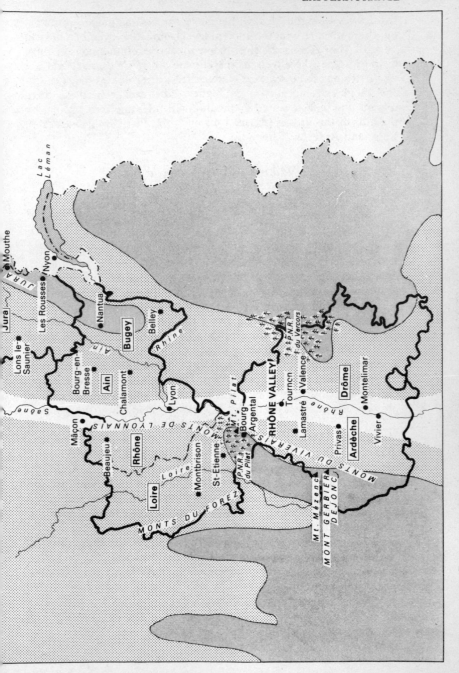

Mouthe

Lac Léman

Nyon

Les Rousses

Nantua

JURA

Jura

Lons le-Saunier

Bugey

Belley

Ain

Bourg-en-Bresse

Chalamont

Rhine

Mâcon

Beaujeu

Rhône

Saône

Lyon

MONTS DE LYONNAIS

Loire

Montbrison

St-Etienne

MONTS DU FOREZ

P.N.R. du Pilat

Mt. Pilat

MONTS DU VIVARAIS

Bourg

Argental

RHÔNE VALLEY

P.N.R. du Vercors

Tournon

Lamastre

Valence

Rhône

Privas

Ardèche

Drôme

Montélimar

Vivier

Mt. Mézenc

MONT GERBIER DE JONC

bank, away from the Alps, with warm summers and golden autumns, but the snow arrives at the 1000 m level from late November and can lie until May. Across the river below the more mountainous country of the Drôme, the effects of the climate are more marked and the weather tends to be severe. Overall it gets drier as you move south, and more extreme as you go higher. The walker in these three regions will be best suited by medium altitudes and in particular by the hills of the Vosges (Alsace-Lorraine), the Jura (Franche-Comté), Loire and Ardèche (Rhône-Loire).

Walking in the *Départements*

Since there are so many *départements* in these regions, fourteen in all, I will, for this chapter, tackle the walking on a regional basis, but describe the best *départements* in depth.

Alsace-Lorraine

Alsace-Lorraine consists of six *départements,* Bas-Rhin, Haut-Rhin, Meurthe-et-Moselle, Meuse, Moselle, and Vosges. The best walking here undoubtedly lies in the Vosges, especially around Gérardmer. The Ballon d'Alsace (1247 m), lies to the west of Mulhouse and from there the Vosges run north over the Col de la Schlucht (1138 m), to the Col du Donan (1009 m), to Saverne on the *Route des Crètes.* Saverne is the best centre for walking in the north Vosges and is at the southern end of the Vosges Park. Darnay is another good centre, but the entire Vosges is excellent and full of good walking facilities provided or initiated by the local walking group, the *Club Vosgien.*

To the north-east, between Nancy and Metz in the *départements* of Moselle and Meurthe-et-Moselle, there is good walking along the river, from Pont-à-Mousson, over to Verdun and St Mihiel. Dom-rémy-la-Pucelle, incidentally, is the birthplace of Joan of Arc.

This entire region is delightful but, however much you love the countryside, don't neglect the towns. Strasbourg, ancient capital of the Holy Roman Empire, is beautiful and full of canals. Nancy is a gem and Epinal on the Moselle is also attractive.

The Moselle and the Meurthe are lovely rivers, the banks forested or cloaked with vines. Nancy is surrounded by woodlands, and from any part of Alsace-Lorraine some section of the Vosges is accessible and less than an hour away.

Franche-Comté

This region has three complete *départements*, and the little *territoire* of Belfort, a fortress on the Swiss frontier in the one part of *Haut-*

Rhin which was not annexed by the Germans in 1871. The three *départements* of Haute-Saône, Doubs and Jura are all excellent for walking but the chief attraction in the region must be the Jura hills, which come in from Switzerland below the Vosges. There are some beautiful river valleys like those of the Ognon, the Doubs and the Loue, and hundreds of lakes. Good walking can be found everywhere in these regions, from such centres as St Hippolyte, for the Montagnes du Lomont, the upper Doubs, or towards Switzerland. Pontarlier, on the Swiss frontier, is surrounded by hills at the 1000-1500 m mark and excellent for walking to Montbenoit in the Sauget, Ornans on the Loue, Les Rousses on the GR 5, and along the Grande Traversée du Jura (GTJ), a long cross country ski-trail. Arbois, in the wine country, or the region south of Lons-le-Saunier, are also attractive. The southern Jura, in the *département* of Jura itself, is less well known, and any walker can get right off the beaten track in the east of this *département*. No one I've met here speaks much English, so a phrase book will be useful.

Rhône-Loire

In the Rhône-Loire region, outside the Alpine *départements,* the wise walker makes at once for the Ardèche, west of Valence. Looking at the 1:250,000 map the division between Rhône and Alps is very clear, the wide valley of the Saône and Rhône sweeping south to divide the mountains to west and east. It is an interesting exercise to lay the four North-South Série Rouge maps 1:250,000, Nos. 104, 109, 112 and 115, on the floor and study them as a whole, for the topographical configuration of eastern France is then very distinct: Vosges, Jura and Alps to the east, the vallies of Saône and Rhône as a division, and then the matching but generally much lower hills to the west of the valley, Ardennes/Côte d'Or, Mâconnais, Beaujolais, Vivarais and Cévennes. The Vivarais, now embraced by the *département* of Ardèche, is one of my favourite places in the whole of France.

Much of this western region is forested, and generally I'm not too fond of forests which tend to block the views, but the Ardèche country opens up to the north and west. The Monts du Vivarais run to the south and west from Pilat for over 100 km and never drop below the 1000 m mark, providing superb walking country with marvellous open, grassy land to the west. The main peaks are Mt Mézenc (1753 m), an extinct volcano, and the Gerbier de Jonc (1551 m), below which lies the source of the river Loire, in beautiful country. The ideal way to enter this region is either from Le Puy or, to stay within the Rhône region, by moving west from Valence.

Liamastre is the ideal centre for day walking, but the Loire *département* is more suitable for backpacking and long-distance walkers.

Further to the south-east, and one of my favourite off-the-beaten-track areas, lies the plateau du Coiron. This is much lower, at the 800 m mark, but there is a marvellous ridge walk (I am addicted to ridge walking) from the Pic de Chenavari above Montélimar of about 40 km, west to the Col d'Escrinet and down to Privas. I have done this several times on my own and never met another soul on the way.

Between this southern region and the Monts du Lyonnais lies the *Parc Naturel Régional du Pilat* (1370 m). The Pilat is marvellous for day walking and backpacking.

The Monts du Lyonnais lie on the Rhône *département* and run north into the Beaujolais. Between the Beaujolais and the Jura lies the *département* of the Ain, centred on Bourg-en-Bresse. Much of this is flat, and given over to rearing poultry, but east of Bresse, the country crinkles up into typical Jurassic folds and there is fine walking, north to south if you want to walk along ridges or along the Gorges of the Ain and to the Lac de Nantua. The country north of Pérouges (a medieval town), and around Chalamont, abounds with lakes and Pérouges itself is well worth a visit.

These three regions offer a variety of walking suitable for all types of walker. The ideal areas for the committed walker, while still offering a choice of terrain, are the hills of the Vosges and Jura, the Ardèche and the Loire *départements,* and in any of the several national parks. Having said that, since walking should be a way to get away from the popular regions, I recommend Ardèche, the Beaujolais, or the valleys of the Doubs *département.*

National Parks

Parc Naturel Régional des Vosges du Nord: This is a new park, heavily forested on the gentle slopes of the northern Vosges. Close to the German frontier, this area is full of little undiscovered villages, ruined castles, and is best reached from Saverne. This is a good area for day walking or short backpacking trips, and the little village of La Petite Pierre is my own personal choice as a centre.

Parc Naturel Régional de Lorraine: This is a large, well spread out park in two separate sections, one of which begins a little way south of the battle-scarred landscape of Verdun, and runs from the east bank of the Meuse as far as Metz on the Moselle. Then follows a gap and the park begins again up near Château-Salins, on the GR 5:E4 footpath. This park has hundreds of kilometres of footpath and plenty of accommodation, ideal for day walking in very moderate terrain.

Parc Natural Régional du Pilat: Created in 1974, the Parc du Pilat, south of St Etienne, is in marvellous country, between the infant Loire and the fully flowing Rhône. It is high country with snow cover from late November until May, with Mont Pilat at 1370 m and the Crète de la Perdrix at 1432 m being the highest points. This park is not particularly large, but would be the ideal centre for a one- or two-week trip by long-distance walkers or backpackers. Bourg-Argental in the south is a good centre, but Le Bessat, a ski resort in the Grand Bois, is more convenient for day trips. Details of the Park are available from the Park Office, Moulin de Vivieux, 2 Rue Benay, 424100 Pélussin — another good walking centre.

Footpaths

Local Footpaths

The three regions contain thousands of miles of footpaths, and a great many organisations devoted to the further development of local footpath networks. All three Regional Parks have waymarked trails, and details may be obtained from local *Syndicats* or Park Offices. There are also many footpath groups. Chief among these, and one of the foremost walkers' organisations in France, is the Club Vosgien, based in Strasbourg, which has waymarked many miles of footpaths and published numerous guides to the Vosges and Rhine areas. Recommended day-walking areas here are the valley of Munster, west of Colmar, where the cheese comes from, with over a hundred waymarked paths; Saverne, with many trails; the Ballon d'Alsace and Bussang in the south, which is excellent day-walking country; and in the Sundgau, near Franche-Comté.

Details on walking in Alsace-Lorraine and the Vosges are obtainable from the *Comités du Tourisme*, local *Syndicats*, or the Club Vosgien, 4 Rue de la Douane, 67000, Strasbourg.

Franche-Comté has the Jura, which is almost entirely perfect for day walking, with the little-known Bugey district in the south being especially well organised with twenty waymarked trails. A booklet is available from the *Syndicat* at Belley, and the *Comité du Tourisme* in Haute-Saône has a booklet covering walks within that *département* and available from local *Syndicats*. In the Jura massif, Les Rousses, Montbeliard or Mouthe are excellent centres, but normally under snow until April.

Any park is excellent for walking and Pilat is no exception. A booklet *Au Coeur du Pilat* lists many walks and is available from Librairie Plaine in St Etienne. They also have guides to other walks in Pilat and this bookshop is a good first stop on your way to Ardèche.

The *Comité du Tourisme* have their own title, *Circuits Pédestres dans le Rhône*, available from bookshops and *Syndicats*.

Ardèche has a great many footpaths, as has the Loire, and anywhere in the upper Loire valley, along the gorges, but especially Montbrison, would be a good centre, for this has access to the Monts du Forez, a little-known area, full of good trails. This is undiscovered country, with excellent walks, well wooded with chestnut and beech, plenty of lakes, and some splendid castles, notably at Bastie d'Urfe near the Lyonnais. There is a walk which runs across the *Forez* from Montbrison to Thiers in Puy-de-Dôme — a fine trip.

The eastern Ain is another excellent walking area, with many waymarked trails, and day walking around the Ain gorges would make an excellent holiday.

Towpaths

The region has a number of towpath walks, which are particularly interesting routes, in the Alsace-Lorraine area. The Canal Marne-Rhin runs from Strasbourg, a city which, like quite a lot of places, has been called the 'Venice of the North'. The Moselle, the Marne and the Meuse are all attractive rivers and have maintained towpaths. Franche-Comté has several rivers worth following, notably the Ognon and the Loue, while the Doubs, especially to the north, is a very attractive river.

Long-distance footpaths

In such a vast region, there are many long-distance trails and the area is large enough to allow for many weeks of walking.

GR 42 Sentier de la Rive-Droite du Rhône: This is a splendid walk, from the Loire *département* across the Ardèche down to St Gilles-du-Gard, 277 km of the most splendid country in France and a route not to be rushed. Ten days would be sufficient but fourteen days would be even better. **Grade 3.**

GR 420 Tour du Haut Vivarais: The ancient Vivarais is now mostly the *département* of Ardèche, and this 208 km walk around the *département* would be my choice as *the* walk in this chapter. A good ten-day trip in a two-week holiday would be ideal. **Grade 3.**

GR 5 Sentier Hollande-Méditerranée: One of the great French footpaths, and one which, if the walker has the time, will lead him or her from the Channel down to Menton.

Four northern sections of GR 5, starting east of Luxembourg, lead across these three regions:

GR 5 Luxembourg, Moselle to Ars-sur-Moselle: 325 km in all, but only half that in Alsace-Lorraine. **Grade 1.**

GR 5 Ars-sur-Moselle to Abreschviller (Lorraine): 177 km in the north. This leads into the Massif du Donon (1099 m), in remote wooded country. **Grade 1-2.**

GR 5 The Vosges from Abreschviller to Fesches-le-Châtel: 290 km down the line of the Vosges, a splendid walk in moderate terrain, which could be accomplished in two weeks with ease, and I recommend this section. **Grade 2.**

GR 5 Fesches-le-Châtel to Nyon: 260 km, across the Doubs and Jura, into Haute-Savoie. Good walking at the 1500 m mark. **Grade 2-3.**

From here the GR 5 continues south and we shall pick it up again later. The GR 5 is well walked and well organised, with adequate accommodation, many *gîtes d'étape* and sensible stages, but it is definitely a route for the fit, committed backpacker or walker. The stages are not too arduous but all are quite long, and there is very little level ground; 25 km a day will be quite adequate while allowing a chance to meet the people and enjoy the scenery.

GR 53 Sentier Vosges du Nord: In the Bas-Rhin *département*, 163 km on the frontier, pleasant undemanding walking country from Wissembourg to Schirmack, on the Bruche south-east of Le Donan. A good backpacking trip. **Grade 2.**

GR 531 Soultz-sous-Forêt — Massevaux: A new route now being opened across the Vosges, Moselle and Bas-Rhin. Topo guide in preparation.

GR 59 Sentier Vosges-Franche-Comté-Bugey: An excellent route of 384 km from the Ballon d'Alsace to Lons-le-Saunier. Three weeks of very pleasant walking across the Doubs. **Grade 2.**

GR 59-559 Lacs et Forêts du Jura: The Jura *département* is full of both lakes and forests. This walk, with a series of *variants,* can be divided into three sections of 240 km, 140 km, or 30 km. Ideal for the long-distance walker. **Grade 2-3.**

GR 590-595 Sentier Loue-Lison: A beautiful walk in the Jura-Doubs, only 105 km, but in splendid country, including a circuit of the Ornans area. This would be a perfect one-week trip. **Grade 2.**

GR 595 Sentier de la Loue: This begins at Besançon, capital of the Doubs, and runs east across the Jura to Pontalier on the Swiss frontier. Only 73 km long but the ideal introduction to the area. Recommended. **Grade 1-2.**

GR 7 Sentier Vosges-Pyrénées: One major section of this great footpath begins in the south Vosges and runs across to Burgundy. Ballon d'Alsace to Serqueux (164 km) is an excellent one-week walk for a fit backpacker. **Grade 2-3.**

GR 740 Tour du Grand Felletin: A new route now being developed in the wild Loire and Ardèche *départements*. No Topo guides yet but probably a **Grade 2-3** walk.

GR 714: A new route from Vittel to Bar-le-Duc in the Vosges and Meuse *départements*. A Topo guide is in preparation.

GR 760 Tour du Beaujolais: This still uncompleted path will consist of several footpaths linked into one tour. **Grade 2-3.**

GR 7-72-72: From Mont Pilat to Mt Aigoual (Lozère) 445 km across some splendid country in Haute-Loire, Ardèche, Lozère and Gard. Allow at least three weeks, for this is rugged terrain and often warm or under snow until late spring. Best attempted in the autumn. **Grade 3.**

GR 9 Sentier Jura-Côte d'Azur: Not yet complete, but one section in this area, across the Jura and the Ain from Rousses to Culoz, is only 125 km but provides up to ten days walking in splendid hilly country. **Grade 3.**

Regional Paths

Somewhere between the GR trails and the local footpaths in length and degree of challenge lie the regional trails, long routes which the regions have established on their own initiative. The Grande Traversée du Jura (GTJ), a cross country ski route in winter, is one of them, and the five-day Traversée des Vosges is another. The Ain offers long walks, of 25 km or more, in the Col de Richmont, or a week's tour in Massif du Mollard de Don, ideal for the long distance walker. Ardèche has two-week tours available on the Haut Plateau, and along the Gorges d'Ardèche, while Loire has a *Tour de la Loire en 5 ans,* a 500 km trip designed to bring you back year after year, unless you have the time to walk 300 miles right off!

Details of these and other trips are available from the *Comités Départementaux du Tourisme.*

Accommodation

As is usual in France, the hotel industry is regulated by local authorities and the Ministry of Tourism. There is no lack of accommodation at all prices and, in addition, these areas are well provided with *gîtes d'étape*. An hotel brochure is available, from the FGTO in London or local *Syndicats*. It is always best to book or in summer find a place to stay by 1800 hrs. *Gîtes d'étape* are plentiful along the main GR trails, especially in the Vosges and Jura. The huts owned by the Club Vosgien are usually open only at weekends and, in theory anyway, reserved for club members, but in practice any walker is welcome, especially if he or she belongs to an affiliated organisation. Since the CV huts are not always open, it is imperative to obtain a list from the Club Vosgien, *Comité du Tourisme* or local *Syndicats,* and book. In the Jura a large group of organisations have banded together to equip the hills with *gîtes* and *refuges,* and there are therefore over a hundred available in Franche-Comté. The excellent possibilities in the Jura hills for Nordic skiing and touring have made this investment worth while. Details can be found in the guides to the GTJ, all Topo guides, and from the *Comités du Tourisme* and *Syndicats.* The Rhône-Loire region possesses twenty-four *gîtes d'étape,* but most of these are in the Alpine *départements.* The Vercors has currently eight, of varying size, and a number of smaller *refuges. Gîtes d'étape* are often found on farms, and information on them is usually to be obtained, if all else fails, from Chambres d'Agriculture.

There are many campsites of all standards and there will be no difficulty in finding a pitch for a walker's small tent. *Camping à la ferme* is also on the increase and this is useful in the various parks where wild camping is not, in theory, permitted. Fire risk and litter pollution are the main reasons why the local people and authorities prefer walkers to either use *gîtes* or campsites. In practice wild camping is possible in all *départements,* although it is as well to ask permission whenever possible before pitching and essential to be careful with fire and litter.

Transport

This entire area is well supplied with transport facilities. There are international flights into Strasbourg, Clermont-Ferrand, Lyon and Mulhouse. The rail links from Paris, Gare de l'Est or Gare de Lyon are fast and frequent to Strasbourg, Colmar, Mulhouse, Besançon, Lons-le-Saunier and so to Lyon. The area is served by two autoroutes, the A4 to the east, and the A6 which runs down the Rhône valley. Both are toll roads and expensive.

Within the regions the local trains and bus services are excellent, and outside the depopulated *départements* of Ardèche and Loire, quite frequent, at least daily and usually operating out from the main local town.

There are a number of useful *trains touristiques.* Along the Vallée de la Dollar in Alsace-Lorraine a steam train runs for 14 km from Cernay. There is another short 10 km journey from Sinones along the Vallée du Rabodeau.

In Ardèche, a steam train, the *Chemin de Fer du Vivarais,* runs from Tournon to Lamastre, and in Loire the romantically entitled *Chemin de Fer de la Loge des Gardes,* runs a steam train from Renaisson to the Grande Ecluse, a wonderful trip. Details from local *Syndicats*.

Maps and Guides

IGN Carte Touristique, Série Rouge covers these regions with three maps, Nos.104 (Lorraine-Alsace), 109 (Burgogne-Franche-Comté), and 112 (Savoie-Dauphiné).

Editions Didier-et-Richard of Grenoble have a number of over-printed 1:50,000 maps in their *Itinéraires pédestres et à ski* series, including No.22 *Des Monts du Vivarais au Pilat*, and Nos.31-34 covering the Jura. These cover the major areas, outside the Vosges. Topo guides are available for all the established GR trails, and there is a large number of local footpath guides, maps and brochures, notably those of the Club Vosgien.

Background reading on the area is rather scanty, since these areas are just that little bit off the beaten track. Michael Shaw's *Eastern France* from Spurbooks covers Alsace-Lorraine and the Vosges. Fred White's *West of the Rhône* from Faber covers the Vivarais and Loire. Richard Wade's *The Loire* from Collins in their Companion Guide series is an excellent read.

Local map and guide stockists are: Tout Pour le Dessin, 13 Rue de la Charité, 69002 Lyon; Cetre, 14 Grande Rue, 25013 Besançon; Montbarbon, Rue Maréchal Joffre, 01000 Bourcy-en-Bresse; Didier-et-Richard, 4 Place de Phillipeville, 38000 Grenoble; Sport des Cévennes, 17-19 Rue Montgolfier, 07100 Armonay (Ardèche); Geroma, 15 Rue des Seours, 67000 Strasbourg.

Wildlife

The Vosges is still wild enough to protect a variety of large mammals, boar and deer, all of which are reserved for shooting. Chamois and marmot can be found in the Jura, and the Alpine foothills. Wild flowers abound, especially in the Jura and Ardèche, and many species of birds find safe habitat in the parks or in the surrounding hills, including peregrine falcons, golden eagles and many owls.

Food and Wine

In its own quiet way, this region has excellent facilities for the gourmet walker and contains, let us remember, the city of Lyon, which has some claim to be the gastronomic capital of France.

Alsace and Lorraine are agricultural areas, where the main animal reared for the table is the pig. Pork and bacon are good and plentiful and Lorraine lends its name to the *quiche,* an egg and bacon flan, which makes a delicious lunchtime meal.

Alsace people, being more Germanic, enjoy eating and this is a centre for *Choucroute* or sauerkraut, a cabbage dish usually eaten with pork. Try the onion tarts or the eel stews. Fish, notably trout, eels and salmon, form the basis of many Alsation dishes, washed down with local beer or the excellent wines of the Moselle. Most Alsatian wines are white, and such familiar names as Riesling, Traminer and Sylvaner are produced and drunk in the area.

Munster cheese comes from the Eastern Vosges, and Strasbourg has its geese, and *pâté de foie gras,* and the *Fourme de Montbrison* from the Loire is a delicious cheese.

I have eaten extremely well in the Jura, and drunk the wines of Arbois. The chief specialities of the region are the Comté and Emmental cheeses and the standard of cooking, even in the small villages, is very high.

Along the Rhône, good food and wine can be found in abundance, especially in the Beaujolais. Poultry from the Ain, trout from the Saône, *quennelles* from Lyon, great cheeses like the *Bleu-de-Bresse, gigot* from the Drôme, *cuisine Dauphinoise* and *cuisine Lyonnaise —* what a feast!

Then there is wine, from the Beaujolais and Mâcon, from the Côtes du Rhône, and the little villages of Ardèche, and even sticky nougat from Montélimar! The wise walker will seek out the little restaurants, to wine and dine well just once a day.

Information Centres

Maison d'Alsace, Champs-Elysées, 75008 Paris; Maison Alpes-Dauphiné, 2 Place du Théâtre Français, 75001 Paris; Comité Régional du Tourisme, Préfecture de Strasbourg, 67000 Strasbourg, tel: (88) 32-99-00; Office du Tourisme de Vosges, BP 5, 88400 Gérardmer, tel: (29) 63-08-74.

Club Vosgien, 4 Rue de la Douane, 6700 Strasbourg. The Club Vosgien is the main source for information on walking in Alsace-Lorraine and the Vosges.

Comité Régional du Tourisme Franche-Comté (also Jura), Office du Tourisme, Place de l'Armée Française, 25000 Besançon, tel: (81) 80-92-55.

The Doubs *départemental* office is in Lons-le-Saunier. *Comité Régional du Tourisme* Rhône-Loire (also Rhône *département*), 5 Place de la Baleine, 69005 Lyon, tel: (78) 42-50-64.

Départemental offices are in Bourg-en-Bresse (Ain), St Etienne (Loire), Privas (Ardèche).

MIDI-PYRÉNÉES

The region of Midi-Pyrénées, like that of Pays de la Loire, is an entirely artificial creation and a mixture of historic provinces. It includes the ancient counties of Quercy and Rouergue, much of the former County of Toulouse, parts of Gascony, the former County of Foix which is now Ariège and the Western and Central Pyrénées.

These disparate historic territories are now absorbed into one vast region, occupying some ten percent of France's metropolitan land surface, and organised into no less than eight *départements:* Ariège, Aveyron, Gers, Haute-Garonne, Lot, Hautes-Pyrénées, Tarn, and Tarn-et-Garonne.

The Pyrenean *départements* of Hautes-Pyrénées and Ariège present their own problems and opportunities but, being mountainous, have been transferred to our Mountain France chapter (chapter twelve). This still leaves a vast area of land, stretching across the country from the Auvergne in the north-east, down to the Basque country in the south-west with Languedoc-Roussillon as the border in the south and east.

This is an area of particular interest to the walker. It has a great deal of wild and remote terrain, excellent weather for much of the year, and is, in spite of the size, virtually unknown to foreign walkers. The red city of Toulouse is the capital and the fourth largest town in France, with a population of half a million, but the other major towns, Cahors, Rodez, Albi, Montauban, Auch, Foix and Millau, are little-known and off the popular circuit for the British tourist.

Much of this land once belonged to the Counts of Toulouse, but their dynasty was extirpated in the Albigensian Crusade, which took its name, of course, from the town of Albi on the Tarn. Cahors belonged for many years to the Lombards, who built the famous bridge of the Pont Valentré, assisted (so they say) by the devil himself, while Foix was independent. For lovers of medieval history, this area is just perfect, full of old towns and castles.

The Region Today

Apart from the aircraft industry at Toulouse, which is also a major university city, the area depends on agriculture, sheep, for wool and cheese, wine (notably from Cahors), brandy and, increasingly, tourism. Mostly it lives on its memories, a golden dreamy land of small towns and golden stone villages, cloaked in honeysuckle, decked with flowers, shimmering in the sunshine.

Cahors, Figeac and Conques, lie on the GR 65, the Road to Compostelle, and remote little Conques, shrine of Ste Foy, still retains one of the last complete medieval treasures in its vast abbey church. Midi-Pyrénées is rich in such relics, and the wandering walker can ramble endlessly in relics of the past; to Rocamadour and see the Black Virgin, to Moissac with its great tympanum, to Ste Cécile's Cathedral in Albi, the town where Toulouse-Lautrec was born, on to the wild rock chaos of Sidobre near Castres and into the even more remote and vast area of the *Parc Naturel Régional du Haut-Languedoc,* which marks the boundary with the southern province.

Physical Description

When the Pyrénées are excluded, it is the rivers which give this region its main physical features. The eastern *département* of Aveyron abuts the Auvergne and is wooded in the north along the valley of the Olt. The Olt is really the river Lot, but it is called the Olt in the local *patois.* The Olt is overlooked by the 1000 m plateau of the Aubrac (1200-1400 m) while around Millau on the Tarn the

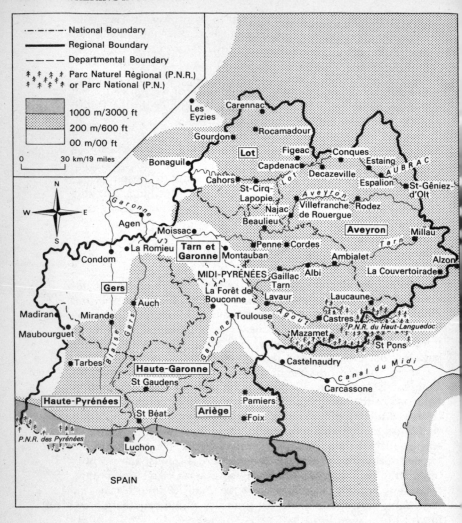

- - - · - - - · National Boundary
━━━━━━ Regional Boundary
- - - - - - Departmental Boundary
♠ ♠ ♠ ♠ Parc Naturel Régional (P.N.R.)
♠ ♠ ♠ ♠ or Parc National (P.N.)

1000 m/3000 ft
200 m/600 ft
00 m/00 ft

0   30 km/19 miles

N
W — E
S

SPAIN

great 1000 m *causses* (plateaux) rear up above the valley. This is
sheep country, and is famous for the cheese of Roquefort.

The Tarn gorges above Millau are famous, and the river flows on
westwards, via Albi, providing a perfect route through the *causses*.
Above Cahors lies Quercy, the ancient province which is roughly
covered by the modern *département* of the Lot. This is rolling, easy
walking country. The high hills begin in the south, around Castres
at Sidobré on the Tarn (700 m), in the foothills of the Monts de Lac-

aune (1259 m) at the Roc de Montalet, and in the ranges of the Espinouse and the Montagne Noire at about the 800-1000 m mark, for which Mazamet is the main centre. Much of this area is covered by the *Parc Naturel Régional du Haut-Languedoc*.

West from Albi the Toulousain plain runs across to the foothills of the Pyrénées, a great flat region, but there is excellent walking country south of the river Aveyron and along the river itself from quaint St Antonin-Noble-Val, across the hills of Rouergue to the medieval towns Bruniquel, Cordes and Gaillac. This is not high country, at around 500 m but remote, depopulated and beautiful. Quercy has the *petites causses* around Cahors, and these run into the Agenais, after which the country flattens out until Auch in the Gers, where the first rumblings of the Pyrénées can be detected. Hautes-Pyrénées has many high mountains but this chapter will cover only the extensive foothills.

South-east of Toulouse lies the country of Pamiers and Foix, in what is now Ariège, good steep walking country dominated by the nearby Pyrénées. Experienced hill walkers will enjoy the Ariège.

Overall, the country is warm, open, full of fine walks and the ideal region for the wandering long-distance walker with an interest in the mediaeval world. It is fairly rugged country, but with no technical difficulties; however, the walker should be fit and used to hot weather if walking in summer. Most of the walks are Grade 3 in summer but 4 to even 5 at other times, depending on the weather.

Climate

This is the Midi and the climate is good: cold and clear in winter, mild to warm in the spring and autumn, but very hot indeed in the summer. Winter temperatures can fall to − 10 °C in the hills. The westerly winds keep Gers and Hautes-Pyrénées green, but it can be dry on the *causses*, and there are regular winter snows on the Aubrac plateau and the higher *causses*. The winter rains flood the rivers, but they fall away rapidly in high summer. For walkers the climate is ideal and the more extreme forms of weather, heavy rain, cold and snow, can be anticipated and are rarely dangerous, a fact aided by the terrain which averages between 500-1500 m everywhere outside the Pyrénées proper. Spring and autumn are the recommended time for walking, until as late as mid-October.

Walking in the *Départements*

Midi-Pyrénées is the country for the backpacker and the long-distance walker, with a few regions worth the attention of the day walker outside the Pyrénéan range. Day walking requires a host of walks available from one centre and of varying lengths. In the vast Midi-Pyrénées there is the urge to move on, but there are good day walking centres as well if you know where to look, and a lot of those little places which could provide a centre for two or three days, before moving on to somewhere else.

Aveyron: This is a very large *département*, roughly contemporaneous with the ancient province of Rouergue. It is ideal for long-distance walking, along the valley of the Olt (which is what they call the river Lot hereabouts), north of Rodez, through St Geniez, Espalion, Estaing, and so to Conques and Figeac. These are all beautiful villages, which live today mostly by the cultivation of strawberries.

The *causses* can be explored on backpacking trips from Millau, a town which is surrounded by the *causses* of Larzac, Sauveterre, Méjean and the Causse Noire. Millau would be a good day-walking centre for the *moyennes* and *grandes causses*, as Souillac or Rocamadour is for the *petites causses* of Quercy further to the north. I recommend walking on the *causses* if you enjoy open windy places, but carry some water for ponds are rare indeed.

Lot: The Lot is a fascinating *département*, well worth a month of anyone's time. It occupies the ancient province of dovecôted Quercy and is full of interesting places. The walker should visit golden Figeac, or settle in for a week and explore the vineyards around Cahors, home of the 'Black Wine of Quercy' which, the locals maintain, brought the Black Prince into France. Rocamadour is an excellent centre, very picturesque, with visits to the great underground cave at Padirac nearby as an alternative excursion if it rains.

Off the beaten track there is good walking along the valley of the Célé, from St Cirq-Lapopie to either Figeac or Cahors.

Tarn: The Tarn is a green, wooded region dominated by the river and centred on the red brick town of Albi, which must be seen. This visited, and after a walk along the Tarn to Ambialet, head south, to Castres and walk into Sidobre, a region of curious rock formations. North-east of Albi, settle in the walled, almost abandoned town of Cordes, a centre for some marvellous open walking country, with access to the great castle of Najac and the valley of the Aveyron river.

Tarn-et-Garonne: This is a small *département* and is heavily farmed. Moissac is an interesting city, with a magnificent cathedral and the best walking is to be found either along the Canal Latéral-de-la-Garonne, from Moissac, or north-west into the Agenais region and Quercy.

Hautes-Pyrénées: This *département*, full of good walking is, as the name implies, mountain country and therefore largely covered in chapter twelve.

Haute-Garonne: This *département,* which contains the capital of the region, Toulouse, is very large and curiously shaped, a wedge pointing south into the Pyrénées at the Val d'Aran. The best walking country is found *anywhere* south of St Gaudens, or near St Béat, *la clé de la France,* a little town which stands on the Garonne. From St Béat there are paths across the frontier into Spain.

Ariège: Foix is the capital of the modern Ariège, a *département* dominated by the Pyrénées and therefore included in chapter twelve.

Gers: Auch, an interesting historic city, is the capital of Gers, a region famous for the production of Armagnac, the only brandy to challenge cognac. Condom and Mirande are two other main centres. Gers is relatively flat country, but divided by the valleys of several rivers: the Baise, the Save, various tributaries of the Garonne and Adour, and the Gers itself. Apart from sheep and poultry rearing, it is wine country, producing the fruity Madiran reds. The towns are small, and this is wandering country, with 1000 km of footpaths to follow among the vines. Auch is the best centre for day walking.

National Parks

There are two parks in this region of which one, the *Parc Naturel des Pyrénées* comes into Hautes-Pyrénées and is dealt with in chapter twelve.

Parc Naturel Régional du Haut-Languedoc: This park straddles the Espinouse and Montagne Noire ranges between the Tarn and Hérault *départements.*

The park can be divided into three regions: Sidobre (900-1200 m), a rocky, green region to the west, the range of the Espinouse (1000 m), running from St Pons to the north-east but on steep rough terrain, and the wooded Montagne Noire (900-1200 m), another long range, overlooking the valley of Carcassonne. The highest peak here is the Pic de Nore at 1211 m. These heights are deceptive for this is the last outcrop of the Massif Central: rocky, steep and tumbled ground, quite hard going, and calling for good boots and some compass work.

There are some beautiful spots within the Park and I particularly recommend the southern slopes of the Espinouse which are perceptibly warmer than the north side. Villages such as Roquebrun on the river Orb, Olargues on the Jaur, St Chinian, where they produce an excellent red wine, really must be visited for they are small, sleepy and very beautiful. This Park is ideal for backpacking and the fit long-distance walker. Details from Parc Naturel Régional du Haut-Languedoc, 13 Rue du Cloître, 34220 St Pons, tel: (67) 97-02-10.

Local Footpaths

The waymarking of local paths, and the provision of maps indicating the routes, is now a major activity for most local *Syndicats*.

Aveyron has a very large number of local routes leading from almost every village: Conques, Estaing, Nant, Rodez, Séverac-le-Château and scores more. There are also a number of more developed local networks (*réseau*) such as the *Sentiers de la Vallée du Tarn; Sentiers de l'Aubrac; Sentier des Trois Vallées,* from Décazeville. The *Syndicats* have the information and the FFRP-CNSGR, Délégation Aveyron, 1 Rue du Bary, 12100 Millau, can supply any technical details.

Haute-Garonne has twenty-four waymarked trails around St Béat and twenty-five from Luchon. In Tarn-et-Garonne, St Antonin Noble-Val is not only a delightful town, but also has nine waymarked trails running out along the Aveyron. There are a further 150 km of waymarked trails around Languepie.

In the Tarn, the little town of Penne has to be visited, with its great castle hanging out over the valley. A 15 km circuit leads from the village to sites in the surrounding countryside. Further south Mazamet is a centre for the Montagne Noire, and St Pons for the Espinouse.

In the Lot, the *Syndicats* at Cahors, Rocamadour, Caberets and Carennac have excellent local trails, exploring the valleys and *causses* of Quercy, and this would be my chosen area.

In such excellent walking country it is not surprising that several companies have organised longer walking tours, from Figeac across Quercy, around Gourdon in the Lot, and in the Tarn, with tours down the valley and in the Forêt de la Gresigne, for two or five days. Details from the *Syndicats* in local towns.

Towpaths

The walker who likes a little history mixed with gentle walking could do no better than follow the course of Paul Riquet's Canal du Midi, built to link the Atlantic and the Mediterranean in the seventeenth century, running south from Toulouse to Carcassonne, and then into Languedoc. This is a beautiful tree-lined path through gentle country.

There are other canal routes in the Midi, notably the Canal-Latéral-de-la-Garonne from Toulouse to Castelsarrasin and Moissac. This takes the walker into the back country with plenty of passing entertainment on the canals and the chance of a lift by *peniche* (barge) to the next lock if your feet get tender. Information from Direction Régionale, 2 Port St Etienne, 31079 Toulouse.

Long-Distance Footpaths

The GR network is only now expanding into this remote area, and most of the trails are concentrated in Quercy or come in from the Auvergne. A number of paths are either not yet complete or lack an official Topo guide. See the appendices for up to date details.

GR 36 Sentier Manche-Pyrénées: One section of a very good one, runs across this region from the great castle at Bonaguil in Quercy, west of Cahors, south to the walled town of Cordes, a spectacular and satisfying walk of 210 km. A good ten day's walking and highly recommended. **Grade 3.**

Please note: A recent map IGN 903 (1979) shows the GR 36 continuing again from St Juery east of Albi, through Ambialet and south across Sidobre, to link up with the GR 7. Parts of this route are waymarked, but there is no Topo guide available at the time of writing. This would be an excellent two-week walk, and the GR 36 continues (according to the map) into the Pyrénées as originally intended. Two Topo guides are in preparation. **Grade 3-4.**

GR 46 Sentier Limousin-Quercy: A long walk from Uzerche in the Limousin, south to Vers, 160 km. A long way but interesting, and suitable for long-distance walkers and backpackers. The GR 46 can be linked with the GR 36 to make a circular tour in the Dordogne for those with more time. This walk goes past Rocamadour and over the *petites causses,* an excellent trip, called locally the Chemin Edmond Michelet. **Grade 2-3.**

GR 6-60 Sentier Alpes-Pyrénées: This path runs across the region from Meyruis in Lozère to Figeac, 215 km with a 70 km tour in the Lot. An excellent walk through some of my favourite places, the Aubrac, Cirques and the Olt. **Grade 3.**

GR 60 Sentier La Grande Draille: A fine 96 km walk on a *draille,* or drove road, from Peyaret to Tréviers. **Grade 3.**

GR 62-62A Sentier de la Causse Noire, Plateau du Levezou Rouergue: What a walk! 186 km. I have done the first section, across the Causse Noire and can only urge walkers to go south at the first possible moment and try this marvellous route for themselves. This walk can begin at Conques in the Rouergue and run south, but going the other way, to finish at the little statue of Ste Foy in Conques, is more satisfying and opens up with the Causse Noire and La Couvertoirade. Either way, it's a fine route. **Grade 3.**

GR 6-64: Another interesting walk, north to south, from Les

Eyzies in Périgord, across the Dordogne to Figeac, 133 km with an 86-mile circular tour in the Dordogne for those with more time. This walk goes past Rocamadour and over the *petites causses*. An excellent trip. **Grade 3.**

GR 65, 65-651 Sentier de Saint Jacques de Compostelle: This is the most historic footpath in Western Europe, a route Christian pilgrims have been following for over 1500 years. Four Topo guides cover the sections in Midi Pyrénées.

Aubrac to Montredon	111 km
Montredon to Montlauzun	58 km
Cahors to Eauzé	218 km
Eauzé to Roncevaux	200 km

There is a route here for every taste and time scale and every walker in France should, at some time, walk all or part of the Road to Compostella. There are also short circular *variants* between Figeac and Cahors, ideal for day walkers. **Grade 3-4.**

GR 600 Tour de l'Aubrac: No Topo guide yet but the Aubrac above the Olt valley is a marvellous region for walking in, say, late spring or from May to October. **Grade 3-5** (in winter).

GR 652: From Gourdon to La Romieu via Agen. A beautiful route of 179 km and an excellent two-week trip across Quercy and the Agenais. **Grade 2.**

GR 653: 223 km in Gers from Colomiers, via Auch to Maubourguet. A long walk across the Armagnac country, off the usual tracks. **Grade 2.**

GR 7-74 (E4): From Mont Aigoual in Lozère (1565 m), to the Montagne Noire, 268 km. Rough, wild country, but very beautiful, and leads through such places as Olargues, along the Jaur valley. A fine three-week walk for the fit traveller, calling for full backpacking equipment and good boots. May to October only. **Grade 3-4.**

GR 71 Sentier Cévennes, Haut-Languedoc: This is an interesting route of 163 km, a *variant* of the GR 7, over some testing country from the Cévennes Park, into the Parc du Haut-Languedoc, l'Esperou to Angles. Ten days should be sufficient to do it comfortably at a pace which allows time to see the country and visit the Templar fortress at La Couvertoirade on the Causse Noire. **Grade 2.**

GR 71C Chemin des Templiers et Hospitaliers: 80 km. This is a new, marvellous route, a tour of the Causse de Larzac, south of Millau, on the *drailles* and medieval routes once patrolled by the Knights Templar and Hospitallers. **Grade 3.**

GR 710: A new route across the Espinouse. No Topo guide as yet. **Grade 3-4.**

Historic Paths

The GR 65 *Sentier St Jacques de Compostelle,* is the most historic footpath in the world. This section, once off the Aubrac, leads to the shrine of Ste Foy at Conques in the Rouergue. The reliquary of Ste Foy is very historic, and was stolen, incidentally, from the monks of Agen. Ste Foy is the patron saint of captives, and the altar screens are forged from fetters.

La Couvertoirade, on the GR 71C, is a little walled town, once a Commanderie, or garrison, of the Knights Templar, and later of the Hospitallers.

Rocamadour in Quercy, is a fantastic town. Built clinging to a rock face, and having one of the very rare Black Virgins in the shrine of St Amadour, it ranked after Compostelle as worthy of a pilgrimage. All these places lie on GR Routes and are fitting objectives for a walk.

Accommodation

The region has a wide variety of accommodation and, most usefully, a very friendly population. I have arrived in Cahors in high summer, failed to find a bed in a heavily booked town and, after ten minutes conversation in a café, been offered a room. The people of the Midi are amiable and invariably helpful, but it still pays to book ahead. Hotels and *auberges* are plentiful and details can be obtained from local *Syndicats* and the FGTO in London. There are plenty of *gîtes d'étape* in the region, mostly along the GR trails. Details are available from the *Comité de Tourisme,* and from CORAMIP, 3 Rue du Taur, 31000 Toulouse.

Camping and *Camping-à-la-Ferme* sites are plentiful. Wild camping is permitted, or at least not actively prohibited, within the precincts of the Parc Régional du Haut-Languedoc, but there are plenty of village sites. Water is not a problem here in the valleys but it can be a problem on the *causses,* where the main water supply is from springs, or from *lavogne* or dew ponds. This is a fairly wild region outside the main towns and so the facilities if plentiful are somewhat spartan.

Transport

All communications centre on Toulouse. There are international flights by Air France and British Airways into Toulouse. Dan Air and Air-Inter fly into Montpellier, an ideal starting point for the Causses and the Espinouse.

There are excellent rail links from Paris, notably an express train, *La Capitole,* which takes only six hours from Paris. There are also good fast road links. Bus and train services within the region are good and operate from the main towns to all the small towns and villages.

There are also two tourist trains. The line from Cahors operates a service throughout the year from Cahors to Capdenac (72 km along the valley of the Lot), and is an excellent way to sample Bas-Quercy; details from the station at Cahors. Lovers of old trains, with engines dating from 1917 to 1947, can take a ride across the Agout, from St Lieux-les-Lavaur, east of Toulouse. Details from the *Syndicat* in Toulouse.

Maps and Guides

In such a vast area it is essential to read a few guide books and study large scale maps before setting out, in order to choose a suitable centre. IGN 1:250,000 Série Rouge covers the area with four maps, No.110 (Bordelais-Périgord), 111 (Auvergne), 113 (Pyrénées-Orientales) and 114 (Pyrénées-Languedoc). These will indicate the walking areas.

The 1:100,000, which shows more relief, covers the area in six maps: Nos.57, 58, 63, 64, 70 and 71. The IGN 310 map covers the Parc Régional du Haut-Languedoc also on 100,000 scale. A separate 1:25,000 scale map, No.412, is available for the Forêt de Bouconne, west of Toulouse. The IGN map No.354 covers the Cévennes, but also shows much of the Causses and the Tarn gorges.

There are 1:50,000 and 1:25,000 map sheets available for the entire region, and the 1:25,000 for the Espinouse and Montagne Noire is the best for this mountain region.

For such an area, a good guide is essential. Freda White's *Three Rivers of France* is an excellent book on the area, and three guides from Spurbooks cover the area: *The Dordogne, Beyond the Dordogne* and *Languedoc Roussillon,* all by Neil Lands. These give a great deal of history and introduce many out of the way spots in the back country.

The *Sentiers et Randonnées* series from Fayard has a title on Quercy and there are Michelin 'Green' guides to *Périgord, The Dordogne* (in English), *Causses* and *Pyrénées.*

The Road to Compostella by W.F.Starkie is a classic on the subject, and *Fastness of France* by Brian Morgan also explores the *arrière-pays. The Albigensian Crusade* by Johnathan Sumption (Faber) explains the history of this tragic period.

Topo guides and maps can be obtained from: Maison de la Cartographie, 25 Rue Cafarelli, 31000 Toulouse; Librairie Rencontres, 36 Rue Hôtel de Ville, 81100 Castres; Deloche SA, 21 Rue de la République, 82000 Montauban.

Wildlife

The pastoral nature of farming in the Midi, the extensive vineyards and afforestation, have limited the wildlife in the Midi-Pyrénées region. Extensive shooting has hardly helped. The mountains do nevertheless contain a good number of large mammals, deer, sanglier, wild goats and, above all, birds. The birdlife is prolific, and the wild flowers on the causses and in the Espinouse are quite remarkable. Vipers are common in the Park, so a snake bite kit is advisable.

Food and Wine

One of the great attractions of Midi-Pyrénées is the fact that this is a country of surprises. It has a great mixture of scenery and a variety of life styles, which vary from the busy student quarters of Toulouse to the wandering shepherd in the empty *causse*.

This is not a great gastronomic region, but good food is not hard to find. *Cassoulet,* a thick stew with sausage and beans, is the dish of Toulouse, although actually created in Castelnaudary. *Foie-Gras* is a major industry in Gers, the cheese of Roquefort is sublime, the *canard magret* delicious, and in season there are crayfish and trout from the rivers. At St Géniez on the Olt they give away a free basket of strawberries on the first Sunday of the picking season to every passing visitor. The cuisine of the Tarn is well spoken of and the region is awash with very good but little-known wine.

There is red Madiran from the Gers, black Cahors from Quercy, sparkling white Gaillac from the Tarn, good *rosé* from St Chinian and, of course, Armagnac. In the Haute-Garonne, the favourite aperitif is the *pousse-rapière,* the 'sword-thrust', which is sparkling wine enriched with a tot of Armagnac, and fairly lethal!

Prices in the country restaurants are extremely reasonable, and this, plus the local cheese and fruit for the mid-day picnic, just adds to the many attractions of this area.

Information Centres

Comité Régional du Tourisme (Midi-Pyrénées), 3 Rue de l'Esquile, 31000 Toulouse, tel: (61) 23-22-05. Walkers should also contact CORAMIP (Comité de Randonnée Midi-Pyrénées), 65 Rue du Taur, 31000 Toulouse.

Départemental offices are at: Rodez (Aveyron); Toulouse (Haute-Garonne); Auch (Gers); Cahors (Lot); Tarbes (Hautes-Pyrénées); Albi (Tarn).

AQUITAINE AND LIMOUSIN

The two regions of Aquitaine and Limousin offer the walker a wide range of opportunities and an even wider choice of terrain. Together these two regions span France from the south-western edge of the Massif Central in Cantal, to the foothills of the Western Pyrénées in the *pays Basque*, in all a vast green stretch of country which contains as a central gem the Dordogne river and *département*.

Historically, and even pre-historically, the regions are fascinating. The Mesolithic caves of Lascaux lie in the Vézère valley, at Les Eyzies in the Dordogne. Even the Romans could not fathom out the origins of the mysterious Basques, and it was the Romans who named the province *Aquitania*, the 'land of waters'. After the fall of

Rome and centuries of comparative anarchy, Aquitaine came back into prominence in the twelfth century as one of the great dukedoms of France, comprising then an area much larger than it does today.

The dukes of Aquitaine controlled Gascony, Poitou and the Limousin, and when Duchess Eleanor of Aquitaine married Henry II of England in 1160, she brought her husband a tract of land which, added to his possessions in England, Normandy, Maine and Anjou, made the Plantagenets the greatest territorial monarchs in Christendom, and also laid the basis for the Hundred Years War, much of which was fought in this region. However, the region marked the Plantagenet dynasty even before that.

Richard Coeur de Lion was killed while besieging Châlus in Vienne. His brother, the Young King, Henry Fitzhenry, died of plague at Martel in the Dordogne, after sacking the Shrine of Rocamadour in Quercy. Bertrand de Born, the troubadour, lived at Hautefort and composed those lyrics which kept King John on his toes. The French King John was captured at Poitiers and the last battle of the Hundred Years War was fought at Castillon, on the banks of the Dordogne. Henry of Navarre's great counsellor, Michel de Montaigne, composed his essays, in scarcely less happy times, from his tower beside the river near Libourne, and this whole region, in spite of the sunny smiling aspect it wears today, was once a place of strife.

The traveller in Aquitaine will find many relics of those warring days, for the land is rich in castles and towns of war, especially in the *bastide* country, south of the Dordogne where, during the thirteenth century, the English and French kings erected a number of little walled towns, *bastides,* to help re-populate the devastated frontier.

The Regions today

Limousin today consists of three *départements:* Creuse, Haute Vienne and Corrèze. Aquitaine has five: Dordogne, Gironde, Lot-et-Garonne, Landes, and Pyrénées-Atlantique. This last *département,* although not very mountainous, holds the Western Pyrénées, and will be covered in chapter twelve.

The regions are prospering today, thanks to sensible investment and a broadly based economy. Limoges, the capital of the Limousin, still manufactures porcelain, but has a sound industrial base across a range of commercial activity. The countryside is rich, and noted for cattle and horse breeding.

Tourism is a major source of income, and the region has many outdoor activities available, often based on the rivers, Creuse, Vienne,

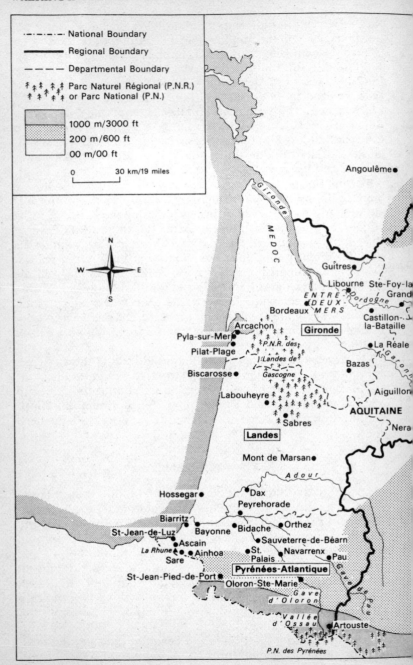

National Boundary
Regional Boundary
Departmental Boundary
Parc Naturel Régional (P.N.R.)
or Parc National (P.N.)

1000 m/3000 ft
200 m/600 ft
00 m/00 ft

0   30 km/19 miles

N
W   E
S

Angoulême

Gironde
MEDOC

Guîtres
Libourne   Ste-Foy-la
ENTRE-   Grand
DEUX-   Dordogne
Bordeaux   MERS
Castillon-
la-Bataille
Arcachon   Gironde
Pyla-sur-Mer   P.N.R. des
Pilat-Plage   Landes de   La Réale
Biscarosse   Gascogne   Bazas
Labouheyre   Aiguillon
AQUITAINE
Sabres   Nera
Landes
Mont de Marsan

Adour
Hossegar   Dax
Peyrehorade
Biarritz   Bidache   Orthez
St-Jean-de-Luz   Bayonne   Sauveterre-de-Béarn
Ascain   Navarrenx
La Rhune   Ainhoa   St.   Pau
Sare   Palais
Pyrénées-Atlantique
St-Jean-Pied-de-Port   Gave de Pau
Oloron-Ste-Marie
Gave
d'Oloron
Vallée
d'Ossau   Artouste
P.N. des Pyrénées

Corrèze and so on, which cross the region and give their names to the *départements*.

Aquitaine is equally fortunate. The capital, Bordeaux, is a wine centre, *entrepôt* for the vineyard-smothered hinterland, and a major port, but here again alternative industry has been allocated to the area and it is now a major industrial and commercial centre. Inland lies the former County of Périgord, a mecca for lovers of good food and wine.

South, along the coast, lie the great forests of the Landes, and the coastal strip is currently being developed into a series of modern, custom-built resorts, to provide for the Atlantic those facilities which the Languedoc-Roussillon resorts provide for the Mediterranean, although the Basque resorts of Biarritz and St Jean-de-Luz still retain their old world charm.

Tourism is important in Aquitaine, as indeed it is everywhere in France, and the region offers the visitor a great variety of scenic attractions, from long beaches to high hills and plateaux. There are many fine little towns and beautiful undiscovered villages and, whatever their particular interests, walkers in Aquitaine and Limousin can never be bored, particularly if the visitor can blend an interest in history with an enjoyment of fine food and wine.

Physical Description

Taken together, these two regions span France from the Massif Central, south and west to the Western Pyrénées.

Starting in the north-east, in Creuse, the *département* is wooded and fairly hilly, with many rivers. The Limousin region has much open moorland, and is nowhere particularly high, Mont Bessou at 977 m near Ussel in Corrèze being the highest peak, standing on the plateau de Millevaches, a name which, incidentally, does not refer to a thousand cows but to many local springs. The Millevaches is a beautiful area for long-distance walking and backpacking.

From the Millevaches the land drops steadily to the south-west, and is down to only 300 m in the regions around Brive-la-Gaillarde, although the hills, if small, are still steep. The Limousin is interesting country for the walker, requiring no great tenacity while being quite challenging, especially in high summer.

Aquitaine is a much larger province, and even if we exclude the mountains of the Pyrénées in the Pays Basque (see chapter twelve) the range of terrain is still significant. Périgord in the north, now embraced by the *département* of the Dordogne, is very beautiful, green rolling countryside. Further south, in Lot-et-Garonne, the countryside is wilder. The western Landes are covered with forests and edged with long open beaches. To exclude the Basque country, we will stop this chapter along the line of the Adour River, east of Bayonne, but anywhere north of this line, around and to the east of Dax, is open country, ideal for the roving backpacker and virtually unexplored.

Overall the two regions, Limousin and Aquitaine combined, offer hill country to the north, gradually declining and levelling to the west, into the Landes, but becoming hot and rugged again south of the Dordogne. The steady decline in height is broken up several times due to the action of the rivers which, over milleniums, have carved out deep valleys in what was formerly a vast plateau. The *causses,* or plateaux, which such effects produce, really begin a little to the south-east of the Dordogne, in Quercy.

The day walker will find plenty of opportunities from centres in Limousin and Dordogne, while the backpacker and long-distance walker, apart from several long-distance GR trails, notably the GR 65, will find more challenge in Lot-et-Garonne or the southern Landes.

Climate

The climate throughout Aquitaine and Limousin is generally warm and sunny in summer, and crisp and mild in winter. Having said that, it is only fair to add that I am writing this in June, in a tent by Les Eyzies in the Dordogne, and it is pouring with rain outside. I have also seen snow in the Millevaches in April, and the cool green of the Basque country, a freshness unexpected this far south, is due to frequent rain from the Atlantic Westerlies. However, the weather is usually warm and sunny from May to October, ranging from 20 °C in July to around 13 °C in December.

The walker can travel here at any time except perhaps in January and February which tend to be wet and cold. Apart from shorts and suncream in summer no 'extreme' stores are necessary. Light boots or walking shoes would be adequate footwear.

Walking in the *Départements*

Limousin

Creuse: Guéret is the capital of the Creuse *département,* and an excellent walking centre, notably for the Vallée des Deux Creuses to the north. Aubusson, apart from its tapestries, has good green countryside and access to the northern end of the plateau des Millevaches (953 m) which must be visited, and west towards the forested country and Bellegarde-en-Marche, the centre for the Combrailles, another green and picturesque region.

The lake region around Vassivière is very beautiful, with many campsites and short waymarked trails. A walk around the shore would make one challenging excursion. Overall, apart from Mille-vaches, this is a good *département* for day walking.

Haute-Vienne: Haute-Vienne lies to the south and west of the Creuse, and contains the region's capital, Limoges. This is a land of vast views and great skies, not particularly high (300-600 m) richly forested, but with rugged hills and with deep river gorges cut in the granite.

The Mont d'Ambazac, north of Limoges, is good walking country, and there is beautiful scenery around Meuzac, Pompadour, a horse breeding centre, and St Yrieux-de-Perche.

Eymoutiers, near Vassivière, is also attractive, with scope for long weekend walks along the Vienne River.

Corrèze: As you may have gathered, I have my favourite *département* in every region, and in Limousin I must recommend Corrèze. I really like walking in the more remote areas, and much of the green Millevaches lies in Corrèze. The village of La Courtine is a good centre, and the walker or backpacker can foray out from here for a day or several days and never take the same trail twice.

Below Argentat lies another favourite walking country, the Xaintrie. This wild country lies between the valleys of the Maronne and the Dordogne. The *Syndicat* in St Geniez-ô-Merle has way-marked over forty kilometres of footpaths, but there are many more and a tour from, say, St Privat to St Geniez, up to the ruined castles at the Tours de Merle, and then west to Beaulieu on the Dordogne, would be an ideal trip. The Corrèze is impossibly romantic. The castle at Ventadour, for example, was once the home of the trouba-dour Bernard de Ventadour, *'who was handsome and adroit, who sang songs and loved ladies'*. Good for him!

Tulle is a neat little town, and was once a centre for the weaving of those fine lace veils beloved of Edwardian ladies.

The *causses* begin in Corrèze, and the Causse Corrèzienne, around Turenne, is a foretaste of the open plateaux of Quercy to the east.

Aquitaine

Dordogne: The Dordogne is a large *département* with hundreds of miles of footpaths, many campsites, and tens of thousands of tour-ists. The terrain is fairly hilly but by no means severe, and very beautiful. The *Périgord Blanc,* north of Périgueux, is hillier than the

Périgord Noir, east of the Vézère. The Dordogne is quite heavily wooded, and vineyards creep up the river as far as Bergerac. The best walking is to be found in the centre of the *département* east of the Trémolat Cingle, a bend in the river, and then as far as Souillac, and up the Vézère.

Another favourite region is the *bastide* country, south of the river. Go from Eymet, through Beaumont, Monpazier, Biron, Villeréal and finally up to Domme over the river, which makes a spectacular end to a week's walking. The *causses* begin to the east of Domme and the walker can follow the river east to Rocamadour in Quercy. Of all the Aquitaine *départements* this one is the best for every kind of walking.

Gironde: This *département* is dominated by the region's capital, Bordeaux, a very fine city, and by vineyards. Vines are particularly abundant in the Médoc on the banks of the Gironde at St Emilion, and in the tongue of land between the Dordogne and Garonne Rivers, which, because of its position, is called Entre-deux-Mers.

There is good walking here among the vines, and you won't go thirsty! A good centre would be La Réole, on the Garonne, or at Bazas, where the forests of the Landes begin. There is also fine coastal walking from the Bay of Arcachon. Arcachon is a good centre for walking into the Parc National Régional des Landes de Gascogne, and apart from the tourist villages the region is very underpopulated and the woodland paths are empty.

Lot-et-Garonne: Lot-et-Garonne is a small *département* of the Agenais, ideal for the backpacker and for the day walker who likes to camp in a small village and explore the hills round about.

The backpacker, or lightly equipped walker, could roam north from Agen to Penne, and across the Lot to Bonaguil and then to Cahors, up the bastides to Villeréal and so to Bergerac. Day walkers could settle in Nérac, anywhere along the Lot, or in the Agenais, preferably at Penne.

Landes: The Landes of Guyenne are vast, flat, sandy and forested. Indeed, this is the largest (800,000 square hectares) forested area in Europe. Personally, I prefer more open country and, apart from a long walk down the coast from Pilat-Plage to Bayonne, I would recommend walkers to hurry through the forests to Dax. This is a very old town, still with a Roman wall, and an excellent centre for walking into the Chalosse region to the east, or over to the coast at Hosségor, a lovely walk in the spring when the mimosa lightens the inevitable firs. Mont-de-Marsan, the capital of the Landes, is another good centre.

At Dax we reach the l'Adour, and this river, which marks the boundary of the Pays Basque, would be an excellent walker's route to follow from Bayonne to Pau, through the towns of Bidache and Orthez.

Pyrénées-Atlantiques: Much of this *département* in the Pays Basque is dominated by the Pyrénées, which will be covered in Mountain France (see chapter twelve).

There is, however, much excellent walking outside the hills of this beautiful green *département,* where the unique and interesting Basque people live, who from some dim antiquity have preserved their language, culture, costume and architecture intact.

The modern *département* of Pyrénées-Atlantiques holds the Basques in an unlikely embrace with the people of Béarn, but for walkers who wish to keep inside the Basque country, anywhere along the Adour, or south of Bayonne as far as Hasparran, or to the caves of Oxocelhaya, will provide a taste of this region without any need to venture into those green mountains now looming up to the south.

National Parks

Parc Naturel Régional des Landes de Gascogne (Val de l'Eyre): This lies to the south of Bordeaux as far as Mont-de-Marsan, and includes most of the vast pine forests of the Landes. The Park was established in 1967 and as well as many kilometres of footpaths contains several smaller parks of interest to the naturalist and ornithologist, notably the *Parc Ornithologique* at Teich, which over the year contains over two hundred different species of birds, in passage or nesting, and the *Eco-Musée* at Marquèze, a living museum showing local building styles and representations of a way of life which has only just disappeared.

The deep forests are seamed with footpaths, but because of the fire risk camping is not permitted and smoking actively discouraged. Information from Park Offices at the *Préfecture,* Mont-de-Marsan.

Footpaths

Local Footpaths

As always, some areas are more suitable than others for day walking, and there are also short GR routes for the more athletic.

The Limousin has many good areas, and a programme of waymarking local footpaths is now far advanced, while in Aquitaine every *département* has hundreds of waymarked trails.

Corrèze: The *Comité du Tourisme* has produced a booklet, *Guide des Sentiers Pédestres en Corrèze,* listing ninety circuits in the *département* and available from any *Syndicat* or the *Comité* in Limoges, price currently 10 francs.

There is also a leaflet, *Promenons-nous en Xaintrie,* published by the *Association pour la Sauvegarde de la Xaintrie,* or available from the *Syndicat* at St Geniez-ô-Merle, listing thirty-five kilometres of waymarked trails in this area. This is my recommended area.

Creuse: The recommended area here is the Marche at Combrailles, around Aubusson. A folder, *Haute Marche et Combrailles,* is available from the Town Hall (*Mairie*) in Auzances. Bellegarde is the ideal centre for this region, but (again) do not forget Millevaches.

Guéret, the capital of the Creuse, is another excellent centre with plenty of waymarked trails, while the trails around the Lac du Vassivière are also often waymarked.

Haute-Vienne: A folder showing twenty-four waymarked footpaths, *Circuits Pédestres en Haute-Vienne,* is available from *Syndicats* throughout the *département,* or from the *Union Touristique de Haute-Vienne.*

Recommended areas are at Bersac sur Rivalier, north-east of Limoges, and at Cussac to the south-west of the capital. This last would be interesting for the British visitor, for it allows visits to the castle at Châlus, where Richard Coeur de Lion was fatally injured, and for the more adventurous there are excursions along the GR 4-E3 which runs a little way to the west and up to Limoges. Further west lies the ruined village of Oradour-sur-Glane, scene of a frightful massacre by the 2nd SS Division in 1944.

A very large number of towns and villages in the Limousin have waymarked their local paths, and folders (*dépliants* or *fiches*) are available from the *Syndicats.*

Dordogne: In spite of the fact that we are moving south, the countryside stays green due to the Atlantic Westerlies, but it does get perceptibly warmer.

The official publication on leisure activities in Aquitaine lists eighteen towns or villages in the Dordogne area alone with waymarked local paths, but I know at least two other villages with waymarked trails which are not listed, so wherever you go in the Dordogne there are sure to be waymarked trails.

Recommended areas, apart from simply saying anywhere in the Dordogne, must be Domme, Beaumont-en-Périgord in the bastide country, Trémolet for a view of the great Cingle — where the river bends in a huge loop — Les Eyzies for the caves, and the Médoc country for wine. I personally recommend the central Dordogne valley from Limeuil to Souillac. This is full of great medieval castles like Beynac and Montfort.

All information on walking in the *département* can be obtained from the *Office Départemental du Tourisme* in Périgueux. This office is a useful first stop for any visitor to the Dordogne and they also produce a booklet *Randonnées Pédestres en Périgord,* price currently 10 francs.

Gironde: This *département* is largely dominated by the National Park, where there is any amount of day walking. The region around Arcachon, near Pyla-sur-Mer on the GR 8, would be interesting. Information is available from the *Comité Régional* in Bordeaux, and the Médoc or Entre-deux-Mers regions are excellent in September and October, during the vintage.

Lot-et-Garonne: This *département* has good walking country and is wilder than the Dordogne. The Agenais is excellent, and (again) no walker should fail to visit Penne and Bonaguil, a huge castle once sold for a bag of walnuts! The walk along the GR 69, when completed, will be superb. There are at least thirteen towns or villages in the *département* with waymarked trails and details are available from Tourisme Pédestre, Centre Ledru-Rollin, Rue Ledru Rollin, 47000 Agen, tel: (58) 66-54-92.

Landes: Mont de Marsan or the coast have to be the two recommended areas. The *Syndicats* have plenty of relevant information. I also favour Peyrehorade, Dax for forays south towards Bidache, and would also recommend a walk up the *gave* du Pau towards Orthez.

All information from the *Comité Départemental* in Mont-de-Marsan or local *Syndicats*.

Pyrénées-Atlantiques: If we exclude the Pyrénées proper until a later chapter, we also exclude the GR 10 and the Trans-Pyrénéan Haute Route, and much fine walking around the Basque villages of Sare and Ainhoa, but I must mention them here just to mark how very fine they are. This still leaves the excellent country along the Adour, around Bidache and through St Palais, a pilgrim site on the GR 65. Oléron Ste Marie is a fine centre and there is excellent walking to the north of Pau and in the vineyards of Juraçon.

Sauveterre-en-Béarn is one of my favourite towns and one well worth visiting, while for the hard walker Navarrenx has 130 km of local waymarked trails, lies on the GR 65, and is noted, incidentally, for salmon fishing.

For the day walker, there is a brochure, *Itinéraires balisés en Béarn,* available from *Syndicats* in the eastern *Béarnais* (part of this *département*), and from the *Maison de Tourisme* at Pau. From the esplanade at Pau you can see the Pyrénées, a taste of things to come.

Long-distance Footpaths

Both regions contain a number of excellent long-distance footpaths.

Because of the heat in summer some pre-training would be advisable before attempting a long backpacking trip, but there are plenty of opportunities and facilities for this, and also for the long-distance walker who will have no trouble finding accommodation, outside the popular Dordogne.

Limousin

GR 4 Sentier Méditerranée-Océan: This trail enters the region at the Simpoux and passes through a number of historically interesting places: Aubusson, Bourganeuf — where the Turkish Prince Zim-Zim was imprisoned by the Knights Hospitaller — and Limoges. The GR 4 here forms part of the Trans European E3. The part around Aubusson experiences snowfalls in winter. Three Topo guides cover the sections in the Limousin: St Flour to Aubusson, 267 km, enters the Limousin. Aubusson to Limoges 131 km, Limoges to Angoulême 141 km. Either of the last two would be a good week's walk. **Grade 2.**

GR 41 Vierzon in the Cher to Evaux-les-Bains in Creuse: Topo guide in preparation.

GR 44: This is currently being waymarked and runs off the GR 4, south of Bourganeuf, across the plateau de Millevaches, and to Bort-les-Orgues. A beautiful walk when completed. No Topo guide as yet, but the total distance will be around 50 km. **Grade 2-3.**

GR 440 Tour de la Montagne Limousine: A backpacking trip in Millevaches, of 130 km. Snow can be anticipated in the winter, but it would be a good week's trip anytime from May to the end of October. Recommended as enjoyable seven-day trip. **Grade 2-3.**

GR 46 Sentier Limousin-Quercy: The GR 46 is still unconnected and in several separate parts, but the Uzerches to Vers section is now open for 160 km. This is a beautiful walk south, and highly recommended. **Grade 3.**

The GR 46 Turenne to Banize section, 128 km, is also interesting. **Grade 3.**

GR 460 Sentier Triangle des Combrailles: Currently waymarked, with a Topo guide in preparation. This is a circular walk in the Creuse, near Bellegarde. **Grade 1-2.**

GR 446 Circuit Maronne et Céré: This is a *variant* in Corrèze from the GR 480, and runs from Turenne to Lamativie Gare. The distance is 130 km and this walk includes a section of the Dordogne Valley, and the Xaintrie. Recommended to all lovers of green and lovely scenery. **Grade 3.**

Apart from the CNSGR in Paris, much useful up-to-date information on the region can be obtained from CHAMINA, 5 Rue Pierre le Vénérable, 6300 Clermont-Ferrand, tel: (73) 92-82-60.

Aquitaine

Aquitaine has a great number of official, waymarked GR trails, and infinite possibilities for long distance walking without much official assistance. Apart from being large enough to include many complete walks, Aquitaine contains sections of several trans-France paths. Most GR trails are concentrated in the north of the region.

GR 36 Sentier Manche-Pyrénées: This long trail enters Aquitaine at Laroche Beaucourt and exits south at Bonaguil in Quercy. A beautiful route in two sections of 98 km (Angoulême to Périgueux) and 178 km (Périgueux to Bonaguil). **Grade 2.**

GR 436: A long weekend or three-day trip in the Dordogne, 65 km, from Brantôme to Pensol. The walk, from the Abbey on the river Dronne, north across the hills, would make a pleasant finish to a day walker's holiday. **Grade 3.**

GR 461: A short but interesting day walk in the Dordogne; 20 km from Montignac to Terrasson on the Vezère, an old pack-horse route which ends at Terrasson bridge. **Grade 2.**

GR 480 Circuit de la Céré et de la Maronne, 303 km. **Grade 3.**

GR 6 Sentier Alpes-Océan: Another long-distance trail with 75 km in the region from St Foy la Grande to Trémolat. Interesting and a challenge. **Grade 2-3.**

GR 636: A 68 km *variant* of the GR 36 in the Dordogne from Bonaguil to Monbazillac. Links GRs 6 and 36, and offers the chance to see the bastide at Villeréal, the castle at Biron, and sample the sweet white wines of Monbazillac. A very good trip indeed. **Grade 3.**

GR 6 and 6-64 Sentier Alpes-Océan: This is a walk for historically-minded grastronomes. It begins here at Trémolat, and follows the Dordogne east as far as Souillac. Take in the little *variant* through Les Eyzies, home of Cro-Magnon man, 95 km in all, and enjoy the best week's walking you could wish for. **Grade 3.**

The GR 6-64, another *variant,* has its own Topo guide, and gives two good routes, Figeac to Les Eyzies 133 km, and Les Eyzies to Pont Le Peyne, 86 km. All three routes are excellent summer walks.

Grade 3.

There are in addition the GRs 64A and 64B, both short single day 20 km trips from Domme and Groslejac on the south bank of the Dordogne in beautiful country.

GR 65 Sentier de St Jacques de Compostelle: The old pilgrim trail passes through Aquitaine only in Pyrénées-Atlantiques, where it terminates the journey through France at St Jean-Pied-de-Port. The section from east of Orthez to St Jean-Pied-de-Port is recommended for there are many reminders of the medieval pilgrims along the way.

Grade 2-3.

GR 65 (Variant) Sentier de St Jacques de Compostelle: The GR 65 is the great pilgrim way, but this section from Aire-sur-Adour is a *variant* off the main trail, most of which actually skirts Aquitaine. This *variant* takes in some pleasant country, and the vines of Madiran. **Grade 2.**

GR 652 (Variant): Another section of the GR 65. When complete it will cover the Agenais, and offer 120 km of good walking between the Lot and Gers rivers. This is little-known country and well worth exploring. **Grade 2.**

GR 69: As yet incomplete, but a recommended route from Aiguillon to Penne d'Agenais of about 50 km. Penne constantly intrudes in this chapter, for it is a beautiful spot, and a fine centre for walking to other castles such as Bruniquel. Topo guide in preparation. **Grade 2-3.**

GR 8 Sentier des Landes: This is a coastal walk running north from near Biscarosse below Arcachon along the *étangs* to the Médoc. You can cross the bay of Arcachon by ferry. The distance is currently about 100 km but the path will almost certainly be extended. **Grade 1-2.**

Both Aquitaine and Limousin are suitable for long-distance walking and the GR network is developing fast. Any walker planning a trip in this region is strongly advised to check on fresh GR developments with the FFRP-CNSGR, Paris, and with the *départemental* and regional tourist offices.

Towpath Walks

Rivers and canals are a good way to explore any region and these two are no exception. The Dordogne can be followed from Bort-les-Orgues, but only becomes attractive after Beaulieu, although the Creuse and the Corrèze are attractive in their upper reaches.

Aquitaine has some great rivers, such as the Garonne, and a tour of the Gironde estuary in Entre-Deux-Mers is an attractive project. The Canal du Midi and the Canal Latéral-à-la-Garonne are also well worth exploring in the country north-west of Agen, while on the northern borders of the Pays Basque the Adour, inland from Bayonne, is a very beautiful river, especially if the *gave* de Pau tributary is followed to Orthèz.

Walking Holidays

Aquitaine's Tourist Offices offer two trips which could interest the walker. The Dordogne has a trip of up to several days, around the village of St Alvère, where all the equipment is carried on a donkey (shades of Robert Louis Stevenson). Evening halts are made on *camping à la ferme* sites and the price is currently around 110 francs per day. Details from the Tourist Office in Périgueux. The trip around Sarlat is also recommended. Guided trips are also available from Agen and Navarrenx. Details from the local *Syndicats*.

Accommodation

Accommodation of all types is plentiful throughout these regions, and taking full backpacking equipment is therefore a matter of personal choice. While wild camping pitches can be found almost everywhere, wild camping is prohibited in the Landes forests and on the Millevaches plateau because of the fire risk.

Advance booking of hotel accommodation is always advisable, especially during the high season in the Dordogne and around Arcachon, but elsewhere there is no real difficulty. A list of hotels is available from FGTO, London, and the *Guide des Logis et Auberges Rurales de France* will be useful.

Gîtes d'étapes are still not common, probably because there is plenty of alternative accommodation. There are two '*Gîtes-de-Groupes*' in Haute-Vienne designed for parties, which would accommodate the casual walking visitor. Information on *gîtes d'étape* can be obtained from the FFRP-CNSGR in Paris or the local CNSGR representative, but it is noticeable that they are most common in the Pays Basque.

Campsites are plentiful throughout the regions with two hundred or more in the Limousin, and over five hundred in Aquitaine.

Camping à la Ferme sites are very well developed, and signs indicating such sites are displayed everywhere.

Chambres d'hôtes are a little scarce, with only three so far in Aquitaine, and about twenty in Limousin. This service will undoubtedly grow and is worth bearing in mind for the future.

Transport

Access to both regions is easy. The roads south are improving and one autoroute runs as far south as Poitiers, another towards Limoges, and a third south to Bordeaux and then east along the Garonne to Toulouse. The train journey from Paris to Périgueux takes five hours, and there are good local connections throughout the regions. There is an international airport at Bordeaux, served by Air France, Air Inter and British Airways. Local bus and coach services are also adequate and there are in addition *Trains Touristiques*. These are an excellent way of getting into the *arrière pays*.

The *Parc des Landes et Gascogne* (Val de l'Eyre) can be explored via the line from Labouheyre to Sabres, the 35 km of track ending at the Eco-Musée. There is a 30 km track from Guitres to Marçenais, north of Libourne.

Walkers wishing to reconnoitre the Pyrénées in comfort could take the train up from Ascain to the top of La Rhune (900 m) or the train up the valley of Ossau to Artouste, said to be the highest rail route in Europe, reaching 1950 m. These mountain trains only run in summer. Information on departure times from the *Syndicats* in Artouste and Ascain.

Maps and Guides

A useful map to start with is the newer edition of the Michelin Yellow 1:200,000 (1 cm = 2 km) *avec relief*. In fact it shows very little relief but it does show many of the GR trails and the most minor roads into the better walking country.

IGN Red Cartes Touristiques No.111 (Auvergne), No.110 (Bordelais-Périgord), and No.113 (Pyrénées-Occidentales), Scale 1:250,000 (1 cm = 2.5 km) indicate points of interest but the Green (Série Verte) 1:100,000 maps (1 cm = 1 km) are more useful to the walker. The whole area is covered by IGN 1:25,000 and 1:50,000 map sheets. The 1:50,000 scale should be adequate for the terrain is not difficult.

Topo guides are available for most of the GR trails, although I found only the GR 6-36 guide readily available locally. The nearest stockist of the complete Topo guide range is in Bordeaux.

Fayard have a *Sentiers et Randonées en Périgord* for local footpaths, and the local *Syndicats* have a variety of brochures, booklets and maps giving details of the local trails.

In an area with such rich history, much of the true flavour will be lost if the background to the region is unknown.

Freda White's *Three Rivers of France* covering the Dordogne, Lot and Tarn is the basic title. Aquitaine is covered in the Collins Companion Guide series, while *The Dordogne* and *The French Pyrénées*, both by Neil Lands from Spurbooks, cover much of the region. *The Hungry Archaeologist in France*, by Glyn Daniel, not only describes the coming of Cro-Magnon man, but also describes the local food, and both should interest the walker. Roger Higham's *Road to the Pyrénées* is a delightful book. Edmund Penning Rowsell's *Wines of Bordeaux* from Penguin Books is a useful source book to the fine local wines.

Local stockists of maps and Topo guides are: Lavauzelle, Rue de la Filature, 87350 Panazol; Mollat, 15 Rue Vital Charles, 33000 Bordeaux; Librairie Parisienne, 14 Rue St Louis, 64000 Pau; La Randonnée, 14-16 Rue Sentini, 47000 Agen.

Wildlife

In a well populated, heavily cultivated area, large wild animals do not survive. There are *sanglier* in the woods, and deer in the forests, plus a variety of smaller mammals, but the main attraction for the visiting naturalist will be the wild flowers, and the birdlife. Ornithologists should be interested in visiting the sanctuary at Le Teich in the *Parc Naturel Régional des Landes at Gascogne (Val de l'Eyre)*. This is a well organised reserve, with a number of hides, but it is necessary to arrange a visit through the Park Office.

Food and Wine

The food of Périgord is famous in France, and based upon three elements, the goose, the truffle, and walnut oil. Dishes cooked *à la Périgourdienne* will be prepared in walnut oil and flavoured with truffle, a dark fungus which attacks the roots of young oaks. They resemble lumps of coke, and are found and grubbed up by trained truffle hounds, or more often by a questing pig. Added to an omelette or a pâté, the flavour is memorable. The goose, or *oie*, and of course *pâté-de-foie-gras*, will be found on every menu in Périgord, and with the local pâtés or ham, an *omelette aux cèpes*, some cheese, and a good red Bergerac, it makes a meal fit for a hungry walker.

The Limousin is more noted for pretty girls than fine cooking, but the hams and omelettes are delicious, and *tripoux*, a dish of veal and mutton, is an excellent filling meal at the end of the day. Further south, in the Pays Basque, the *piperade* makes its appearance. Try *jambon piperade*, a dish of ham with a cheese sauce and chopped peppers.

When it comes to wine, the walker has an embarrassment of riches. The great wines of Bordeaux are here in abundance of course, but they tend to be expensive. I recommend Cahors, Bergerac, or the white wines from Duras, as a less expensive alternative. In Aquitaine, the Juraçon whites and the Madiran reds are both excellent.

Information Centres

Limousin: Maison du Limousin, 18 Bvd Haussmann, 75009 Paris, tel: (1) 770-32-63; Délégation Régionale au Tourisme, 41 Bvd Carnot, 87000 Limoges. *Départemental* offices are in Tulle (Corrèze), Guéret (Creuse), and at the Place Jordan, Limoges (Haute-Vienne).

Aquitaine: Maison du Périgord, 30 Rue Louis le Grand, 75002 Paris, tel: (1) 742-09-15; Délégation Régionale au Tourisme, 24 Allées de Tourny, 33000 Bordeaux. *Départemental* Offices are at Périgueux (Dordogne), Mont-de-Marsan (Landes), Agen (Lot-et-Garonne), Pau (Pyrénées-Atlantique), and at 12 Cours du 30 Juillet, Bordeaux (Gironde).

LANGUEDOC-ROUSSILLON

Moving South from the Massif Central the climate becomes increasingly Mediterranean and the countryside more arid. The South of France, which lies below the Massif and Haute-Provence, between the frontiers with Spain and Italy, is divided roughly in two by the waters of the Rhône. The region to the west of the Rhône, now called Languedoc-Roussillon, is an area of great natural beauty, and a paradise for those walkers and backpackers who enjoy exploring the lesser-known and more remote places. I have given this region a chapter to itself for the simple reason that there is much to discover there (and I love it).

Languedoc-Roussillon is a new and somewhat disparate region,

formed in the 1960s by combining parts of the medieval County of
Toulouse, or Languedoc, with the *département* of Pyrénées-
Orientales, which is all that now remains of French Catalonia, or
Roussillon. The Languedoc was once much larger, and in the early
Middle Ages covered most of the country south of the Loire.

The County of Toulouse was overwhelmed in the Albigensian
Crusade (1208-44) when the knights of the Ile de France, led by
Simon de Montfort (father of that other Simon de Montfort who, as
Earl of Leicester, founded the English Parliament) invaded the
Languedoc to extirpate the Cathars, an heretical Christian sect
which was then well established in the region. The Crusade and the
longer-lasting presence of the Franco-Spanish frontier has endowed
the province with a uniquely rich legacy of castles and fortified
towns, of which walled Carcassonne and Aigues-Mortes are the best
known examples.

The Crusade virtually destroyed the romantic troubadour culture
of the Languedoc. One major town, Béziers, destroyed in the Crusade, only really recovered in the seventeenth century with the
opening of the Canal du Midi, a beautiful waterway which links the
Atlantic and the Mediterranean, and provides in addition an excellent towpath walk.

Roussillon, which makes up the rest of this modern region, was
part of Spain until the signing of the Treaty of the Pyrénées in 1659,
an act which established the Franco-Spanish frontier on the present
line. The people of Roussillon remain Catalans, who have their own
language, culture and traditions, and maintain close links with the
people of Spanish Catalonia on the other side of the frontier. They
dance the *Sardane,* the great folk dance of Catalonia, and the Catalans are still very much a people apart.

In the reign of Louis XIV, the Cévennes, in the north of the
present *départements* of Hérault and Lozère, saw an uprising by the
Huguenot Camisards, who stayed to defend their homes after Louis
XIV revoked their religious freedom with the Edict of Nantes, in a
struggle which lasted until the Revolution. The Cévennes is still a
stronghold of the Protestant faith in France, and is marvellous walking country, full of rugged hills, abandoned farms and villages.

The old language of the south, the *langue d'oc,* is rarely heard now
although you may find that the old people still use it among themselves, but Catalan is a living language, and has accented the local
French tongue sometimes to the point of making it almost unintel-
ligible. That difficulty apart, the people are hospitable, curious
about visitors, and very proud of their history and traditions. As you
travel about their country you will soon see why.

A turbulent past has left this region with a rich store of castles, with golden medieval fortresses beetling down from almost every crag and some of them, like Salses on the borders of Roussillon near Perpignan, or the Cathar fortresses in the Corbières, are in excellent preservation. On the road to Toulouse stands mighty Carcassonne, the best preserved medieval *cité* in Europe, while on the edge of the Camargue, in the Rhône delta, stands Aigues-Mortes, a walled city built by St Louis as his port for the Seventh Crusade.

The Region Today

Languedoc-Roussillon today is made up of five *départements*. They are, from the east: Gard, Lozère, Hérault, Aude and Pyrénées-Orientales; the latter including most of the former county of Roussillon.

Commercial activity in the region is almost entirely dependent on wine production and tourism, although there is some market gardening. A small farm is known here as a *'mas'*. The wines of the region are steadily improving in quality and those of the Côtes de Roussillon and Fiton are already graded a prestigious AC. Except for the high plateau of the Cerdagne, which, as a Pyrénéan area, is covered in chapter twelve, the entire region is carpeted with vines. The town of Sète is the largest wine port in France with exports exceeding even those of Bordeaux.

Since the early 1960s the French Government has been encouraging tourism in the area by financing the construction of a series of purpose-built holiday resorts along ninety-five miles of beach in the littoral of the Gulf of Lions. This encouragement also included eradicating the mosquitos which formerly swarmed in the *étangs* or salt water lakes. La Grande-Motte, Port-Leucate, Barcarès and Cap-d'Agde are just four of these new towns. Cap-d'Agde and Port-Leucate also have naturist villages, created especially for nudists.

These modern developments are so far restricted to the coastline, and have not overshadowed the charm of such older resorts as Sète, Valras-Plage, Le Grau-du-Roi and gem-like Collioure. Inland there are scores of red-roofed towns and villages, each the perfect base for a walking tour, and seemingly a million miles from the tourist packed beaches on the nearby coast.

The cities in the area are attractive. Perpignan, the capital of Roussillon is dominated by the red castle of the Kings of Majorca, who lived here from 1294 to 1344, while Montpellier has been a university city since the eleventh century. Other attractive towns include Béziers, capital of Hérault, which has a wine festival on 18 August, a day when wine flows freely from fountains; Pézenas,

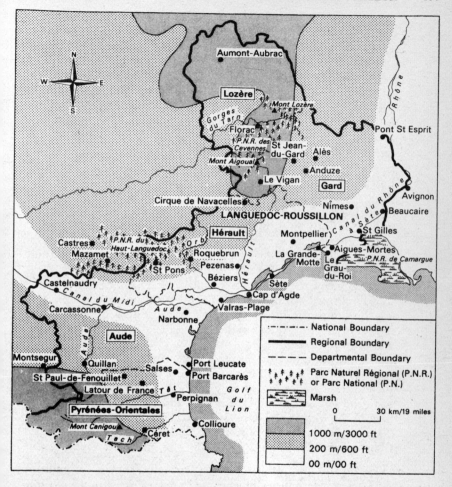

where Molière lived and wrote, a pearl of sixteenth and seventeenth-century architecture; Narbonne, a city established by the Romans; and the walled cities of Carcassonne and Aigues-Mortes. These last two towns are situated by, or near, the waters on the beautiful Canal du Midi, built by Riquet of Béziers in the seventeenth century, and still used today by commercial barges and holiday cruisers.

Physical Description

Starting in the north-eastern part of the province, the extreme north is buttressed by the Cévennes. These are high forested hills, threaded with rivers and extremely beautiful. Mt Aigoual (1565 m) is the highest peak, and there are several others over the 1300 m mark. The Cévennes has good day-walking centres but will appeal particularly to backpackers.

South of the Cévennes lie the *Grandes Causses*, a plateaux region divided by a series of rivers, notably the Tarn, the Doubie, and the Vis. The *causses* are open, high, limestone plateaux, largely devoted to sheep. There are four *Grandes Causses*, those of Sauveterre, Méjean, Noir and Larzac, and three *petites causses*, Began, Campestre and Blandas. All average around 1000 m in height. Water can be scarce and is usually found in *lavogne*, or dewponds. The *causse* Larzac, which is the largest, runs steeply up to 900 m from the river Tarn far below. The town of Millau, which lies just beneath the *causse* Larzac, is at only 353 m. Once up on the *causse*, though, the walking is fairly level. Boots are advisable for walking in this region and it gets very hot in summer. The *causse* country is marvellous for solitary walking, for the villages have often been abandoned and only the sheep and the eagles move across the landscape.

South, below the *causses*, the country is hilly and broken but often thickly covered with dwarf oaks and brushwood called *'garrigue'*, which is impenetrable except along tracks. Fire is an ever-present danger in the *garrigue* and wild camping therefore highly inadvisable and often forbidden.

The coastal littoral is flat and open, running for 224 km from Aigues-Mortes by the Rhône to Collioure beyond Perpignan, where the eastern Pyrénées are already in sight. This coastal plain is not wide and is overlooked between Sète and Narbonne by the mountains of the Montagne Noire (1031 m) and the Espinouse (1091 m). These are the last outcrops of the Massif Central and are divided from the foothills of the Pyrénées by the Minervois valley, a wine region which runs from Narbonne up through Carcassonne, to Toulouse. This valley has many streams but no major rivers except the Agly, all sources being tapped to feed the Canal du Midi. Roussillon has two major rivers, the Têt and the Tech, which flow from Mont Canigou, while the Aude, Hérault and Gard *départements* are all named from their principal river.

Three rising ranges of foothills, largely carpeted with vineyards and *garrigue*, now bar the way to the Pyrénées. The Corbières hills (1230 m on average) run inland from Salses to Quillan on the Aude. Then comes the Fénouillades (1342 m) and finally below Mont Canigou (2784 m) the last major mountain of the Pyrénées, the lesser hills of the Albères in the Aspres range (684 m on average). All three ranges have attractive walks or could provide a lateral tour, and are rolling rather than steep.

Languedoc-Roussillon, therefore, has a wide variety of terrain, but the 1:250,000 IGN map shows the broad outline; mountains in the Cévennes, the Espinouse and the Montagne Noire; open plains in the high *causses* and along the littoral; the high foothills of the Asprès, Albères and Corbières. The region is intensely cultivated and where cultivation ceases there lies *garrigue* and, above that, afforestation and steep cliffs. Open walking is barely possible in much of this region and the traveller should stick to waymarked paths or farm tracks. This said, I know of few regions with so much to offer the walker, and the warm sun and the near-blue sea are just additional advantages. These walks are Grade 2-3, reaching perhaps 4 in early spring or late autumn.

Much of Roussillon is dominated by the Eastern Pyrénées, but these will be covered in chapter twelve.

Climate

Since the region is large it can also offer a variety of climate. It is warm and windy, and the weather tends towards extremes. Storms are frequent in the hills, even in summer, but the humidity is usually low and the air invigorating. The snow arrives on the Pyrénées and Cévennes as early as October and can stay until May. I have seen deep drifts on Mont Lozère in April. Summers on the Gulf are long and warm and the mountain rivers, which are dangerous torrents in winter, shrink to shallow placid streams in the summer, unless they are suddenly swelled by flash thunderstorms. One feature of the region, especially on the frontiers and along the coast, are the winds, which can make double-guying of tents a perpetual possibility.

The *tramontane* blows from the Pyrénées, and the *mistral* sweeps down the Rhône. From the east comes the *grec*, and from the south the *marin*, while across the Montagne Noire comes the *vent du Nord*. Winds are the most memorable factor for the camper, and double-guying is advisable.

Shorts and boots are advisable in summer, and windproofs an additional necessity in autumn and winter. The walker should plan his trip for between April and June or between early September and the end of October. The summers are very hot and the shade infrequent. After October the weather can break and, although the winters are mild by British standards, the weather is unreliable and can reach extremes of cold at heights. A close study of heights and contours is therefore advisable. Any hill route over 650 m high should be avoided between mid-October and the end of March, unless the walker is fit, well equipped, and skilled in the use of crampons and ice-axe.

Walking in the *Départements*

Each *département* has areas of special interest to walkers, and I recommend the following:

Lozère has the Aubrac plateau around Aumont-Aubrac, the Parc National des Cévennes, and the Tarn gorges. This is a wild rugged *département,* ideal for backpackers.

Gard has good country west of Alés, but I recommend the serious walker to explore the wild country on the borders of Ardèche, based on Pont-St-Esprit, or the bush country, or *garrigue,* north of Nîmes around St Martin-de-Londres.

Hérault has the marvellous *cirque de Navacelles,* a deep gorge on the river Vis. The plateaux or *causses* country around Le Vigan and Millau is marvellously remote and there is a fine walk down the rivers Orb, Hérault or along the Canal du Midi. The Espinouse and Montagne Noire mountains are steep and tough, where the picturesque village of Roquebrun would be the ideal centre.

Aude has the lower vine-cloaked hills of the Minervois region around Carcassonne and green wooded hills around Quillan. The river Aude can be followed up from Quillan to the Cerdagne plateau. The Fenouillèdes hills, near the deep cleft of the Galamus gorge are dotted with castles, each the perfect target for a long-distance walk.

Even without counting the marvellous mountains of the eastern Pyrénées, Pyrénées-Orientales is full of good walks, notably around Céret and Latour-de-France, in the Vallespir and Conflent areas. The valleys of the Têt and Tech are beautiful in the spring, for the trees start blooming in February and the peach orchards are thick with blossom by mid-March.

National Parks

Parc National des Cévennes: This was created in 1970 and is the largest park in France. With a population of only some five hundred inhabitants it is also quite deserted, seamed with rivers, very beautiful and full of paths. St Jean-du-Gard is the best centre, and there are good trips to Florac, across the windy *corniche des Cévennes,* and along the gorges of the Tarn.

Parc Naturel Régional du Haut-Languedoc: This is a new park on the borders with the Midi-Pyrénées. The area embraces the rugged granite Espinouse mountains, the Montagne Noire and the curious rock formations of Sidobre, inland from the littoral at just over the 1000 m level. Castres, St Pons or Mazamet are good centres for this area.

Parc Naturel Régional de Camargue: This is mainly a nature reserve, full of white horses, black cattle and pink flamingoes. Visitors to the Nature Reserve need a written permit. Apply to the Directeur de la Réserve Nationale, 1 Rue Stendhal, 13200 Arles.

Footpaths

Local Footpaths

There are waymarked local paths in the Cévennes, based on St-Jean-du-Gard, Anduze, the Corniche des Cévennes, St-Jean-du-Bruel and Saint Maurice-de-Navacelles. A guidebook, *Sentiers Pédestres en Cévennes,* is available from the Office du Tourisme in Alès. The walks are for a day or half-day and cover all parts of the hills. The *département* of Gard publishes a book, *Randonnées Pédestres en Languedoc,* and the Cévennes Park Office in Florac has a good foot-path brochure, and has laid out many local trails.

Editions Fayard publish a guide to *Sentiers du Roussillon,* which lists walks, varying in length from half-a-day to two days. Bookshops and the *Syndicats* will also have guides to local walks, and the day walker will find excellent walking areas in the Cévennes, in the *causses* around Florac, along the rivers Tarn, Doubie and Jonte, and on Mont Lozère. Waymark Travel Ltd offer walking holidays to the Cévennes.

Towpaths

Languedoc-Roussillon is rich in towpaths, for it possesses that great man-made waterway, the Canal du Midi, which was built by Paul Riquet, a native of Béziers, in the seventeenth century, and is still in use. This runs from Castelnaudray to the Étang de Thau near Sète, and to walk the distance would take the long-distance walker or back-packer a pleasant two weeks. The total distance is 240 km.

The Canal du Rhône à Sète runs from Beaucaire to Sète, and takes in such historic places as St Gilles, ancestral home of the Counts of Toulouse, and St Louis' Crusader city of Aigues-Mortes. This is a marvellous route across the Camargue, with egrets and pink flamin-goes wading in the lakes beside the path.

Long-distance Footpaths

Languedoc-Roussillon has many long distance paths, offering a wide selection of terrain, but a long trip here requires a fit and experi-enced walker. However, shorter trips are possible by using GR *vari-ants.* There are also a number of *drailles* or drove roads on the *causses.*

GR 36 Sentier Manche-Pyrénées: Three sections of this path cross Languedoc-Roussillon in Tarn, Aude and Pyrénées-Orientales — 245 km in total, but it can be done in stages. Topo guides for two sections in Languedoc-Roussillon, Albi to Mazamet and Mazamet to Mont Canigou, are now in preparation. The Montagne Noire will be difficult in winter. **Grades 2-3-4.**

GR 42 Sentier Rive Droite du Rhône: One section in Gard. Bessat to Beaucaire on the Rhône, and on to St Gilles 291 km in total, but the Beaucaire to St Gilles section is quite short. **Grade 1-2.**

GR 43 Draille (Drove Road) de la Margeride: Across Lozère and then north on the GR 7 and GR 4. May to November only, 50 km. **Grade 3-4.** A very exciting trip.

There are many other *drailles* on the *causses,* notably on the Causse Méjean.

GR 62 Sentier de la Causse Noire from la Pierre Plantée (Cévennes) to Conques in Aveyron: A classic route through marvellous wild country and a highly recommended 186 km two-week trip. **Grade 3-4.**

GR 62A Sentier de la Causse Noire: Meyrueis to Montpellier-le-Vieux, 25 km. This crosses the open Causse Noire country and you can visit the Templar fortress at La Couvertoirade. Montpellier-le-Vieux is a rock chaos, not a town. Recommended. **Grade 2.**

GR 63 From the col de la Cabane Vieille to Avignon (Vaucluse): 133 km over good country in the Gard. **Grade 2-3.**

GR 66-66A Sentier du Tour de l'Aigoual: Various footpaths, 91 km, linked up around Mt Aigoual, 1565 m in the Cévennes Park — an excellent one week trip for backpackers. **Grade 3.**

GR 67-67A Sentier du Tour des Cévennes: A good route for the backpacker or long-distance walker — 158 km and two weeks long. Alternatively there is the shorter 28 km *variant* in the Vallée des Gardons. **Grade 3.**

GR 68 Sentier du Mont-Lozère: This circles Mont-Lozère by linked GR trails, a 110 km route and the ideal one-week trip. **Grade 3-4.**

GR 7-74 Sentier Vosges-Pyrénées: One long section Mont Aigoual to the Montagne Noire. End April to early October only, 268 km. Other sections take in the Grandes Causses and would be excellent in summer. **Grade 3.**

GR 71 Sentier Cévennes-Haut-Languedoc: Various footpaths. Probably April to October only at the height, 196 km. Also *variants* l'Esperon via Alzon to Le Caylar, 803 m — 51 km. **Grade 3-4.**

GR 71c Chemin des Templiers et Hospitaliers: A new guide to a new route 80 km across and around the Causse Larzac south of Millau, on the old routes once patrolled by the Knights Templar. **Grade 3.**

GR 72-73 Tour du Beaujolais: One section, Ardèche to Lozère from

Bez to Barre-les-Cévennes, 79 km. Also *variants* taking in Mont Aigoual. A short but challenging trail with lots of opportunities. **Grade 4.**

GR 74: Across three *départements,* Gard, Aveyron, Hérault, to St Maurice de Navacelles to Lodève through the *garrigue,* 83 km. On the way see the great valley of the cirque de Navacelles. **Grade 3-4.**

GR 77 Sentier Sommail, Minervois, Corbières: Across the Espinouse and Minervois to the Corbières, south to Signal d'Alaric, 102 km, a very warm walk in summer but a good ten days at any time. **Grade 3-4.**

The GR 10 (*Sentier des Pyrénées*) also crosses this region but is covered in chapter twelve. The Aubrac plateau (1000 m) in the north of Lozère has a GR *Sentier du pays Tour de l'Aubrac,* **Grade 3,** organised by ADECA, the local outdoor group, in 1980-81. This offers a circular tour in the Aubrac of 168 km.

Sentier Européan No 4 also crosses the region along the GR 7 at Mont Lozère and crosses the Franco-Spanish frontier at Mont Canigou. Most of these routes have short sections, circular tours or *variants.* See the Topo guides or the IGN 903 for details of these and other GR trails running into the region.

Please consider the effect of summer temperatures when walking in this area.

Historic paths

The Robert Louis Stevenson Trail enters Languedoc-Roussillon at the monastery of Nôtre-Dame des Neiges (Our Lady of the Snows) near La Bastide Puylaurent, and crosses Mont Lozère to Florac on the Tarn and then to St Jean-du-Gard by La Pierre-Plantée. This path follows the route taken by Stevenson and his donkey in 1878.

The GR 74 section through St Guilhem-le-Désert follows one of the Roads to Compostella from Italy, and take in many out-of-the-way places.

This region is rich in history and the independent walker could use the 1:50,000 map to explore Romanesque churches in Roussillion, or those frontier castles, collectively called the 'Sons of Carcassonne', in the Corbières. These are, from the east: Aguilar, Queribus, Peyrepertuse, Puivert, Puilaurens and finally, in Ariège, Montségur. This tour is a magnificent hill walk across wild country, and would take two weeks or more.

Accommodation

Tourist facilities are well developed in Languedoc-Roussillon, but still relatively inexpensive. Youth hostels can be found in the larger towns. Most villages will have at least one small hotel, but in high summer they will be full so always ring ahead and book. The village cafés often have simple rooms to let. The number of *gîtes d'étape* is increasing and they can be found all along the various GR routes. Pyrénées-Orientales estimate that by 1981 they will have 150 *gîtes* in their *département* alone. Information on *gîtes d'étape* in Languedoc-Roussillon can be obtained from the Association de Tourisme de Randonnée (ATR), Chambre Régionale d'Agriculture, Place Chaptal, 34076 Montpellier, tel: (67) 92-95-94. Information on campsites and *gîtes* can also be obtained from the Maison du Tourisme in Perpignan, or from the *Service des Gîtes Ruraux*. For Languedoc *départements* the addresses are:

Aude: Service des Gîtes Ruraux, 70 Rue Aime-Ramon, 11000 Carcassonne, tel: (68) 25-24-95.

Gard: Service du Tourisme, Place des Arènes, 30000 Nîmes, tel: (66) 21-02-51.

Hérault: Chambre d'Agriculture, Place Chaptal, 34076 Montpellier, tel: (67) 92-81-88.

Lozère: Relais du Gîtes Ruraux, Place Urbain, 48002 Mende, tel: (66) 65-34-56.

Gîtes d'étape are frequently found on farms and the Chambres d'Agriculture will often have information on new developments. The *gîte* network is growing very rapidly as are *camping à la ferme* sites.

There are over six hundred campsites in Languedoc-Roussillon, plus countless *camping à la ferme* pitches. Wild camping is not permitted in the National Parks and should be avoided in high summer in the forest regions and *garrigue* because of fire risks. Smoking is discouraged for the same reason.

Transport

Getting to Languedoc-Roussillon is relatively simple. There are national or international flights into Toulouse, Perpignan, and Montpellier. Major airlines servicing this region are Air France, Air Inter (via Paris) and Dan Air. Good rail links exist from Paris to Narbonne, Nîmes, Béziers and Toulouse, with a good lateral service along the coast and out into the *causses*. A coach service reaches many of the smaller towns. Drivers can reach the area on routes nationales or down the A6 autoroute which veers off on the Spanish autoroute, the A9, across the Languedoc littoral.

The train ride along the coast from Narbonne to Perpignan is a must, for this runs across the *étangs*, which are full of flamingoes, while from Perpignan another little train, *le petit train jaune,* takes walkers up to the Cerdagne plateau.

Maps and Guides

1:250,000 Touristique Série Rouge, Pyrénées-Languedoc No 14 will do for the initial survey, and the 1:100,000 Série Verte Nos 72, 65, 58 show paths. 1:50,000 and 1:25,000 scale sheets are advisable for walkers in the Cévennes and the Espinouse.

Good general guides are George Savage's *Languedoc,* from Barrie & Jenkins, Freda White's *West of the Rhône,* and Neil Lands' *Languedoc-Roussillon* from Spurbooks. *Travels with a Donkey in the Cévennes* by Robert Louis Stevenson is a necessary read, and the 1908 edition can be obtained from most public libraries. *The Albigensian Crusade* by Johnathan Sumption (Faber) is another good background title. I recommend reading something of the background to this beautiful historic and unknown country, for you will then enjoy your visit far more, and can make a point of seeing the sights you might otherwise miss.

Maps and guides are available locally from: Pontain, 5 Grande Rue, 34000 Montpellier; Librairie Rive Gauche, 29 Quai Vauban, 66000 Perpignan; Librairie Rencontres, 36 Rue de l'Hôtel de Ville, 81100 Montauban; Buholzer, 13 Bvd Victor Hugo, 30000 Nîmes.

Wildlife

The naturalist will have a field day in Languedoc-Roussillon. Wild horses and bulls wade in the Camargue marshes, there are izard, the Pyrénéan chamois in the foothills of the Aspres, and wild boar and deer in the Cévennes. Apart from mammals, the birdlife is also prolific. Flamingoes and egrets can be found in the *étangs* all along the littoral from Perpignan to Nîmes and there are eagles and vultures in the Pyrénées as well as hosts of migrating birds in spring and autumn. A good fieldguide and a pair of binoculars will add to your enjoyment. There are no dangerous animals except for vipers. A snake bite kit is sold in most pharmacies and would be a worthwhile purchase in summer.

Food and Wine

In such a diverse region the food, while lacking something of the quality of Provence or Burgundy, lacks nothing in variety. The seafood is magnificent and a visit to the quayside restaurants of Sète or Collioure is recommended. Wild boar is served at St Jean-du-

Gard, and in Roussillon grilled snails form the basis of the Catalan *cargolade*. The area has many fine cheese, the *Bleu de Causse*, *Roquefort* from the causses near Millau, the black-skinned *Pyrénéan* cheeses, and *chèvre* or goat's cheese, which is excellent and available everywhere. *Cassoulet*, a thick stew of bacon and beans, was invented in Castelnaudary, and the *tielles* or fish pie at Sète is another delicious local dish.

A typical meal would consist of four or five courses: soup, main course of meat or fish, cheese, fruit, dessert, accompanied by wine and followed by coffee. The fruit is excellent with peaches and oranges straight from the trees, table grapes from Clermont on the Hérault, cherries and apricots from Céret and melons from the Roussillon plain.

The region is awash with wine and, apart from the AC Côtes de Roussillon, the VDQS Minervois and Corbières, I recommend the wines of St Chinian and the Listel *gris-de-gris* dry rosé wines from Aigues-Mortes. Local wines are often served in a *pichet*, a small jug.

Information Centres

There are *Syndicat* offices in all towns and most villages, but the following addresses will be useful to campers, backpackers and walkers: Comité Régional du Tourisme, 12 Rue Foch, 34000 Montpellier, tel: (67) 72-15-62. Other *départemental* offices are in Mende (Lozère), Carcassonne (Aude) and Nîmes (Gard).

Association de Tourisme de Randonnée Languedoc-Roussillon (ATR), Place Chaptal, 34076 Montpellier, tel: (67) 92-95-94 (Contact them for information on *gîtes d'étape)*; Chambre d'Agriculture de l'Hérault, Place Chaptal, 34076 Montpellier, tel: (67) 92-95-94; Office de Tourisme des Cévennes, BP 226, 30103 Ales, tel: (66) 52-21-15; Maison du Tourisme, Palais Consulaire, Quai Lattre de Tassigny, 66000 Perpignan (This office is always very helpful to walkers in Roussillon and the Eastern Pyrénées); Club Alpin Français, 4 Rue de l'Académie, 66000 Perpignan; Association pour le Développement de l'Aubrac (ADECA), 48130 Aumont Aubrac, Lozère (This office also has information on *drailles)*.

The South of France
PROVENCE, CÔTE d'AZUR, CORSICA

The South of France, whatever your reason for going there, has a touch of magic about it. We think of troubadours and St Tropez, girls and gambling and glamour, while, if we think of Corsica, we think of Napoleon, *maquis* and *mafiosi*. Walking can hardly predominate in a region with such multifarious attractions but if, as walkers, we regard all this as a colourful background, then walking in the South of France can provide attractions not readily found elsewhere.

All three areas came to France late. Provence, to the east of the Rhône, was annexed only in the fifteenth century, Corsica came reluctantly in the eighteenth, and the *comté* of Nice only in the last century. Monaco still remains a nominally independent principality.

The eastern area has only been firmly French since 1947 when the towns of Tende and La Brigue voted to rejoin France having been once annexed by Italy. The northern boundary of Provence lies east of the Rhône and south of a line drawn from Pont-St-Esprit. Below this you are firmly in the Midi, where the Mediterranean influences climate, customs and thought.

Provence was a Roman possession, and takes its name from the title *Provincia Romana,* but there are palaeolithic sites at Nice and Monaco dating from long before that.

Hannibal marched his elephants through here in the Second Punic War and, when the Roman Empire fell, it was the Visigoths and not the Teutonic Franks who first gained possession of the region. Charlemagne took Provence in 776 but for much of the Middle Ages Provence owed allegiance not to France but to the Holy Roman Empire.

Successive Popes lived in Avignon for a hundred years, from 1309, and it was not until 1481, when 'Good King René', Count of Bar and King of Naples died that Provence came to France. It still remains distinctly 'Provençal', and treasures linkes with the Languedoc. The Côte d'Azur, the Blue Coast, runs from Fréjus, east to the Italian border and, while the Italian influence has sunk under mass hedonism, Nice is an Italianate town.

Corsica lies 100 miles out into the Mediterranean, and was in turn Greek, Roman, Ostrogothic, Genoese, and independent, before becoming a province of France in 1769, just in time for a young man called Napoléon Bonaparte, who was born in that year in Ajaccio, to call himself French. In Corsica, the island's hero is not Napoléon, but Pascal Paoli, 'General of the Corsican Nation', who fought the Genoese and then the French in a vain bid to keep the island independent, and even today Corsica (*Corse*) makes claims to autonomy.

The Regions Today

Provence today is composed of six *départements* of which the coastal four are, from the west: Bouches-du-Rhône, Vaucluse, Var, and Alpes-Maritimes; this last *département* and the two other Provençal *départements,* Alpes-de-Hautes-Provence and Hautes-Alpes, have been largely covered in 'Mountain France' (chapter twelve), but some walks in the flatter parts of Alpes-Maritimes will be included here. Corsica has two *départements,* Haute-Corse and Corse du Sud.

The regions live by tourism, wine, commerce of all sorts, agriculture related to sheep, olives and lavender, fruit and flowers. Industry includes hydro-electricity, salt distillation in the Camargue, per-

N
W — E
S

Hautes-Alpes

Nyons
Pont-St-Esprit
BARONNIES
Mont Ventoux 1909 m.
Orange
Sault
Carpentras
Montagne de Lure
Sisteron
Digne
P.N. de Mercantour
Tende
Mercantour
Vaucluse
Alpes-de-Haute-Provence
Puget-Théniers
Alpes-Maritimes
Avignon
PROVENCE
Apt
Entrevaux
Verdon
Castellane
COTE d'AZUR
Sospel
Menton
Châteaurenard
P.N.R. du Luberon
Gorges du Verdon
Vence
Nice
Beaucaire
St-Rémy
Les Baux-de-Provence
Alpilles
Grasse
Monaco
Arles
CRAU
Aix-en-Provence
VALENSOLE
Drauguignan
Cannes
P.N.R. de Camargue
Bouches-du-Rhône
Var
Théoule-sur-Mer
Stes-Maries de la Mer
St-Maximin-la-Ste-Baume
Fréjus
Aubagne
La Ste-Baume
Maures
St Tropez
Toulon
Bormes les-Mimosas
Le Lavandou
Iles d'Hyères

----- National Boundary
━━━ Regional Boundary
----- Departmental Boundary
Parc Naturel Régional (P.N.R.) or Parc National (P.N.)
Marsh

3000 m/9000 ft
1000 m/3000 ft
200 m/600 ft
00 m/00 ft

0   30 km/19 miles

Bastia
Ile-Rousse
Calvi
Calenzana
Haute-Corse
Mt Cinto 2707 m
Corte
P.N.R. de la Corse
Vizzavona
Bastelica
CORSE
Ajaccio
Corse du Sud
Zicavo
Zonza
Conca
Porto-Vecchio

CORSICA

fumes from Grasse, and the mining of ochre and bauxite. Nice and Aix-en-Provence are university towns.

Physical Description

The estuary of the great river Rhône, and that powerful wind, the *mistral,* dominate the Bouches-du-Rhône, notably in the marshlands of the Camargue, an area famous for bulls and horses. To the east of the Camargue lie the stony flatlands of the Crau, but it is not long before hills begin to appear. First, the chaine des Alpilles, east of Les Baux, low but of fantastic shapes, at around 300 m. Then, to the north-east, the long ridges of the Montagne du Lubéron, rising from 600 m to 1125 m at the Grand Lubéron near Apt. Mont Ste Victoire (1011 m) near Aix is the main local peak.

Beyond Aix lie great tracts of walking country, anywhere north of the N7 road which runs from Aix as far as Draguignan in the Canjuers, and onto the vast plateau of Valensole. The great challenge walk here is along the Gorges du Verdon. This lies south, near Aubagne, now the home of the Foreign Legion, in the Massif de Sainte Baume (994 m).

Between Toulon and Fréjus, inland from St Tropez, lies the Massif des Maures, a superb walking range, within sight of the sea, at between 300 and 600 m, with views over the splendid Le Lavandou coast to the Iles d'Hyères.

As you move inland from the coast, so the countryside becomes more open, and climbs steadily to real outdoorman's country. In the north of Vaucluse, on the border with the Drôme, lie the Baronnies and that great mountain of Provence, Mont Ventoux (1909 m). This lies east of the Roman city of Orange, which is the perfect base for walking. The whole region of Ventoux is marvellous, while the town of Sisteron and the Montagne de Lure (1826 m) are always worth a visit.

The next *département* to the east, the Var, has the great gorges of the Verdon and Var, south of Castellane, with excellent hard walking, while in Alpes-Maritimes, Grasse — a centre for the manufacture of perfumes — is overlooked by ranges of open hills at around 1200 m.

St Martin-Vésubie is a truly Alpine village and this is a frontier zone now, with formidable peaks and stiff walking. The Vallée des Merveilles, nearby, lies at around 2000 m. Mont Neillier at 2785 m, and the Mont du Grand Capelet at 2934 m, actually on the Italian frontier, are just two of the many peaks in this rugged region, for which St Dalmas-de-Tende is the best centre.

Provence-Côte d'Azur, offers a vast range of walking, from the flat, sea-level Crau, in the south-west, rising steadily as we move north-east into the tangled masses of the Alpes-Maritimes. This ends as hill walking country, just below the Alpine chain and, while the warm weather and late snows can affect them, the gradings are from 2 to 4 in most areas.

Corsica

Corsica 'Isle of Beauty' is indeed very beautiful. It lies one hundred miles south of the Riviéra, fifty miles from the Italian peninsula and eight miles north of Sardinia. It is one of the largest islands in the Mediterranean, 184 km long, and 80 km wide, a vast area of land, mountainous and very sparsely populated; half of the 220,000 population live in the two main towns of Ajaccio and Bastia. Napoléon said that he could tell Corsica even when blindfolded from the smell of the *maquis*, the thick myrtle bush, heather and gorse, which covers most of the island. There is 1000 km of coast and the mountains rise to 2600 m and average about 700 m. Corsica is perfect walking country but more suited to the fit, well-equipped, experienced backpacker, at the Grade 4 to 5 level.

Climate

This whole area has a Mediterranean climate, but the different heights can produce quite severe extremes. Walking in summer over the rocky open plateaux can be scorching, while snow remains late in the hills and sudden thunderstorms are not uncommon. The *mistral* blows heavily in March and regularly in the winter, often for days on end.

In summer, temperatures of around 30 °C are common. Spring comes early, the mimosa blooms in February and spring and autumn are the best times for walking, especially in Corsica, where the *maquis* is in bloom from mid-April to mid-June. In winter beware of snow and mist anywhere over 800 m. Below that, in Provence the air is clear and cold, and in Corsica the spring temperatures, at about 16 °C, are ideal for long stiff walking. Corsica has at least three climates at any one time, depending on the altitude. There is little rain between June and October but, that said, the walking is best in the periods April to June, or September to October, outside the hot crowded holiday months.

Walking in the *Départements*

The climate, as well as the terrain, should influence the selection of a walking area, for from May until September this area can become very hot indeed.

Provence

Bouches-du-Rhône: The Bouches-du-Rhône is not good walking country, being low-lying, hot and humid, somewhat mosquito infested, and swampy. That said, it is an extremely interesting area, with the Camargue National Reserve, the beaches and gypsy camps near les Stes-Maries-de-la-Mer and such historic sites as Avignon, the Roman city of Arles and the rocky outcrops of Les Baux. However, there is *some* good walking anywhere in France if you know where to look, so I recommend Châteaurenard as a centre for visits to lots of historical places, and as a starting point for a walk along the Canal de Provence to Aix. The Rhône-Sète Canal can be followed right across the delta to the walled town of Aigues-Mortes, in Languedoc-Roussillon, but the mosquitos are vicious.

Vaucluse: Vaucluse, and especially the Ventoux, is perfect Mediterranean walking country, the only rival in this part of the world to my beloved Sisteron area.

Vaucluse contains Mont Ventoux, Mont Victoire and the Lubéron, and from Sault de Vaucluse, the perfect centre, there is access to both Ventoux and the open country towards Sisteron. I am always surprised at how few people walk into this splendid country. There are scores of towns to serve as starting points or objectives but between them you can be all alone. It is well worth exploring the square of country between Nyons, Carpentras, Apt and Sisteron.

Var: The Var offers the walker a great choice of terrain. Stay close to the sea and you have the Riviéra at hand and excellent walking at about the 700 m mark just inland, along the Massif des Maures. La Garde Frénet is small but very central, and I like Bormes-les-Mimosas and not just for the name. North of Draguignan, the country is higher and more open, and this great plateau of Valensole is bounded on the north by the gorge or 'canyon' of Verdon, a classic two-to-three day route, south from Castellane. Details on this quite difficult trail are available from the *Syndicat* in Castellane.

Alpes-Maritimes: The eastern section of the Alpes-Maritimes is pure alpine, the last link in that massive chain of mountains which curls south from Switzerland and is covered, therefore, in chapter twelve 'Mountain France'. There still remain sections, outside the Vésubie, which are less demanding, and two new trails running east-west across the *département* which any walker would enjoy.

Puget-Théniers, or just about anywhere east or west of the Gorges du Loup, north of Vence, would be ideal for the walker. The terrain is open and, at about the 1200 m mark, perfect for a two-week wander off the beaten track. Use the *Chemin-de-Fer-de-Provence* from Nice to get into the back-country.

Corsica

Walking in Corsica can be rough, grade 4 to 5. The island contains that great footpath, the GR 20, which is probably the nearest European equivalent of the great wild American routes. The Corsican Tourist Board asked me repeatedly to stress that walking in the Corsican hills is not for the unfit or inexperienced, and walkers I have consulted, who have completed or attempted the GR 20, all bear this out. You have been warned! The highest peak is Monte Cinto, 2707 m in Haute-Corse, east of Calvi, and there are plenty of peaks at the 2000 m to 2500 m mark.

Good walking centres are at Corte, Vizzavona, Bastelica, and Zicavo. Zonza, in the Corse de Sud *département*, is also excellent.

The paths themselves are easy to follow, but endlessly steep, and there are a few glaciers. Snow and mist can be inhibiting from November to May, and I have seen snow on Monte Cinto in August. Walkers travelling in Corsica would do well to arrive in Bastia, and make their first call at the Club Montagne-Corse, 1 Bvd Auguste Gaudin, 20 Bastia, or in Ajaccio visit the *Syndicat* in the Bvd Paoli.

National Parks

There are four national parks in the region.

Parc Naturel Régional de la Camargue: The Camargue is a region of salt flats and marshes, in the delta between the two arms of the great river Rhône, which divides below Avignon. The actual Park is quite small, and bordered on the east by the Alpilles and the Crau, a paradise for pink flamingoes, egrets, black bulls and white horses, herded by the *guardiens,* the cowboys of the Camargue. Much of the Park is a bird sanctuary, open only to ornithologists or parties of bird watchers accompanied by a guide. Apply to M. le Directeur de la Réserve Nationale, 1 Rue Stendhal, 13200 Arles, for permission to visit.

Parc Naturel Régional du Lubéron: This lies in Vaucluse, between Marseilles and Mont Ventoux, 75 km of green forested hills, scented with lavender and wild flowers. Walking is possible everywhere in the Lubéron, and the old shepherds' huts still stand, although the villages where the shepherds used to live are becoming increasingly deserted. Apt is the best starting point, being situated almost centrally on the northern edge of the Park.

Parc Naturel du Mercantour: Lying in the east of the Alpes Maritimes, this Park is described in chapter twelve.

Parc Naturel Régional de Corse: This vast Park occupies most of central Corsica and runs north-east to south-west between Calvi and Porto Vecchio. The GR 20 runs across the Park and can be walked in about twelve days 'by experienced walkers as a high degree of energy is required', as the brochure delicately puts it!

Footpaths

Local Footpaths

The tourist authorities everywhere in Provence, Côte d'Azur and Corsica are very keen to promote walking in the *arrière-pays,* and the local *Syndicats* are waymarking many interesting routes. Aix, capital of Provence, has waymarked many walks on nearby Mont Ste Victoire, grading them in degrees of difficulty. A map is available from the *Office du Tourisme* in Aix.

One simple method of finding good walking is by train. Take *le Train du Sud* from Nice, and buy a copy of *50 Randonnées Pédestres* from the booking desk and you have both access and a guide to hundreds of kilometres of walking right across Provence.

The same thing can be done in Corsica by taking the little railway that runs from Ajaccio for 145 km through Corte to Bastia. This is a beautiful ride even if you don't get off the train at the end.

In the Côte d'Azur, there is excellent day walking from Sospel, north of Menton, where the *Syndicat* has waymarked over twenty trails, taking anything from two hours twenty minutes to nine hours thirty minutes to complete, and giving adequate variety for a two week stay.

Tende and St Dalmas-de-Tende offer walks into the Vallée des Merveilles, which I heartily recommend, but there are more trails from St Etienne de Tinée and Auron, although these lie higher.

Apt is the ideal centre for Lubéron, and Carpentras gives access to Mont Ventoux, while for day walks the canyon de Verdon and Castellane are ideal. In Corsica, Corte is a good centre for day walking, as is the Cap Corse peninsula, north of Bastia.

Towpaths

In a region where enjoying the warm weather can be marred by endless climbs and descents, some gentler towpath walking can be pleasant. The canals lie off the Rhône, and there are several worth exploring. The Canal de Provence, which leads east from the Rhône, is not yet fully completed. The Canal des Alpilles is best reached at St

Rémy-de-Provence, and more accessible than either is the Canal Rhône-Sète, which is used to water the Crau, and which leads to the walled town of Aigues-Mortes, giving three days lazy walking from Beaucaire to the medieval port founded by St Louis. Walkers should be aware that some canals shown on the maps are just glorified culverts, bringing in hydro-electric power by tapping the mountain rivers. Towpath walking is permitted by grace of the canal authorities, but I have never been turned back.

Long-distance Paths

The long-distance walks in these areas are challenging, largely because of the weather, and range in difficulty from the relatively simple GR 9 on the Lubéron to the GR 20 in Corsica. A number of trans-France routes have stages in Provence—Côte d'Azur.

GR 4 Sentier Méditerranée-Océan: This very long path begins in the Alpes-Maritimes, near Grasse, runs up to Entrevaux and west to Lubéron, before turning north. This section, Grasse to Pont St Esprit, is a highly recommended route of around 160 km across beautiful country. Two Topo guides are available. **Grade 3.**

GR 5-52 Sentier Hollande-Méditerranée: A timed route. This runs south from Larche to Nice or Menton, across the Mercantour Park. There are two routes, dividing at St Sauvern-Sur-Tinée. The distance either way is around 150 km across tough country, and ten days walking would be necessary to complete the distance. **Grade 4-5.**

GR 6 Sentier Alpes-Océan: This runs across Vaucluse from Sisteron to Beaucaire on the Rhône. An excellent route of 280 km which can be walked enjoyably in fourteen days. That's how long it took me but I wish it had taken longer. **Grade 2-3.**

GR 9-92-97 Sentier Vaucluse-Tour du Lubéron: This Topo guide contains details on three GR trails, including a highly recommended 160 km Tour of the Lubéron. This last would make a perfect ten day trip. **Grade 4.**

GR 9-98 Sentier Var, Bouches-du-Rhône: Two trails 220 km and 70 km respectively, taking in St Tropez, Marseilles, Ste Baume, and the beautiful bays or *calanques.* Apart from Marseilles, this is a route for hedonists, taking in the 'bustier' beaches. **Grade 2-3.**

GR 91 Sentiers Vercors-Ventoux: This trail runs across the Drôme and Hautes-Alpes but begins, or ends, at Mont Ventoux, 170 km of excellent walking across the beautiful wild and unexplored Barronnies up to Vercors. A good two-week trip, highly recommended for backpackers, but as usual it helps to be fit. The Ventoux is always windswept, and the summer temperatures on the top can be up to 20

°C lower than in the valleys! **Grade 4-5.**

GR 20 Sentier de la Corse: From Calenzana to Conca, 173 km of tough walking. Requests for information elicited comments like 'Don't try it in winter'. 'Don't try it in April'. 'It's all up and down'. 'We gave up'. Clearly this is a route for fit people with time on their hands. The walk is in remote country, much of it over the 2500 m mark, and crosses only four roads in the entire route. Food will be a problem and supplies will have to be carried, as provision points are few and far between, only Vizzavona and Bavella being actually on the route. Three weeks would be a reasonable time to allow for the trip with around eighteen days of walking. I have checked this out with experienced walkers and all agree that this a route well worth doing, but not to be undertaken lightly. Because of the terrain, Corsican distances are deceptive, so be warned! **Grade 4-5.**

In addition to these GR routes, the mainland region hs a very active outdoor organisation, the *Association Départementale pour le Développement de la Randonnée dans les Alpes-Maritimes,* called, thank goodness, ADDRAM for short. ADDRAM has waymarked two excellent routes east-west across the Alpes-Maritimes, *Le Sentier des Balcons de la Côte d'Azur. Sentier GR de Pays:* This footpath, 160 km in length, is waymarked in red and yellow, and runs from Carnolles, west of Menton along the escarpments of the pre-Alpes to Théoule-sur-Mer, West of Cannes. The average height is around 650 m, the views are excellent and, as there is adequate accommodation on the way, this route is suitable for all types of walker.

The second path, *Le Sentier de Six Vallées,* is not yet complete. Full details are available from ADDRAM, Villa Taema, Monta Leigne, 06700 St Laurent-du-Var. More ADDRAM footpaths are being developed.

Historic Paths

St-Maximin-la-Ste-Baume once held the relics of Mary Magdalene which were transferred to Vézelay for safe keeping and never returned. Les Saints-Maries-de-la-Mer is the place where Mary Magdalene, Mary, mother of James and John, and Mary, sister of Lazarus, came ashore after fleeing from Palestine. The gypsies believe in this and come from all over Europe to pray there on 24th May.

Accommodation

The facilities available in this region vary considerably. Since the economy largely depends on tourism it is easy to assume that there will be adequate hotels and campsites, but *tourisme vert* is still developing, and the accommodation inland is often fully booked. Camping is always possible, but pre-planning is still advisable.

A list of hotels can be obtained from the FGTO, London or local *Syndicats*. In the smaller villages the walker may have to rely on *Chambres d'Hôtes* or cafés for accommodation.

Gîtes d'étape are found mainly in the eastern Alpes-Maritimes where the CAF has built a number of huts along the GR trails or to give access to climbing areas; details from the CAF or from Topo guides. There are plenty of campsites and wild camping is usually permitted outside the Parks, with due warnings about fire risk. Fire is a great danger in Provence and Côte d'Azur, and even smoking in the hills is firmly discouraged.

Corsica is a very popular holiday resort for the French, and therefore very crowded in July and August. Outside these months the problem of accommodation is not acute. The main towns lie on the coast and inland the hotels are fewer. There are only two *gîtes*, or rather *refuges*, on the GR 20, so you will have to camp. Campers are welcomed in Corsica, providing they are careful with their stoves. Open fires, however, are not permitted. There is plenty of water even in the mountains in summer and campers can pitch their tents anywhere, though checking with the local people would be courteous and advisable. Local details from FRHPA, 34 Cours Napoléon, Ajaccio. It is forbidden to light fires in the forests and even smoking is frowned upon. When a carelessly dropped match can and has led to the destruction of millions of trees, this is not unreasonable. Any fires seen should be reported at once to the Gendarmerie.

Transport

Thanks to tourism, transport into and within these regions is plentiful. There are daily flights into Marseilles, Nice, Nîmes, Bastia and Ajaccio by Air France, British Airways and Air Inter.

Rail connections from Paris, Gare de Lyon, run down the Rhône Valley to Avignon, Marseille and Nice, and there are night sleepers to Avignon available from the Channel ports. Car and passenger ferries of the SNMCM (*Société Nationale Maritime Corse Méditerranée*) run to Corsica from Marseilles and Nice, and seats can be booked via P & O Ferries in the UK. These ferries arrive at Ajaccio, Bastia, Calvi or Propriano. The crossing takes from two to five hours, depending on the route.

In Provence and Corsica, there are bus services into the back-country, serving the villages, generally once a day. Bus tours are available, organised by the *Service d'Autocars de la SNCF*, and bus schedules can be obtained from the *Syndicats*.

These regions possess two marvellous *Train Touristique* rides, which walkers would be wise to employ.

In Corsica, the train ride from Ajaccio through Corte to Bastia, is 232 km of scenic railway, climbing across the mountains, crossing valleys on high viaducts, plunging through tunnels. This is the ideal way to gain access to the centre of the National Park, or pick up the GR 20. A shorter line runs along the north coast between Calvi and Ile-Rousse.

In Provence, the *Chemin de Fer de la Provence* operates a single track line across the Alpes du Sud. This line was opened in 1892 to serve the back-country, and still (just) functions today from Nice to Digne. The train makes frequent stops and a connecting bus service runs even deeper into the hills, off the valleys of the Var, Verdon and Tinée. The railway reaches its highest point 1012 m, north of Annot. This line gives the walker access to splendid country and the trip is an adventure in itself.

Maps and Guides

Good maps and guides are absolutely essential in both areas, but especially when exploring Corsica. A 1:25,000 scale IGN sheet and a compass are highly advisable, for walking in Corsica and the eastern Alpes-Maritimes.

To begin with a general map, the IGN red Carte Touristique No.115 (Provence-Côte d'Azur) for the mainland, and No.116 (Corse) will help in the selection of an area. Michelin Yellow maps 1:200,000 (1 cm = 2 km) No 81, 84 and 90 (Corse) give further information and show *drailles* and certain footpaths. A Michelin Green map (1 cm = 1 km) is available for Côte d'Azur and Alpes-Maritimes.

Thereafter 1:25000 or 1:50000 IGN are advisable, or the over-printed walking maps from Editions Didier-et-Richard. No 1, (St Ediénne-de-Tinée) and No 9 (Haut Pays Niçois), are very good. The IGN publishes two maps on walking in the Canyon du Verdon.

A number of walking guides exist, notably *Sentiers et Randonnées de la Côte-d'Azur* (Fayard), and *50 Randonnées Pédestres avec le Train du Sud* published by the SCFP. The latter can be bought at station booking offices.

A great deal of walking information is also available from the Tourist Offices and the local *Syndicats*.

Visitors would be well advised to read some more general guides to the area, for Provence is rich in history and Corsica is a unique island, not entirely French and well worth studying.

Archibald Lyall's *The South of France* (Fontana) or A.N.Brangham's *Provence* (Spurbooks) are excellent. Michelin Green guides are available to the French Riviéra-Côte d'Azur (in English), Provence (English) and Corsica (French). There are Blue guides to Corsica, but a strange lack of good English guide books, although Garry Hogg's *Corsica* is very readable.

Maps and guides can be purchased locally from: Rontani, 5 Rue A Marie, 06000 Nice; Faure, 81 Bvd St Roufe, 84000 Avignon; Hachette, 1 Place Foch, Ajaccio, Corse; Costa, Bvd Paoli, Bastia, Corse.

Wildlife

Excessive shooting in the past has decimated the wildlife hereabouts, which is only now recovering. Ornithologists will enjoy the flamingoes, ospreys and egrets of the Camargue delta, and the Mercantour has deer, wild sheep, chamois, marmots, and a host of birds, especially raptors. Corsica has plenty of deer, boar and mountain sheep, still intensively shot at, but somehow surviving, and a rich birdlife, especially in the spring and migration months, when duck, woodcock and seabirds arrive by the thousands.

Food and Wine

Provence has produced many dishes of international repute, while the Côte d'Azur has restaurants which rival Paris, and Corsica takes pride in the quality of its regional cuisine.

Olive oil, garlic and herbs flavour the dishes of Provence. *Bouillabaisse,* a fish stew, is included on every menu at a reasonable price, and fish, either from the sea or the mountain rivers, is a feature of every Provençal meal. There is *Brandade de Morue* (cod in cream with garlic) or *loup de mer* (sea bass), trout of course, *filet de porc,* in red wine, herbs and garlic, the inevitable *salade niçoise,* with egg and anchovy, and further west, snails from the Camargue.

Good wine flows from the Côtes de Provence, or the great strong reds of the Côtes du Rhône, Châteauneuf-du-Pape, Gicondas, and Taval rosés. As usual the wise and economic walker chooses the smaller restaurant, off the main street, and eats from the 'menu'.

Corsica has some local dishes and makes a feature of *saucisson,* sausage. Try *coppa,* smoked pork, or *pigatelli,* from pig's liver. Seafood is good, also the game, especially woodcock and grouse, is especially fine, and there are several cheeses, notably *Ponte Leccia.* Corsica has a considerable wine trade and the Ajaccio wines, graded AOC, are very drinkable as are the *patrimonio* wines from Bastia.

The mountain people also drink a type of *eau de vie,* or *marc,* made from myrtle berries. It's an experience!

Information Centres

Comité Régional du Tourisme, Côte d'Azur Alpes-Maritimes, 55 Promenade des Anglais, 06000 Nice, tel: (93) 82-10-55.

Départemental offices are in Marseilles (Bouches du Rhône), Gap (Hautes-Alpes), Avignon (Vaucluse), Digne (Haute-Provence).

Office du Tourisme de Nice, Gare SNCF, Avenue Thiers, 06000 Nice, tel: (93) 82-08-04); ADDRAM, Villa Taema-Montaleigne, 06700 St Laurent-du-Var, tel: (93) 31-76-64; Comité Régional de Tourisme, Région Corse, BP 162, 38 Cours Napoléon, 20178 Ajaccio.

Mountain France
THE ALPS AND THE PYRÉNÉES

The two main mountain regions of France need a chapter to themselves, for the mountains are different. In a country like France, which offers such a variety of terrain, it would be possible to walk for years and rarely stray from the horizontal. Possible perhaps, but a great pity, for some of the finest walking in France lies in the mountain areas.

In this chapter we shall explore the facilities available in the two major regions, the Alps and the Pyrénées. Technically, there are many mountains also in the Massif Central, with peaks of 2500 m or more, but the mountains, as the term is commonly understood, are mostly found in the Alps and the Pyrénées, and it makes sense to gather these two regions together into one chapter because, although geographically far apart, they present the walker with similar problems and opportunities and the information available for these regions is often produced in a similar form. To give an example, while Topo guides to GR routes generally give both times and distances, those for the mountains give time only, for the very good reason that *'as the crow flies'* is hardly relevant in the mountains, where the steep terrain can make even short distances very time-consuming. Moreover, in an effort to balance out the regional economies, the French have bracketed together in the regions many *départements* where the terrain differs from flatland to mountain peak. The mountain sections present their own challenges and must, therefore, be treated separately.

The French Alps consist of the Savoie, Dauphiné and Provençal Alps between Lake Léman (Geneva) and the Mediterranean in the *départements* of Haute-Savoie, Savoie, Isère, Drôme and, in Provence, parts of Hautes-Alpes, Alpes-de-Haute-Provence, and Alpes-Maritimes. This totals seven *départements* which together contain the major peaks on the eastern frontiers with Switzerland and Italy. This range includes Mont Blanc at 4807 m, the highest peak in Western Europe.

The French Pyrénées span the neck of the Iberian peninsula and, although the southern slopes run far out into the plains of Catalonia and Aragon, the northern French side is much steeper. A bare 50 km will take our flying crow from the watershed of the Pyrénées down to the northern plain, but here again, to make up the administrative region, large tracts of lowland have been grafted onto an otherwise mountainous region.

We will therefore concentrate on those parts of the four Pyrénéan *départements,* Pyrénées-Atlantiques (Pays Basque and Béarn), Hautes-Pyrénées (Bigorre), Ariège (Foix), and Pyrénées-Orientales (Roussillon), which are mountainous, and ignore the flatter sections, or the foothills, which are covered elsewhere in the chapters on Aquitaine, Midi-Pyrénées, or Languedoc-Roussillon.

Mountains served one major useful purpose in former times. They acted as barriers to invading armies, and provided secure frontiers. Apart from that they were useless, providing a poor livelihood, and sheltered only the shepherd, and outlawed men. Agriculture relied on the *transhumance,* the twice-yearly treck of farmers and their livestock, from winter shelter in the valley up to summer pasture on the shoulders of the mountains. To a greater or lesser extent the *transhumance* still goes on, but the mountains' prime historic role, as a frontier, has become established. They are also now commercially useful as skiing areas.

For much of history the Alps and the Pyrénées presented no political or indeed military barrier whatsoever, for the simple reason that the frontiers of an expanding France met that of her surrounding neighbours well inside the present encircling mountain walls.

This acounts for a number of anomalies, many local customs, and more than a few decidedly un-Gallic preoccupations in these areas. The walker will soon realise that mountain France is different.

Most of the Alps belonged, until well into the last century, to the Italian Kingdom of Savoy, and only became part of France in 1860. Dauphiné provided the income, a rather lean one, I imagine, for the French King's eldest son, the Dauphin.

In the Pyrénées, the Basque kingdom straddled the frontier in the west up to Bayonne. Ariège belonged to the princely Counts of Foix, who shared the sovereignty of Andorra with the Spanish Bishop of Urgel, while, until 1659, Roussillon was a fief of, successively, the Counts of Barcelona, the Kings of Aragon, and the Hapsburgs. These mountains contain people who to some extent regard the word 'French' as an adjective. They are French Catalans, French Basques. They speak their own language and dance to their own music. Much of this is a hangover from the past but it provides the mountains of France with much interest and local colour.

The Region Today

Both regions, Alps and Pyrénées, have suffered from a massive depopulation since the end of the Second World War. Industry is obviously lacking, and the main occupations are tourism, especially skiing, pastoral farming, and a limited amount of employment in the hydro-electric industry, public works and in the management of national parks and outdoor facilities.

The French Government and the regional authorities are anxious to develop summer tourism in the mountains without destroying that quality of life on which the main attractions of the region depend. The emphasis therefore is on reliable and adequate facilities for walkers, climbers, and outdoor activities of every kind. This programme has been growing for a number of years and the facilities now available to walkers in Mountain France equal those to be found anywhere in the world.

Physical Description

The Alps are the frontier between France and neighbouring Switzerland and Italy, running in a series of steps from Lake Geneva, or Lac Léman as the French call it, for some 400 km across six *départe-*

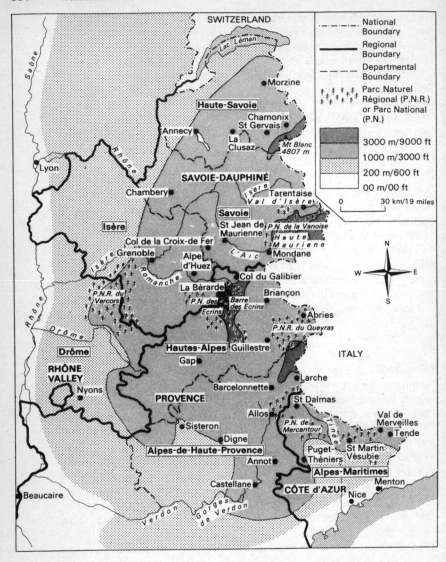

ments, down to the Mediterranean sea. This range contains the highest peak in Europe, Mt Blanc (4807 m), and scores more at the 3000-4000 m mark. This is, of course, tremendous climbing and skiing country, where even the walker would be well advised to take ice-axe and crampons in any season except high summer, and where a degree of scrambling is required on many routes. It also contains much walking of the less extreme variety, and many excellent long-distance routes around the National Parks or the main ranges. The route of the *Grande Traversée des Alpes Française*, Grade 4-5, will serve to provide a general outline of this range.

Beginning in the north, by Lac Léman, the mountain region climbs at the Dent d'Oche to La Chapelle d'Abondance, then over the ski slopes of Morzine and Avoriaz (1800 m) to Brévent (2526 m).

East of Brévent lies Chamonix, a great walking centre, at 1035 m in the valley of the Arve. Chamonix is encircled by mountains, Mont Blanc itself, the Grandes Jorasses (4208 m), the Aiguille du Midi (3842 m), the Aiguille de la Guere (2852 m), and scores more. Several glaciers flow down from Mont Blanc slopes where a guide might be advisable. There are 310 km of waymarked trails as well and the challenging *Tour du Mont Blanc* for the really fit walker.

South of Mont Blanc and the steep Taréntaise in Isère, the Vanoise National Park offers splendid walking at the 2000-2500 m mark, with peaks up to 3852 m at La Grande Casse, while south again are two more Parks, Les Ecrins at about 2000 m in the Massif du Pelvoux (Mt Pelvoux 3946 m), and Queyras to the east at the 2000-3000 m level.

The mountains of Haute-Provence are around the 2000 m mark, and after crossing the new Park of Mercantour, averaging about 2000 m, the range and the *Traversée* Path descends at last to the sea at Menton.

This follows the main chain of the French Alps, but the range is buttressed along the route by several smaller massifs, or pre-alpes, those of Vercors in the Drôme *département* and Lubéron in Vaucluse, being two good examples. The Alps is a high granite chain, snowbound from late October until May, and, given fitness and certain basic skills, perfect walking country for the day walker, the long-distance walker, but above all the backpacker.

Every walker who explores the Alps has a favourite region, but any of the three great Parks, or around Chamonix, would be the perfect centre for the first-time visitor.

The French Pyrénéan chain covers about the same distance as the French Alps, some 400 km, but they are not so high. The Pic d'Aneto at 3404 m is the highest peak, and this actually lies in Spain. There are, however, eighty-four summits over 3000 m in height, and the range must be considered a challenging area. The walking is of all grades but mainly 3-5.

Although the Pyrénées are often regarded as one continuous chain, there are in fact two separate ranges, one starting in the Pays Basque and running south and east to the Val d'Aran, the second starting a

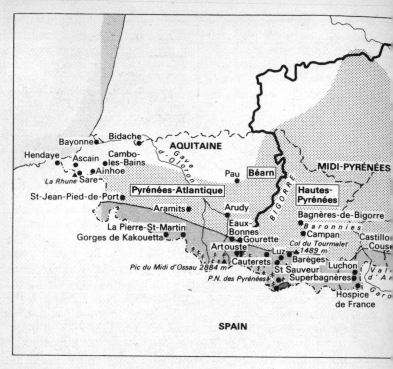

little north of this gap and running east to the Mediterranean. Through the gap of the Val d'Aran, the river Garonne, called here the Garona, which rises in Spain, flows over into France. We are concerned here with the French Pyrénées, that part of the range lying north of a frontier which, with a number of exceptions, follows the watershed from the Bidossoa river east to the Cap Cerbère.

This is a vast area seamed by deep valleys, long walls and *cirques*. It begins gently enough in the Pays Basque, at La Rhune (900 m), rises to over 2000 m in Bigorre at the Pic du Midi d'Ossau (2884 m) and, with a final thrust at Mont Canigou (2784 m) the pride of Roussillon, descends rapidly to the sea.

The French Pyrénées are steep, wild and windy, with snow on the tops from mid-October until May or June, and in winter studded from end to end with ski resorts. The region also contains a great Park and many excellent but little-known walking areas.

Climate

Both regions are mountain areas and, as always in such areas, it is essential that the walker obtains regular weather information. This is

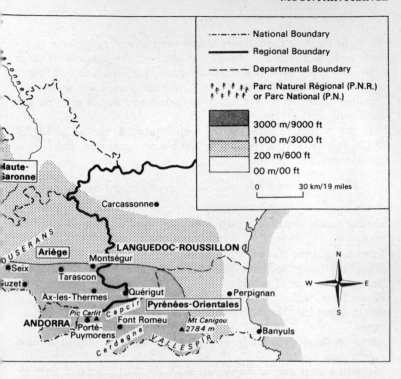

Key:
- ·—·—·— National Boundary
- ——— Regional Boundary
- ————— Departmental Boundary
- Parc Naturel Régional (P.N.R.) or Parc National (P.N.)
- 3000 m/9000 ft
- 1000 m/3000 ft
- 200 m/600 ft
- 00 m/00 ft

0 ____ 30 km/19 miles

usually available from the hotels and *gîtes*.

Snow cover is also a problem for the walker, for I have seen snow in both areas as early as mid-October, and lying as late as July. Mist and low cloud can also be expected, so skill with map and compass is essential anywhere, even on a low-level local trail. I dislike labouring points of skill and safety, but it has to be said that if you want to really explore the mountains you need to know the basic outdoor skills.

The ideal walking months in both areas are from mid-May to mid-October but if you intend to go high the time scale must be reduced to between mid-June and end of September. At either end of the scale, ice-axe and crampons (and the knowledge of how to use them) will be essential, and no one will laugh if you carry them at other times as well. Thunderstorms are not uncommon in mid-summer, and since the days are hot an early start is advisable.

Glacier trips, ice-climbing and rope-work are outside the scope of this book, but where such skills are deemed necessary in local guidebooks, then the services of a mountain guide are advisable, at least on the initial trips.

Safety

Much as I dislike those books which harp on endlessly about safety and imply that only a fool would venture off the *autoroute* without crampons and a sack of Kendal mintcake, the mountains of France are remote, high, wild and potentially hazardous, claiming up to a hundred victims every year, most of them killed largely or in part by their own carelessness.

If the walker is experienced, well equipped and WEATHER WISE there is very little danger, but please remember, and follow, the Mountain Code.

The Mountain Code

Be Prepared
Do not tackle anything which is beyond your training and experience.
Ensure that your equipment is sound.
Know the rescue facilities available in the area you are in and the procedure in case of accidents.
Know First Aid.
Avoid going into the mountains alone unless you are very experienced.
Leave word of your route and proposed time of return. Always report your return.
Make sure your map and compass skills are well practised. Rely on your compass.

Consider Other People
Avoid game shooting parties.
Lead only climbs and walks you are competent to do so.
Enjoy the quiet of the countryside; loud voices and radios do disturb.
Do not throw stones and dislodge boulders.
Do not pollute water.
Choose a climb which will not interfere with others or wait your turn.

Be Weather Wise
Know the local weather forecast.
Weather conditions change rapidly. Do not hesitate to turn back.
Know the conditions on the mountain; if there is snow or ice only go out when you have mastered the use of ice-axe and rope.

Respect the Land
Keep to footpaths through farm and woodland. If in doubt, ask.
Camp on official sites or obtain permission of the landowner.
Dig a hole to make a latrine and replace the turf.
Remember the danger of starting a fire.

Take all your litter home.

Avoid startling sheep and cattle.

Help Conserve Wildlife

Enjoy the plants, flowers and trees but never remove or damage them.

Avoid disturbing wildlife.

If an accident does occur, help is available from the *Gendarmerie de Montagne* — dial 17 on the nearest telephone — or from the *Club Alpin Français*. French mountains are not as crowded as those in the UK and a party in trouble may have to rely on their own resources for a long time before help arrives. Mountain Insurance is highly advisable and available from the British Mountaineering Club.

Walking in the *Départements*

The Alps

Mountain walking calls for skill. The walker should be fit, well equipped, shod in boots and able to use map, compass, ice-axe and crampons. It is of course perfectly possible to manage for a while without any of these, but not for far and not for long.

While the entire Alpine region is mountainous, there are considerable variations within the range and scope therefore for all sorts of walking and backpacking.

Haute-Savoie: Centred on the lakeside town of Annecy, Haute-Savoie is extremely mountainous, but there is gentler walking towards La Clusaz and in the Annecy region itself. Gentler, that is, compared with the peaks in the Chamonix-Mt Blanc area. Those looking for gentler slopes could explore the country around Morzine, walking over into Switzerland to nearby Chambéry, which is one way of getting fit. Between Chambéry and Grenoble lies the Massif of Chartreuse, which one of my correspondents urges me to recommend, and I do so wholeheartedly.

Savoie: The *département* of Savoie is very large and dominated in the east by a string of ski resorts: Tignes, Val d'Isère, La Plagne, and the vast Parc de la Vanoise. The Tarentaise area is ideal for walking.

This is one of the finest mountain areas in the Alps, and yet much less frequented than the Chamonix-Mont Blanc area, which is only 40 km away. Most of the walking is at about the 2000 m mark, but there are many big peaks and glaciers for the more adventurous. Modane in the south, west of Mont Cenis (2083 m), is a good centre for walking into the Park and through the wild Haute Maurienne on the Italian frontier.

Isère: This *département* takes its name from the river which torrents west from the Italian frontier, and Isère occupies much of the former principality of Dauphiné, centred on Grenoble. The eastern edge of this *département*, from the Romanche valley up to the Col de la Croix de Fer and the Grandes Rousses area, is superb. Alp d'Huez, an 'old' (pre-war) ski resort, is an excellent summer walking centre.

Drôme: The Park of Vercors, at around 1500 m, lies in the south-west of Isère and across the frontier with the Drôme. The Vercors plateau, just above Grenoble, is perfect for day walking or for a back-packing tour. Villard de Lans is a good centre. The Baronnies district, above Ventoux near Nyon, is another good region in the south of this *département*.

These four *départements* contain the highest of the high mountains of France, and will appeal to all lovers of high, wild and beautiful places.

Hautes-Alpes: In this *département* we leave the Italianate influence of Savoie and enter the former province of Provence. Provence is beautiful, carpeted with lavender and studded with golden villages.

The *département* contains two Parks, the Ecrins and the smaller Queyras, and is ideal walking country, at altitudes marginally lower than those to the north, around 2000-3000 m, although the Barre des Ecrins is at 4102 m, and there are plenty of peaks over 3000 m. There is more sunshine than in the Northern Alps, thanks to the Mediterranean influence, but the area is snowbound from late October until May with many glaciers.

Queyras is lower, sunnier, rather less well-known and runs across to the Italian frontier. Outside the Parks there is good walking north and west of Briançon, towards the Col du Galibier, the Col du Lautaret (2058 m) and south around Gap.

Alpes de Haute-Provence: I have walked extensively in these hills and recommend for day walking the area around Digne or Annot, and from any of the little stations along the *Chemin de Fer de Haute-Provence*. The country north of this railway line is high (2500 m), wild, empty and good for backpacking.

The country east of Sisteron is ideal for wild camping and back-packing, while those seeking a thrill could descend the Canyon de Verdon from Castellane, a trip which requires a head for heights and care with your footing.

Alpes-Maritimes: The *arrière-pays* of the Alpes-Maritimes has been rather over-shadowed by the attractions of the Côte d'Azur. The Alpes-Maritimes offer a great deal of good walking, most of it hilly but not all of it mountainous. The mountain walker will find what he or she seeks in the new Park of Mercantour, and good day walking is to be found around Tende. The Vallée des Merveilles is a must, for apart from the picturesque rock carvings it is a spectacular route with access into Italy. Other areas in the Alpes-Maritimes with walking below the 1500 m mark and the east-west trails into the Var, are covered in chapter eleven. Most of the mountain villages have waymarked local trails.

The Pyrénées

I have had some good times walking in the Pyrénées, outside the main holiday season, and in the remoter areas. The Pyrénées offer a great variety of walking country and some real challenges to the fit committed walker, notably the 700-plus km of the GR 10 from Hendaye to Banyuls, and the higher Haute Route.

Pyrénées-Atlantiques: This is a large *département,* and absorbs the Pays Basque and part of Béarn. These western Pyrénées are not particularly high at around 900 m; they are very green, but they climb steeply towards Béarn and Bigorre.

Three provinces of the ancient Basque kingdom of Navarre still remain, as districts of the Pays Basque: Labourd on the coast, Navarre around St Jean-Pied-de-Port, and Soule around Mauléon. Historically-minded walkers will follow the GR 65 Road to Compostelle through St Jean. Day walkers will settle in Sare or Cambo-les-Bains, while the backpackers will head for the haute Soule between the Pays Basque and Béarn. La Pierre-St-Martin or the Vallée d'Aspe will satisfy the mountain men, while Aramits and the country towards Pau, the capital of Béarn, will entertain the long-distance walker. Artouste, near the National Park, is beautiful and the lakes and forests of eastern Béarn, near the *pays des gaves,* are delightful.

Hautes-Pyrénées: The Hautes-Pyrénées, which embraces most of the former province of Bigorre, contains some classic walking areas, and if this were my first trip to the Pyrénées this is the area I would choose, heading at once for the *pays Toy* near Barèges, and the country around Luz-St-Sauveur. Here lies the great wall of the Cirque de Gavarnie, the steep Col du Tourmalet, much of the Pyrénéan National Park and, for something more gentle and off the beaten track, the Barronies region and the valley of Campan. This region is immensely historic, and almost anywhere will give excellent walking. Kev Reynolds recommends the Vignemale, Néouvielle, and the seven hour tour of the Pic du Midi d'Ossau as just a few of the many gems in this *département.*

Haute-Garonne: Most of this *département* lies outside the brief for this chapter, but the area does include the *Pays de Luchon* and this cannot be left out, because from Luchon the wise walker heads south over the Porte de Venasque, past the ruins of the old Hospice de

France, and into Spain for the Maladeta range and the Pic d'Aneto. This is a classic and indeed historic route across the mountains.

Keen day walkers will find Luchon extremely well organised to meet their requirements and, all in all, if you have only a little time to spare, then Luchon is just the place to get a taste for the Pyrénées, while the hills of Comminges, a little to the north, are good for long-distance walking from village to village.

Ariège: Ariège is a very large *département,* and all of it is hilly. I have walked across it from Seix in the Couserans, up to Guzet and eventually to Ax-les-Thermes. I recommend this route to backpackers; Ax-les-Thermes is good for day walkers, and the region east of Tarascon for those who fancy long-distance walking from village to village or some strenuous day trips. A visit to the great Cathar castles, such as Montségur or Quérigut, would be a good objective for a backpacking trip at the grade 3 level. Ariège is an excellent area and well worth exploring.

Pyrénées-Orientales: This, the home of the French Catalans, has some fine mountain walking. Day walkers should take the *petit train jaune* from Perpignan and go to the Cerdagne, there to walk in the lake country around Mount Carlit, down the Capcir valley or across the watershed into Spain. The GR 10 and Trans Pyrénéan Haute Route also cross this area and should interest the backpacker, while long-distance walkers can explore the Vallespir, the Canigou massif, or circle the villages of the Cerdagne plateau.

It is worth mentioning that many trails in the French Pyrénées can, and often do, lead the walker into Spain. The frontier is rarely marked, and I have yet to be asked for my passport (although I had it with me) or have French money refused. However, Spanish maps and a few Spanish words can be useful to the Pyrénéan walker.

National Parks

These two ranges, Alps and Pyrénées, contain no less than six National Parks, each offering the perfect centre for a walking holiday. One reliable piece of advice for anyone contemplating a visit to Mountain France is to go to a National Park. The walking facilities are excellent and, naturally enough, the Parks are set in areas of great natural beauty.

Parc National de la Vanoise: This was the first French National Park, opened in 1963, and it now includes the nature reserve of Tignes and Iseran. It lies in the east of Savoie, to the south of the town of Bourg-St-Maurice, and borders the Italian park of Gran Paradiso.

It includes the valley of the Isère and l'Arc with Val d'Isère as a good centre. The heights run between 1200 m up to the 3852 m of the Grande-Causse. There are 80 km of glacier, and the climate is sunny and mild, the air dry even in winter. Modane is the best walking centre, followed by the Plan d'Ammont. The *Tour Pédestre de la Vanoise* is a marvellous route from the Tarentaise across to Maurienne, using ski stations as summer stops. The ideal route for long-distance walkers.

There are over 500 km of waymarked footpaths in the Vanoise, and many refuges along the GR 5, GR 55, and the Grande Traversée des Alpes. Details on walking in the Park are available from the *Syndicat* at Modane, Val d'Isère, Bourg-Saint-Maurice, or from the Maison du Parc, 135 Rue du Dr Julien, BP 105, 73003 Chambéry, tel: (79) 62-30-54.

Parc National des Ecrins et du Pelvoux: This new park lies in Dauphiné, across Hautes-Alpes and Isère. Briançon is the main town although Gap, to the south, is an excellent access route. This is a fairly high massif with Ecrins at 4102 m and Mont Pelvoux at 3946 m, but there is plenty of walking at a lower level and this park is much greener than the Vanoise.

The region is noted for the abundance of alpine flowers, with over two thousand different kinds within the confines of the Park, as well as much wildlife, chamois, marmot, mountain hare and great eagles. Camping is permitted only on the periphery of the Park. Inside there are *refuges,* but wild camping is discouraged and frequently actively forbidden. Details from Maison du Parc, 05290 Vallouise, or Parc National des Ecrins, 7 Rue Colonel Roux, 0500, Gap.

Parc Naturel Régional du Queyras: Queyras is an even smaller park, east of the Ecrins, and at a lower level, around the 2000 to 3000 m mark. Guillestre is the best centre.

Parc Naturel Régional du Vercors: I have a great affection for the Vercors plateau which, apart from the walking possibilities, is perfect ski-touring country. This park lies near Grenoble, at the 2000 m level, and overlooks the Drac and Drôme valleys. The park is heavily forested with long open glades and high ridges.

Details are available from the Maison du Tourisme, Grenoble.

Parc National du Mercantour: This is another new park which opened in the face of considerable local opposition in 1979. It lies in the Alpes-Maritimes, 70 km north of Nice, along the Franco-Italian frontier, at the very end of the main Alpine massif. The height is around 3000 m, dropping in parts, near say St Martin-Vésubie, to around 1000 m. This entire park is worth exploring, and special attention should be paid to the lake region of the Vallée des Merveilles near Tende. This is a very beautiful shrine of prehistoric wall carvings. This park is snowbound in winter.

The Pyrénées

Parc National des Pyrénées: This is a vast park running along the Franco-Spanish frontier from Béarn well into Bigorre, and abutting the Spanish Ordesa Park across the frontier. It contains some marvellous walking country in the Aspe and Ossau valleys, the Balaïtous, around the Pic du Midi d'Ossau, near the Pont d'Espagne south of Cauterets, the Vignemale in Gavernie and the Nëouvielle . . . everywhere! There are over 400 km of waymarked trails, many *refuges,* and both the GR 10 Trans Pyrénéan footpath and the more demanding *Haute Route* cross this Park.

The European brown bear is said to survive here in small numbers, and there are izard, the rat-like desman, the Pyrénéan chamois, wild boar, deer, and many species of bird. Details on the Park are available from many sources as well as from Amis du Parc, 20 Rue Saumonzet, 64000 Pau.

Footpaths

Local Footpaths

The essential requirement for local footpaths in mountain areas is that they should display the countryside, be well marked, and capable of completion well before dark. Bearing this in mind, certain areas and centres are clearly to be favoured and I am again grateful to a number of walkers who have written to me suggesting suitable areas.

Haute-Savoie: Chamonix is an excellent area with 310 km of waymarked paths, and a lift network to get the walker off to a good start or down before dark. The Mont Blanc area is full of classic walks of all distances and the *Syndicat* at Chamonix will supply a folder illustrating many routes.

Savoie: Two areas have been suggested here, the Vanoise and the Grande Chartreuse. Modane is the perfect centre for the Vanoise, although Val d'Isère is very central, as is St Jean-de-Maurienne.

La Grande Chartreuse lies near Chambéry, almost in Isère, and has many excellent walks. The pine forest route to the Grand Som (2026 m) is recommended, as it overlooks the Monastery of Chartreuse, where the liqueur comes from.

Walkers can also achieve the summits of Chamechaude (2082 m) and the Dent de Crolles. From here on a clear day you can see across to the Vanoise. The Grande Chartreuse is virtually unknown to British walkers and is well worth exploring.

Isère: The Ecrins Park is highly recommended with many kilometres of footpaths and La Bérade would be a good centre. Briançon is the nearest big town and the place from which to start, but Belle-donne and, of course, the Vercors should also be visited. The Tour-ist Office in Grenoble provides useful information on all these areas.

Hautes-Alpes: The Queyras Park is an obvious choice and as yet far from crowded. Abries or Guillestre are good centres, with adequate campsites. The Durance River flows through this *département,* and anywhere south-west of the Queyras Park offers open terrain and ex-cellent walking country as far as Gap.

Alpes de Haute-Provence: Digne has plenty of accommodation and good paths as well as access to many other little places along the rail-way. Allos and, further west, Sisteron are also excellent centres. One area of which I am never likely to tire is the wild country east of Sis-teron.

Alpes-Maritimes: The *Chemin de Fer de Provence* single track line from Nice to Digne will lead the day walker to plenty of ideal centres. Just alight from the train at any likely spot and walk off in any direction.

Puget-Théniers is excellent, as are the valleys of the Tinée and the Vésubie. The Mercantour Park offers some hard hillwalking, but there is a gentler route into the Vallée des Merveilles through Tende, which is the best centre for this remarkable valley.

The Pyrénées

Like all lovers of the Pyrénées I have my favourite areas, and starting on the Atlantic coast would recommend the following areas in each *département:*

Pyrénées-Atlantiques: The Basque villages of Sare, Ainho or Ascain, are marvellous walking centres, with access to La Rhune (900 m). Many of the footpaths were (and probably still are) smugglers' trails. As a walking centre, Sare could hardly be bettered, and it is said to be the prettiest village in the Basque country.

Bidache, east of Bayonne, has a ruined castle and some easy walk-ing country, but for something more strenuous I recommend the hills of the Arbailles around St Anthony. A walk to the gorge of Kakouetta is a real excursion.

Hautes-Pyrénées: This is a highly recommended area. I would head at once for the *Pays Toy* around Luz-St-Sauveur, for the Cirques of Gavarnie and Troumouse. The circuit of the Pic du Midi d'Ossau, the shapliest of the Pyrénéan peaks, makes a marvellous 6-7 hour walk across several cols, with the certain prospect of spotting izard, the Pyrénéan chamois.

The col du Tourmalet above Barèges is a wild area, but the Lac de Payolle in Bigorre, or the splendid country around Eaux-Bonnes and

Gourette, should not be missed. This region is so full of centres that one can only list them. Cauterets, Bagnères de Bigorre, the Balaïtous, the Vignemale, are all excellent. Just go there and walk.

Haute-Garonne: The choice here is simpler, for few towns anywhere can match Luchon when it comes to facilities. The *Syndicat* has a thick folder of information on waymarked trails. St Bertrand-de-Comminges is worth a visit and the walks around high Superbagnères offer marvellous views. Try and visit the Hospice de France on the footpath into Spain.

Ariège: The Couserans are highly recommended by the local people, and Castillon would be a good centre. The ideal town is Ax-les-Thermes, a spa from which it is possible to visit the Cathar castles, get into Andorra, or make a long trip through Puymorens-Porté, up to the Cerdagne. Andorra is very rocky, quite unexplored, full of possibilities, but not quite French enough for inclusion here.

Pyrénées-Orientales: My favourite area here is the Cerdagne, especially the Carlit area, above Font-Romeu, a region full of lakes and streams, with the chance to climb Mont Carlit (2921 m). A tour of the Cerdagne could take in all the surrounding watershed and include Puigmal (2910 m) on the Spanish frontier.

It is also possible to walk in a day from Font Romeu over the col de Nuria into Spain. Lightly laden, this will take about eight or nine hours, and one can stay the night in the monastery of Nuria and walk back the next day.

Other good areas in Roussillon are the Vallespir, the Capcir and the Canigou massif above Prades or Vernet-les-Bains. The walk to the Romanesque monastery of St-Martin-du-Canigou is particularly fine.

Long-distance Footpaths

The Alps

Every country has its classic walking routes, France has more than most, and these two mountain ranges contain the very best of them. Who would not like to do the Tour de Mont Blanc, complete the Pyrénéan Haute Route, cross the Pyrénées on the GR 10 or walk down from Switzerland to the Mediterranean on the Grande Traversée des Alpes?

La Grand Traversée des Alpes Françaises (GTA): This great route is made up of several GR trails and covered in Topo guides for the GR 5, 54 and 58. The distance is some 400 km and there are ninety-eight *gîtes* or mountain *refuges* along the way. The recommended route would take a fit walker thirty walking days with six or seven hours walking per day, and would include Mont Blanc, Vanoise, Ecrins,

Queyras and Mercantour. A highly recommended route for the fit walker.

Full details are available from the CAF or the CIMES (*Centre Information Montagne et Sentiers*) organisation at the *Maison du Tourisme* in Grenoble. They produce a brochure on the walk and a recent book in French, *La Grande Traversée des Alpes,* published by CIMES in Grenoble, is an indispensable aid at 30 francs.

GR 5 Sentier Hollande-Méditerranée: This long footpath has four sections, each with its Topo guide covering the Alps from Lac Léman to Menton, and they include many *variants.*

The *GR 5 (Lac Léman to the Col de la Croix du Bonhomme)* in Haute-Savoie is a timed route, which would probably take twelve days for a fit walker. **Grade 5.**

The *GR 5-55 in Savoie (Croix du Bonhomme to Modane)* across the Vanoise park, a highly recommended route, would be another two-week trip. **Grade 5.**

The *GR 5 (Modane to Larche)* is an easier country where distances are given. This is 168 km and would take about eight days. **Grade 4.**

The *GR 5-52 (Larche to either Nice or Menton)* would need about ten days. There is a choice of route, 154 km to Nice and 95 km to Menton. **Grade 4.**

The times needed for these walks are hard to judge, for the Topo guides give the stages in hours rather than distances. The estimates given here, as an aid to trip planning, are probably on the generous side.

GR 54-541 Parc National des Ecrins-Tour de l'Oisans: A circular, highly recommended two week trip around the Parc des Ecrins and Isère. There are two shorter *variants,* each capable of being covered in about three days. A Topo guide is available and, although the route is timed, the distance is around 183 km. **Grade 4-5.**

GR 541: This trail follows from the Ecrins and leads east from Ecrins linking to the Tour de l'Oisans. Topo guide in preparation.

GR 56 Tour de l'Ubaye: The Ubaye tour is a short, interesting trail, which runs off the GR 5 below Queyras, goes through Barcelonette in Haute Provence, and returns to the GR 5 at St Dalmas. The best access to it is from Briançon, and the tour takes about seven walking days. Recommended for a good fit backpacker. **Grade 3-4.**

GR 58 Tour du Queyras: This can be reached along the GR 541, or taken as a tour in its own right. Both are included in the Topo guide. The tour is shorter than the Tour des Ecrins, and a *variant* GR 58B goes over into Italy. About a week, or 120 km, of tough going.

GR 6 Sentier Alpes-Océan: Parts of this long trail run across Haute-Provence, from Sisteron to Beaucaire on the Rhône, a marvellous route with easy access and, according to the IGN 901, this route then runs east from Sisteron to the GR 56. The Sisteron-Beaucaire stage is about 280 km. A good two-week walk. **Grade 3-4.**

GR 6-56 St Paul-sur-Ubaye to Sisteron: Topo guide in preparation.

GR 9: Two Topo guides for this trail. Les Rousses to Culoz and Culoz to Grenoble. Either section would be a tough walk.

GR 9-429: Saillans to Brantes, from the Drôme to Vaucluse.

GR 9-91-93-95 Parc Régional du Vercors: This Topo guide covers four trails in and around Vercors Park; 130 km, 85 km, 60 km and 35 km respectively. Ideal for the long-distance walker with a week or two to spare. The GR 9 continues across Provence and we will meet it again. **Grade 3-4.**

GR 94-946 Tour des Pre-Alpes du Sud: Much of this lies in Drôme, but it runs into Hautes-Alpes and touches Sisteron, a recommended area. The distance is 180 km and ten days should do it easily. Excellent country, ideal for backpacking and a highly recommended walk. **Grade 4.**

GR 96 Sentier des Pre-Alpes de Haute-Savoie and Tour du Lac d'Annecy: Back in the north again but an excellent region for a fit walker's first trip to the Alps. Two weeks should cover most of the ground. Topo guide available. **Grade 5.**

TMB — Tour du Mont Blanc: There is a Topo guide available, giving timings and heights. This is a classic route and I am advised that it is an excellent two-week tour 'with plenty of scope for diversifying scrambles', among some staggering scenery. See bibliography for guide books to this route. **Grade 5.**

BLL — Sentier du Balcon du Léman: This is a fine route, quite short at 194 km, on the mountains beyond Geneva, just inside France. Highly recommended for splendid views across the lakes and hills, and would take about ten days. **Grade 4-6.**

BL — Tour du Léman-Balcon Vaudois: This walk, in the same region, is 160 km and would be a pleasant week's walk for the lightly equipped walker in June to September. **Grade 4-5.** New trails are being continually developed in the Alps and there is scope here already for several holidays.

The Pyrénées

I have done a lot of walking in the Pyrénées, a region with a great deal to offer the walker but which, until recently, has been pretty well unknown. This is now being remedied, a fact which we Pyrénée-lovers view with mixed feelings, but after all, good things should be shared.

HRP — The Haute Route: This, like the *Grande Traversée des Alpes* is a classic Grade 5 route. The *Haute Randonnée Pyrénéenne* runs across more than 400 km of hills and mountains and would take the fit walker about forty-five days to complete. The Haute Route keeps as high as possible and involves some scrambling and occasional descents into Spain. An ice-axe is advisable, except in August. It can be broken down into several two week trips, and there are CAF huts along much of the route. A tent and full backpacking equipment is advisable, but the reward is an invigorating expedition, quite dramatic and with superb panoramas.

GR 10 Sentiers des Pyrénées: This spans the range, but travels on lower ground than the HRP. Five Topo guides cover this route from the Atlantic to the Mediterranean, and although as the crow flies it is a distance of 400 km, the GR 10 route is over 700 km from Hendaye in the Basque country to Banyuls on the Mediterranean. This is a well waymarked route and any one of the five Topo guides will give the walker a good two-week trip. To complete the whole trip in one go would take *at least* thirty walking days. **Grade 4-5.**

GR 36 Sentier Manche-Pyrénées: The last link in this trans-France footpath is now complete with the waymarking of the section from Carcassonne, across the Corbières and up to the Cerdagne. This is also the E4 European footpath, which leads on into Spain. I recommend this route to all long distance walkers who like wine and history, for it takes in the walled town of Carcassonne, where you should begin, leads past the frontier castles, over Canigou, and along the crest to the Cerdagne. It has all sorts of terrain, good weather from May to September, and lots of interest. If CAF huts are used backpacking is not necessary. **Grade 3-4.**

GR 65 Sentier de St Jacques de Compostelle: This route, a classic trail, runs through St Jean-Pied-de-Port, and can be followed south into Spain, or retraced towards the north up to Eauzé in Aquitaine. **Grade 3.**

GR 77 Sentier Sommail: A good route across the foothills of the Minervois and Corbières.

Historic Paths

The main pilgrim centre in the Alps is the Grande Chartreuse, where the first Charterhouse was built in 1084. The Monastery of St Bérnard up on the frontier is a further worthwhile objective. The Sanctuary of La Salette, near Grenoble, is set in magnificent mountain scenery and would also make a good objective for a trip.

Accommodation

Since both these mountain regions are suitable for walkers, the facilities are excellent. The accommodation at all levels tends to be simple but adequate, rather than elaborate and expensive.

French walkers rely on *gîtes,* or *refuges,* rather than hotels or camp-sites, and those walkers intending to do the same would be well advised to join the Club Alpin Français immediately on arriving in France, or one of the bodies affiliated to it. This will not only entitle the walker to much reduced hut fees, but will also enable him or her to reserve a place. In the UK the affiliated body easiest to join is the Austrian Alpine Club (United Kingdom Branch), 13 Longcroft House, Fretherne Road, Welwyn Garden City, Hertfordshire, AL8 61Q, tel: Welwyn Garden City (07073) 24835. The British Mountaineering Club (BMC) is said to be working to a similar scheme. I'm not too keen on mountain huts, which often tend to be crowded, noisy and all too often dirty. Give me a small tent and a quiet pitch anytime.

A list of hotels in the various regions, Isère, Savoie, Dauphiné, Provence, and Alpes-Maritimes, can be obtained from the FGTO or by consulting the *Logis de France* guide. Booking is advisable in summer.

Gîtes d'étape are very common in the Alps and Pyrénées, and details on the accommodation available can be found in most Topo guides and from the Maison du Tourisme and the CAF, CIMES, or in the Pyrénées from the *Randonnées Pyrénéennes,* 4 Rue de Villefrance, 09200 St Girons, tel: (61) 66-02-19.

The *Randonnées Pyrénéennes* organisation is *the* group to ask when enquiring about outdoor activities, especially walking, in the Pyrénées. Their brochures, folders and booklets are available from all the major *Syndicats* and *Maisons du Tourisme,* and they also produce a booklet, *Hébergements en Montagne (France-Espagne),* which gives full information on mountain huts and *gîtes* in the French Pyrénées and across the frontier in Spain.

There are plenty of campsites and details are available from local *Syndicats* or the FGTO, London. A walker's tent will often fit in, or even on, a crowded campsite. *Camping à la ferme* is available everywhere, and wild camping is usually possible in the mountains. Within the confines of the Parks the rules vary. In general, wild camping is not permitted within the confines of the parks, but these rules are interpreted differently in each area, and much of the interpretation depends on the size of the tent and the mood of the park ranger. In the Pyrénéan park, camping is tacitly allowed about one hour's walk from the road. In Mercantour no one seems to mind over 1500 m. In Ecrins they direct you to sites on the periphery, in the Vanoise no one seems to care. It is worth pointing out again that a National Park in France means something more like an Area of Outstanding Natural Beauty (AONB) in the UK. People live, work and farm in the parks, and if wild camping is not available then *camping à la ferme* is always an alternative.

Transport

Although mountainous, neither region is truly remote. There are international airports near the mountains at Geneva, Lyon, Marseilles, Nice, Tarbes, Toulouse and Perpignan, all served by regular international flights. From the airports there are bus or coach shuttle (*navette*) services to the nearest towns or railheads, and rural coach or postbus services into the valleys are quite adequate. Rail services to the Alps and Pyrénées are via Paris, Gare de Lyon, Austerlitz, or Gare de l'Est.

Road links are excellent. There is an autoroute, Paris to Perpignan, and Paris to Nice, with a link road east, between Grenoble and Geneva, across the Alps, and many N-roads. Grenoble is the centre point for the Alps and, depending on the chosen region, Annecy, Chambéry, Briançon, Gap, Sisteron, Digne and Nice would all be excellent starting points for a trip to the mountains, easy to get to and good centres for local services.

For the Pyrénées, Toulouse is the central point, and the starting place for trips are, from the east: Bayonne, St Jean-Pied-de-Port, Pau, Lourdes, St Gaudens, St Girons, Foix and Perpignan.

Both regions have a number of tourist trains, *Trains Touristiques*, track railways or single track lines, ideal for getting into the more remote areas. The *Chemin de Fer de Provence* runs from Nice to Digne, while in Perpignan, the *petit train jaune,* the little yellow train, runs up to La Tour de Carol in the Cerdagne.

In Pyrénées-Atlantiques a train runs from Laurens, south of Pau, to Artouste, the highest train track in Europe at 2000 m, and another runs from Sare towards Spain. Both give swift access to remote walking country, and are good trips in their own right.

In Isère, the *Funiculaire de St Hilaire-du-Touvet* lifts the passenger from 260 m to 1000 m (at an 83° angle) and gives marvellous views over the Grand Chartreuse and Mont Blanc, ending in Grenoble; a good way to make a reconnaissance of the area.

The *Petit Train de la Mure* runs for 60 km across the hills and takes the walker into some good areas. Information from the Office du Tourisme, La Mure.

Mont Blanc has its tramway, a one-hour round trip from St Gervais, an ideal way to see just how much snow lies on the tops, while Chamonix has the *Tramway du Montenvers,* which runs throughout the year up to 1909 m, as well as many useful cable cars.

Walkers are well advised to track down these tourist trains. They are often greatly under-used, and save many hours of 'walking in' to the chosen area.

Maps and Guides

The benefits of reading about an area before you go there cannot be overestimated, but in the mountains it is essential.

IGN 1:250,000 Carte Touristique maps are useful for selecting a likely area. The Alps are covered by No.112 (Savoie-Dauphiné), No.115 (Provence-Côte d'Azur). Michelin have a Green map, scale 1:100,000 (1 cm = 1 km) No.195, Côte d'Azur, Alpes-Maritimes, which is also excellent for route planning as it shows relief and footpaths.

In the Alps the best maps are to be found in the Editions Didier et Richard, who have nine 1:50,000 maps *Itinéraires pédestres et ski* covering the Alps. The Didier-et-Richard shop in Grenoble is an excellent map and guide centre, and a place any walker should visit.

Each National Park has a special map, usually overprinted with walking routes and facilities, on scales from 1:100,000 to 1:25,000, except Queyras. Four maps cover the *Parc National des Pyrénées*.

Guide books to the Alps abound, but the walker will find two in English particularly useful: *100 Hikes in the Alps* published by The Mountaineers/Cordee and *The Tour de Mont Blanc* by Andrew Harper (Cicerone Press). *100 Hikes in the Alps* also contains some Pyrénéan walks. Topo guides exist or are in preparation for all waymarked GR routes, and CIMES in Grenoble have published a guide to *La Grande Traversée des Alpes*.

In the Pyrénées, the IGN 1:250,000 Carte Touristique maps are the 113 (Pyrénées-Occidentales) and 114 (Pyrénées-Orientales) 1:50,000 and IGN 1:25,000 maps cover the entire area, and there are four 1:25,000 maps for the *Parc National des Pyrénées*, overprinted with the footpaths, GR routes, and hut details. A similar overprinted map exists for the Cerdagne-Capcir region. The *Syndicat* in Vernet-let-Bains has produced a 1:20,000 map, Massif du Canigou, which is useful, although vague about relief.

The basic walking guides in English are *Pyrénées East, Pyrénées West* and *Pyrénées, Andorra, Cerdagne*, three small books by Arthur Battagel published by West Col. They include the Spanish side of the range.

Fayard have guides to both these and other areas in their 'Sentiers' series, and *Sentiers du Roussillon* and *Sentiers et Randonnées des Pyrénées*, both by Joseph Ribas, are very good. Kev Reynolds' *Walks and Climbs in the Pyrénées* (Cicerone Press) is excellent.

The GR 10 has five Topo guides and the *Haute Randonnée*

Pyrénées (HRP) is covered by a book by Georges Veron, published by the *Club Alpin Français.*

Michelin Green Guides are available for the Alps and Pyrénées, including one in English for Provence, while for a more general introduction to the latter range, Neil Lands' *The French Pyrénées* will be useful, or *Provence* by A.N.Brangham, both published by Spurbooks. *50 Randonées avec le Train du Sud* covers walks from the *Chemin de Fer de Provence* north of Nice.

Walkers in the Pyrénées should consider if maps of the Spanish side are necessary, and if so obtain those published by Editorial Alpina. These show relief, with a 20 m contour interval, but are not, in my experience, always quite accurate. This is true also of maps published by the Spanish *Institute Geographica*, and if they are used a degree of caution is advisable.

I cannot cover all the relevant detail on these mountains in one chapter and must urge all would-be walkers there to study maps and guide books on the region carefully.

Locally, maps and guides can be obtained from: Didier-et-Richard, 4 Place de Phillipville, 38000 Grenoble; Rontoni, 5 Rue a Mari, 06300 Nice; Roc Sport, 12 Rue de Postiques, 74230 Thônes (Haute Savoie); Le Vieille Boutique, 10 Rue Trésorerie, 73000 Chambéry; Librairie Rive Gauche, 29 Quai Vauban, 66000 Perpignan.

Wildlife

In both areas the wildlife, even the larger mammals, is quite prolific. Chamois, or izard as they call them in the Pyrénées, are very common, and wild goats, marmots and sheep are often seen on the lower slopes. The Pyrénées contain such rare creatures as the desman, a large aquatic rat with a short trunk, very rare, thank goodness, but sometimes sighted by patient naturalists near Luchon. Wild boar and deer are common, and the Pyrénéan National Park is said to contain about fifty of the European brown bear, which no one I have talked to has ever actually seen.

The great attraction of the mountains is the bird life, and the flowers. Raptors, and in spring and autumn the migrating birds from Africa, are the major attractions. A good field guide to plants and birds is a worthwhile addition to the kit.

Food and Wine

Neither area can claim to be gastronomic, but there is good sensible cooking in both areas, and hunger is a very good sauce.

Savoie and Haute-Savoie go in for cheese fondue, the *fondue savoyarde*. Fish from the mountain rivers is excellent, as are some stews, and the very drinkable wines from Apremont, Mondeuse, and the Jura. The Pyrénées has a number of little dishes, and there are some regional specialities. *Jambon Piperade*, a spicy omelette, is excellent in the Basque country, the Béarnaise sing of *Poule au pot*, the people of Bigorre offer *garbure*, a thick soup, and *canard magret*, a duck cutlet. The Catalans will force a *cargolade* dish of grilled snails on you if possible. The fish, the ham and goat's cheese (*chèvre*) or the black-skinned Pyrénéan cheese are all excellent. The Catalans have a whole range of vaguely Spanish dishes, and a point worth noting, restaurant prices away from the tourist towns are very reasonable indeed.

In the Pyrénées the wines of Madiran, Juraçon, or the Côtes du Roussillon, Corbières or Minervois are reasonably priced and excellent.

Information Centres

Maison du Tourisme de la Drôme, 14 Bvd Haussmann, 75009 Paris, tel: (1) 246-66-67; Maison Alpes-Dauphiné, 2 Place du Théâtre Français, 75001 Paris, tel: (1) 296-08-43; Maison de Savoie, 16 Bvd Haussmann, 75009 Paris, tel: (1) 246-39-26; Maison des Pyrénées, 24 Rue du 4 Septembre, 75002 Paris, tel: (1) 742-21-34.

Délégation Régionale du Tourisme, Alpes du Nord/Savoie Mont Blanc, 11 Avenue de Lyon, 73000 Chambéry, tel: (79) 69-16-46; Comité Régional du Tourisme (CIMES), Maison du Tourisme, 14 Rue de la Republique, 38000 Grenoble, tel: (76) 54-34-36; Fédération Offices de Tourisme et SI, (Savoie, Haute Savoie, Isère), 4 Rue St Maurice BP 438, 74012 Annecy.

Départemental offices are in Aix (Provence) and Nice (Alpes-Maritimes).

Comité Régional du Tourisme, Antenne Pyrénées, 3 Rue de l'Esquile, 31000 Toulouse, tel: (61) 23-22-05.

Départemental offices are at Foix (Ariège), Tarbes (Hautes-Pyrénées), Pau (Pyrénées-Atlantiques), Carcassonne (Aude).

Maison du Tourisme, Quai de Lattre de Tassigny, 66000 Perpignan; Randonnée Pyrénées, 4 Rue de Villefranche, 09200 St Girons, tel: (61) 66-02-19 the best source of information for the Pyrénées.

The *Club Alpin Français* has branches in many towns and villages in or near the Alps and Pyrénées.

BIBLIOGRAPHY

Regional guide books are listed in the relevant chapters and this bibliography is designed to suggest books of general interest on walking in France, France and the French.

Michelin Green Guides (to all areas) in French or English.

Stevenson, Robert Louis, *Cévennes Journal,* Mainstream Publishers, Edinburgh, 1979.

Stevenson, Robert Louis, *Travels with a Donkey in the Cévennes,* Folio Society, 1978.

Barret & Gurgand, *Priéz pour nous à Compostelle,* Hachette 1978.

Highams, Roger, *Provençal Sunshine,* Dent 1969.

Oursel, Raymond, *Pèlerins du Moyen Age,* Fayard 1978.

Brangham A.N., *The Naturalist's Riviera,* Phoenix House 1962.

Duggan, Alfred, *The Devil's Brood* (The Angevin Family), Corgi.

Wylie, Laurence, *Village in the Vaucluse,* Harvard University Press 1974.

The Conquest of Gaul by Julius Caesar, Penguin Books.

Cunliffe, Barry, *Rome & The Barbarians,* Bodley Head.

Perde, François, *Sur les Routes des Pèlerins en France,* Fayard 1980.

Evans, J., *Life in Medieval France,* London 1957.

Les Très Riches Heures du Duc de Berri, Hallweg.

Brown T. & Hunter R., *Map and Compass,* Spurbooks 1976-79.

Yoxall H.W., *The Wines of Burgundy,* Penguin.

French Farm & village Holiday Guide (Annual, Mitchell-Beazley.

Hamilton, Ronald, *Holiday History of France,* Chatto & Windus.

Davidson, Marshall, *Concise History of France,* Cassell.

Cobham, Alan, *A History of Modern France* (3 vols.), Penguin.

Appendix One
HOW TO REQUEST INFORMATION

Below is a sample letter in English and French that you could copy if you want to send off for information.

English

Dear Sir/Madam,
    I am planning a walking tour in your region and I would be very grateful for any information or illustrated material you could send me on the available facilities for walkers and campers in your area.
    I would particularly like information on the local waymarked footpaths, on campsites and *gîtes d'étapes*. I already have the IGN maps and relevant Topo guides to the Grandes Randonnees. Is there any area you would particularly recommend?
    I enclose a large stamped addressed envelope, together with an International Reply Coupon for the postage. I look forward to an early reply.

Yours faithfully,

A.N.Other

French

Monsieur/Madame,
    J'ai l'intention d'effectuer une randonnée pédestre dans votre région et je vous serais reconnaissant de toute information et brochures que vous pourriez m'envoyer sur les possibilités de randonnée et de camping dans la région.
    Des renseignements sur les sentiers balisés locaux, les campings, et les gîtes d'étape me seraient également utiles; je possède déjà les cartes IGN et les guides topographiques Grandes Randonnées. Il y a certainement des endroits intéressants?
    Je joins une enveloppe à mon adresse et un coupon-réponse international. Dans l'attente de vous lire veuillez agréer Madame/Monsieur mes meilleurs sentiments.

A.N.Other

Appendix Two
USEFUL VOCABULARY

French	English
une carte	map
une boussole	compass
un sac à dos	rucksack
un sentier	a footpath
une balade	a walk
une arrête	a ridge
tout droit	straight on
à droite	turn right
à gauche	turn left
une tente	tent
sac de couchage	sleeping bag
abri	shelter
une boulangerie	baker
une épicerie	grocer
un boucher	a butcher
un terrain de camping	campsite
un gué	a ford
château d'eau	water tower
une pharmacie	chemist
une ampoule	a blister
un coup de soleil	sun stroke
une bière	beer
bière pression	draft beer
un demi	a small beer
le temps	the weather
beau temps	good weather
mauvais temps	bad weather
je me suis perdu	I am lost
Pouvez-vous m'indiquer le chemin de ...	Can you show me the way to ...
je suis fatigué	I am tired
je suis épuisé	I am shattered
quelle est la distance jusqu'à ...	How far is it to ...
un réchaud	a stove
Une cartouche or une recharge	a cartridge (of gas)
l'essence	petrol
la neige	snow

il'y a ...	there is ...
activités de plein-air	outdoor activities
la boue	mud
mouillé	wet
une douche	a shower
une averse	a shower (of rain)

GRANDES RANDONNÉES

NOTE that the second or subsequent figures shown under 'Distance',
indicates a 'variant'. Routes described as 'Tour' are usually circular.

Cat. Ref.	No. of GR	Title	Distance - kms
101	GR 1	Tour de l'Ile-de-France	605
102	GR 11	Sceaux — Neauphle-le-Château	48-31
103	GR 11	Neauphle-le-Château — Senlis	175
104	GR 11	Senlis — La Ferté-sous-Jouarre	145-601-41
105	GR 11	La Ferté-sous-Jouarre — Fontainebleau	170
106	GR 11	Fontainebleau — Neauphle-le-Château	164
117	GR 111	Sentier de l'Essonne (Milly-le-Forêt à Gravigny Balizy)	215
107	PR 1	Petite Randonnée en Ile-de-France	Local walks
116	PR 2	Petite Randonnée en Ile-de-France	Local walks
108	GR 12/12A	Sentier Ile-de-France/Ardennes	302-130
118	GR 120	Tour du Boulonnais	In preparation
109	GR 121/121A	Valenciennes — Boulogne-sur-Mer	250-254
119	GR 123	Carlepont/Hesdin — Pas-de-Calais, Somme, Oise	In preparation
120	GR 124/124A	Folleville/Cire-1.-Mello et Bethlsy-St-Pierre — Oise	In preparation
110	GR 13/132	Fontainebleau — St-Martin-s-Ouanne	162-37
111	GR 13	St-Martin-s-Ouanne — Mont-Beuvray	208
112	GR 13/131	Mont-Beuvray — Signal du Mont	60-54
113	GR 14A	Gagny — GR 11 (Seine-et-Marne)	55
114	GR 14/141	Dormans à Châtel-Crehery, Tour de la Montagne de Reims	288-55
115	GR 14	Boissy-Saint-Leger — Dormans	265
201	GR 2/24	Aix-en-Othé — Val Suzon et 24, St-Dizier — Mussy-sur-Saône; Haute-Marne — Aube — Côte-d'Or	In preparation
212	GR 2/213	Pont-sur-Yonne — Auxerre	196-98
203	GR 2	Triel — Le Havre; Val-d'Oise — Eure — Seine-Marit.	96
204	GR 2	Des Andelys — Le Havre	188
205	GR 21/211	Le Havre — Saint-Valéry-en-Caux	291
206	GR 22	Orgerus — Mamers (Sentier Paris — Mont St Michel)	217
207	GR 22/22B	Mamers — Mont St Michel	223-60
208	GR 221	Pont-d'Ouilly à St-Lô, Coutances	200
210	GR 222	Pont-de-l'Arche — Verneuil	145
211	GR 223	Tour du Cotentin	291-34
215	GR 225	Dieppe — Forêt de Lyons; Seine-Maritime	In preparation
216	GR 226	Conde-sur-Noireau — Carolles; Manche — Calvados	In preparation

Cat. Ref.	No. of GR	Title	Distance - kms
209	GR 23/25	Sentier de la région Rouennaise	233
217	GR 26	Feucherolle — Vernon — Deauville; Yvelines — Eure	In preparation
334	GR 3-3A	Arfeuille — Gerbier-de-Jonc	258-37
301	GR 3	Cosne-sur-Loire — Arfeuille	In preparation
335	GR 3/32	Cosne-sur-Loire — Orléans et d'Orléans — Malesherbes	173-37-93-28
303	GR 3	Orléans — Saumur	255
304	GR 3	Fontevraud — Pont-de-Mauves	188
305	GR 30	Tour des Lacs d'Auvergne	170
307	GR 31	La Nièvre à Vierzon	165
345	GR 31	La Charité-sur-Loire — Chambord; Nièvre — Cher — Loir-et-Cher	In preparation
306	GR 33/331	Saint-Alvard — Pierre-sur-Haute	201
332	GR 330	Tour du Livradois	260
333	GR 34	Vitre — Mont Saint-Michel	144
310	GR 34	Mont Saint-Michel — Barrage de Rophemel	140
339	GR 34	De Treguier à Morlaix; Côtes-du-Nord — Finistère	260
343	GR 34	Saint-Brieuc — Tréguier (Tour de Bretagne — Tro — Briez)	146
308	GR 34	Loudeac — Tréguier (Sentier des Côtes du Nord)	336
007	GR/34/37/39	Tour des Chouans	303
344	GR 341	Loudeac — Paimpol; Côtes-du-Nord	260
313	GR 347	Josselin — Redon	95
314	GR 35	Sentier du Loir	232
315	GR 35/351	Dreux — Senonches et Verneuil — Cloyes; Eure-et-Loir	In preparation
316	GR 36	Ouistreham — Ecouche	130
317	GR 36	Ecouche — Mans	213
318	GR 36	Mans — Parthenay	240
337	GR 36	Parthenay — Angoulême	309
342	GR 36	Périgueux — Bonaguil; Dordogne — Lot-et-Garonne	In preparation
347	GR 36	Albi — Mazamet; Tarn	In preparation
348	GR 36	Mazamet — Canigou; Tarn — Aude — Pyrénées-Orientales	In preparation
320	GR 36	Angoulême — Périgueux	98
319	GR 36A	Saint-Christophe-du-Jambet — Saint Léonard-des-Bois	62
322	GR 36	Bonaguil — Cordes	210
329	GR 360	Jonzac — Saint-Agnant et GR 4 Saint-Laurent — Cognac — Saintes	180
354	GR 364	Tour Gâtine et Bocage Vendéen	200
323	GR 37	Vitré — Josselin	277-58
340	GR 37	Guerledan — Presqu'ile de Crozon; Côtes-du-Nord — Finistère	In preparation

Cat. Ref.	No. of GR	Title	Distance - kms
330	GR 37	Sillé-le-Guillaume — Vitré	157
341	GR 37	Vitré — Plelan-le-Grand (Sentier de l'Argoat)	174
350	GR 371	Loudeac — Saint-Brieuc; Côtes-du-Nord	In preparation
327	GR 38	Baud — Redon (Landes de Lanvaux)	154
326	GR 39/39A	Rennes — Redon	170
328	GR 39	Rennes — Mont Saint-Michel	100
401	GR 4	Grasse — Pont-Saint-Esprit	In preparation
402	GR 4	Pont-Saint-Esprit — Saint-Flour	125-21
403	GR 4	Saint-Flour — Aubusson	267
404	GR 4	Aubusson — Limoges	131
405	GR 4	Limoges — Angoulême	141
406	GR 4	Angoulême — Saintes	118
407	GR 40	Tour du Velay	160
414	GR 400	A travers le volcan Cantalien	146
415	GR 420	Tour du Haut-Viverais	208
416	GR 440	Tour de la Montagne Limousin	130
417	GR 460	Triangle des Combrailles	
408	GR 41	Brioude — La Bourboule	90
409	GR 41	Super-Besse — Evaux-les-Bains	145
419	GR 41	Vierzon — Evaux-les-Bains; Cher — Creuse — Allier	In preparation
410	GR 412	Olliergues — La Chaise-Dieu	54
411	GR 42	Bessat — Beaucaire	277
412	GR 441	Tour de la chaine des Puys	108
413	GR 46	Uzerches — Vers	160
420	GR 46	Tours — Aubusson	In preparation
514	GR 5	Ouren — Ars-sur-Moselle	325
516	GR 5	Ars-sur-Moselle — Abreschviller	177
502	GR 5	Abreschviller — Fesches-le-Châtel	290
503	GR 5	Fesches-le-Châtel — Nyon	260
504	GR 5	Lac Léman au Col de la Croix du Bonhomme	3 weeks
505	GR 5/55	La Croix du Bonhomme — Modane et Prc de la Vanoise	3 weeks
506	GR 5	Modane — Larche	168
507	GR 5/52	Col de Larche — Nice et GR 52 St-Dalmas-Valdeblore — Menton	154-95
501	GR 53	Wissembourg — Schirmeck	167
524	GR 531	Soultz-s/Forêt — Massevaux; Bas-Rhin — Moselle — Vosges — Haut-Rhin	In preparation
522	GR 53/5	(En allemand) — de Wissembourg au Donon et du Ballon d'Alsace à Masevaux	
508	GR 54	Parc National des Ecrins, tour de l'Oisans	183
523	GR 549	Vizille à Chamrousse	
517	GR 56	Tour de l'Ubaye	

Cat. Ref.	No. of GR	Title	Distance - kms
509	GR 58	Tour du Queyras	120
510	GR 59	Ballon d'Alsace — Lons-le-Saunier	384
519	GR 59/559	Lacs et forêts du Jura	240-140-30
518	GR 590	Sentier Loue-Lison	105
512	GR 595	Besançon — Pontarlier	73
601	GR 6	Sisteron — Beaucaire	280
602	GR 6	Beaucaire — l'Aigoual et variants	170-7
619	GR 6/56	Saint-Paul-sur-Ubaye — Sisteron et Tour de l'Ubaye	In preparation
603	GR 6/60	Meyrueis — Figeac	215-70
605	GR 6/64	Figeac — Les Eyzies	133-86
604	GR 6	Eyzies-de-Tayac — Sainte-Foy-la-Grande	92
620	GR 65	Eauze — Roncevaux; Gers — Landes — Pyrénées-Atl.	200
616	GR 600	Tour de l'Aubrac	194
606	GR 62/62A	Sentier de la Causse Noire, Plateau du Levezou, Rouergue	186
607	GR 65	Puy — Aubrac	140
608	GR 65	Aubrac — Montredon	111
617	GR 65/651	Conques — Cahors — Vallée de Cèle	154-58
613	GR 65	Cahors — Eauze	218
614	GR 652	Gourdon — La Romieu	179
621	GR 65	Le Puy — Conques	226
610	GR 66	Sentier du tour de l'Aigoual	78-125
611	GR 67	Sentier du tour des Cévennes	130-28
612	GR 68	Tour du Mont-Lozère	110
	GR 60	Grande Draille, Peyuret — Trevers	96
618	GR 653	Colomiers, Auch Maubourget	223
701	GR 7	Ballon d'Alsace — Bourbonne-les-Bains	164
702	GR 7	Grancey-le-Château — Nolay	129
710	GR 7/76	Nolay — Mont Saint-Rigaud	236-60
709	GR 760	Tour du Beaujolais	
704	GR 7/72/73	Mont-Pilat — Mont-Aigoual	445
705	GR 7/74	Mont-Aigoual — la Montagne Noire	268
706	GR 71	L'Esperou — Angles; Gard — Aveyron — Hérault — Tarn	163
712	GR 714	Vittel — Bar-le-Duc; Vosges — Meuse	In preparation
707	GR 77	Sentier Sommail, Minervois, Corbières	103
009	GR 71C	Tour des Templiers du Larzac	80
801	GR 8	D'Ares — Contaut	75
901	GR 9	Des Rousses — Culoz	125
902	GR 9	De Culoz — Grenoble	149
903	GR 9/91/93/95	Parc Régional du Vercors	
907	GR 91	Vercors — Ventoux; Drôme — Vaucluse	118-40
904	GR 9/429	Saillans — Brantes; Drôme — Vaucluse	

Cat. Ref.	No. of GR	Title	Distance - kms
906	GR 998	Pont-de-Mirabeau — Saint-Tropez et Marseilles — Les Calanques — La Ste-Beaume; Bouches-du-Rhône — Var	220-70
905	GR 9/92/97	Brantes — Pont-de-Mirabeau; Vaucluse	336
908	GR 94/946	Tour des Préalpes du sud	180
909	GR 96	Sentier des Préalpes de Haute-Savoie et du Tour du Lac d'Annecy	2 weeks
1001	GR 10	Hendaye — la Pierre-Saint-Martin	170
1002	GR 10	Sainte-Engrace — Arrens	103
1003	GR 10	Gourette — Melles	Ten days
1004	GR 10	Melles (Haute-Garonne) — Mont-Louis (Pyrénées-Orientales)	Ten days
1005	GR 10	Merens — Banyuls	1 week
		(The GR 10 will take up to 6-8 weeks total)	
2001	GR 20	Sentier de la Corse	240
001	TMB	Sentier International du tour du Mont-Blanc	3 weeks
002	BLL	Sentier du Balcon du Léman (Haute-Savoie)	194
003	BL	Tour du Léman — Balcon Vaudois (cantons du Valais et de Vaud — Ain)	160
005	GR R1	La Réunion	1 week
006	PR	Bretagne	In preparation
008		Tour de Brocéliande — Ille-et-Vilaine	In preparation
010		Tour de la Causse du Cantal; Aveyron	In preparation
011		Tour des Vallées de la Maronne et de la Cére	
015		Tour de la Vallée de la Brenne; Indre-et-Loire	In preparation
024	GR de Pays	Sentiers Ceinture Verte (Paris)	
121	GR 11/11C	Grand Sentier de l'Ile de France	340-20
118	GR 120	Tour du Boulonnais (Pas de Calais)	130
	GR 33/331	Sentier Combrailles-Forez (Traversee Puy de Dome)	201
	GR 341A/341B	Morbihan – Côtes du Nord	277-48-19
348	GR 36	Albi – Canigou	550 (30 days)
016	GR	Tour de Gorges de l'Aveyron	303
021	GR 380	Tour Monts d'Arrée (Brittany)	225
026	GR de Pays	Tour Pays d'Eygurande (Auvergne)	90
023	GR de Pays	Coeur de Gascogne (Gers)	165
022	GR 62A/62B	Causse Noir	186-75
010	GR 620	Horizons du Rouergue (Aveyron)	138
1006	GR 10	Sentier des Pyréneés Hendaye – Arrens	260
017	Sentiers de PR	Littoral Mediterranéean	8 itin.

INDEX